Theories of Practice in Tourism

Tourism research that is inspired by theories of practice is currently gaining in prominence. This book provides a much-needed introduction to the potential applications of theories of practice in tourism studies. It brings together a variety of approaches exploring how theories of practice bridge themes and fields which are usually addressed separately within tourism research: consumption and production; travel and the everyday; governance and policy; technology and the social. The book critically engages with practices as a fruitful approach to tourism research as well as how the particularities of tourism might inform our understanding of practice theories.

This book contributes to conceptual and methodological debates providing insights from authors who have engaged with practice theory as an entry point to researching tourism. It offers a solid starting point for researchers and students alike who wish to learn about, and try, this approach, as well as explore its possibilities and limitations in the field of tourism.

Laura James is Associate Professor at the Tourism Research Unit at Aalborg University, Denmark. She researches regional governance, knowledge dynamics and innovation. She currently explores cross sectoral interactions between food and tourism, developing a practice-based conceptual framework to explore how public and private tourism actors adapt, combine and transform existing practices to produce new tourist experiences related to food production, processing and dining.

Carina Ren is Associate Professor at the Tourism Research Unit at Aalborg University, Denmark. She researches connections between tourism and other fields of the social. With a focus on everyday practices, she explores processes of cultural innovation, knowledge collaboration and value-creation in tourism.

Henrik Halkier is Professor of Regional and Tourism Studies and Dean of the Faculty of Humanities at Aalborg University. His research experience is primarily related to the role of institutions, discourses and practices in tourism and regional development. He is currently working on practices, institutions and networks within the field of food tourism.

Theories of Practice in Tourism

Edited by
**Laura James, Carina Ren and
Henrik Halkier**

Routledge
Taylor & Francis Group

LONDON AND NEW YORK

First published 2019
by Routledge

2 Park Square, Milton Park, Abingdon, Oxfordshire OX14 4RN
52 Vanderbilt Avenue, New York, NY 10017

Routledge is an imprint of the Taylor & Francis Group, an informa business

First issued in paperback 2020

British Library Cataloguing-in-Publication Data
A catalogue record for this book is available from the British Library

Library of Congress Cataloging-in-Publication Data
A catalog record has been requested for this book

ISBN: 978-1-138-06170-5 (hbk)
ISBN: 978-0-367-58977-6 (pbk)

Typeset in Times New Roman
by Taylor & Francis Books

Contents

Illustrations

Figures

Tables

Contributors

Giovanna Bertella is an associate professor at the Tromsø School of Business and Economics, UiT The Arctic University of Norway. She has adopted a practice approach to the study of knowledge and learning in tourism in her PhD dissertation. Practice theory is applied also to several of her recent works. Topics covered in her research include: rural tourism, tourism networking and innovation, tourism entrepreneurship, nature-based tourism, animals in tourism, sustainability. The geographical settings investigated in her research include northern Norway and Italy.

Marcelo de Souza Bispo is an associate professor at the Federal University of Paraíba (Brazil) in the Management Department, co-leader of the Research Group in Learning and Knowledge Studies (NAC-UFPB) and visiting scholar at Kentucky University (2015–2016) in the Sociology Department. He was awarded outstanding reviewer of the Annual Meeting of the Academy of Management (2016–2017) and best paper at the Brazilian Academy of Tourism (2014). He has a PhD in Management from Mackenzie University (Brazil) and a bachelor degree in Tourism from the Methodist University of São Paulo (Brazil). His research interests are Tourism Studies, Practice-Based Studies, Qualitative Research, Organisation Studies, and Education.

Erica Dayane Chaves Cavalcante is an adjunct professor at the Federal University of Paraíba in the Tourism and Hospitality Department and member of the Research Group in Learning and Knowledge Studies (NAC-UFPB). She has a Master in Management and is a PhD candidate in Management at the Federal University of Paraíba. She was awarded best paper at the Brazilian Academy of Tourism (2014). Her research interests are Tourism Studies, Practice-Based Studies, Qualitative Research, and Organisation Studies.

Alessio Cavicchi is an associate professor at the Department of Education, Cultural Heritage and Tourism at University of Macerata (Italy). His main fields of interest and research are consumer food choice, economics of food quality and safety, sustainable tourism and innovation in the agro-food sector. He has experience as an invited expert for several programmes and DGs of the European Commission in the food sector (DG Research, DG Regio-Urbact, DG Agri, Joint Research Center, European Agency for Competitiveness and Innovation).

Timo Derriks is a researcher and lecturer at the HZ University of Applied Sciences, Vlissingen, the Netherlands. While being a member of the Tourism Management bachelor program, he not only concentrates on innovation and strategy of leisure and hospitality organisations but also on tourism destination development in coastal regions. He holds an MSc in Leisure, Tourism and Environment and is currently a PhD candidate at the Cultural Geography Group, Wageningen University, the Netherlands. In this PhD, he is studying the connecting and changing of practices in innovation processes in the state province of Zeeland, the Netherlands.

René van der Duim is Professor at the Cultural Geography Group, Wageningen University, the Netherlands. He holds a PhD on the relation between tourism and sustainable development making use of insights from actor-network theory. He has executed research and educational projects in countries like Thailand, Nepal, Costa Rica, Tanzania, Namibia, Kenya, Uganda, Portugal and the Netherlands. He has co-edited five books and has published his work in journals such as *Annals of Tourism Research, Journal of Sustainable Tourism* and *Tourism Management*.

Christian Fuentes is an associate professor at the Department of Service Management and Service Studies, Lund University and a senior researcher at the Centre for Consumer Research, University of Gothenburg. He is interested in consumer culture and markets and undertakes research in the fields of green marketing, ethical consumption, alternative markets, digitalisation and retail. He often draws on socio-material practice theory and makes use of ethnographic methods to explore how marketing practices and devices shape consumption and markets. His research has been published in outlets such as the *Journal of Marketing Management, Consumption, Markets & Culture, Business Strategy and the Environment, International Journal of Consumer Studies* and *Journal of Retail and Consumer Services*.

Henrik Halkier is Professor of Regional and Tourism Studies and Dean of the Faculty of Humanities at Aalborg University. His research experience is primarily related to the role of institutions, discourses and practices in tourism and regional development. He is currently working on practices, institutions and networks within the field of food tourism. He has extensive editorial experience with edited volumes and special issues for international publishers and journals.

Kevin Hannam is PhD FRGS and Professor of Tourism Mobilities at Middlesex University, Dubai and a senior research fellow at the University of

Johannesburg, South Africa. He holds a PhD in geography from the University of Portsmouth, UK. Previously he held positions as Head of Tourism & Languages at Edinburgh Napier University and Associate Dean (Research) and Head of Tourism, Hospitality and Events at the University of Sunderland, UK. He has edited and authored/co-authored ten books and over 100 academic articles and book chapters. He is founding co-editor of the academic journals *Mobilities* and *Applied Mobilities* (both published by Routledge).

Laura James is Associate Professor at the Tourism Research Unit at Aalborg University, Denmark, and her research focuses on regional governance, knowledge dynamics and innovation. She is currently exploring the links between food and tourism, focusing in particular, on cross sectoral interactions and developing a practice-based conceptual framework to explore the ways in which a variety of public and private actors within the tourism sector adapt, combine and transform their existing practices (individually and in collaboration) to produce new tourist experiences related to food production, processing and dining.

Tanja Knoblauch Nielsen is a PhD fellow in the Department of Design and Communication, University of Southern Denmark. She has a MA in Tourism from Aalborg University. Currently she is doing a PhD in understanding and applying co-designing as an approach that entails a move away from prescribed methods and business models in smart tourism towards co-designing possible smart tourism futures in situations and networks were big/open data, technologies and people meet, align and make each other act. Her research includes studies of co-design projects with tourism professionals, students, researchers, IT and business consultants.

Jonas Larsen is a professor in mobility and urban studies at Roskilde University, Denmark. He has a long-standing interest in tourist photography, tourism and mobility more broadly. More recently, he has written extensively about urban cycling and geographies of running, urban marathons and sport tourism. His latest books are the *Tourist Gaze 3.0* (2011, with John Urry) and *Digital Snaps: The New Face of Snapshot Photography* (2014, with Mette Sandbye). Jonas Larsen's work is translated into Chinese ((both in China and Taiwan), Japanese, Polish, Portuguese and Korean (in process), and he is on the editorial board of *Mobilities, Tourist Studies* and *Photographies.*

Karin Peters is Assistant Professor at the Cultural Geography Group, Wageningen University, the Netherlands. She holds a PhD on the meaning of public spaces for issues of social integration. Her research focuses on leisure, public space, diversity and issues of inclusion and exclusion in the Netherlands and at the European level. She has published her work in journals such as *Leisure Sciences* and *Gender, Place & Culture: a Journal of Feminist Geography.*

Morten Krogh Petersen, MA, PhD, works as Business Development Manager at Gemeinschaft, an anthropological consultancy specialising in urban development. By bringing human actors and organisation together with new technological opportunities, he seeks to co-produce places and properties that can host and create value through different versions of 'the good life'. In doing so, he draws on his previous academic work at Aalborg University Copenhagen within The Techno-Anthropology Research Group.

Outi Rantala, D.Soc.Sc., acts as Associate Professor of Responsible Arctic Tourism at the Multidimensional Tourism Institute, University of Lapland. Her research has focused on nature relationship and rhythms of everyday and holiday through such phenomenon as wilderness guiding, touristic sleep, weather, adventure tourism, and architecture. She also has an active role in developing tourism education within the University of Arctic's Thematic Network on Northern Tourism.

Carina Ren is Associate Professor at the Tourism Research Unit at Aalborg University, Denmark. Carina researches connections between tourism and other fields of the social. Using ethnographic research and focusing on everyday practices, she explores different processes of cultural innovation, knowledge collaboration and value-creation in tourism. She has published in leading tourism journals and is the co-editor of several special issues and books, recently *Co-Creating Tourism Research. Towards collaborative ways of knowing* (2017, Routledge).

Cristina Santini is an assistant professor at Università San Raffaele in Rome, Italy. Her research interests cover: entrepreneurship, small business, business strategy, food and wine industry, qualitative methodology and participatory research methods. Her recent works also focused on methodologies and tools to be employed in order to reduce academicians-practitioners gap.

Theodore R. Schatzki is Professor of Geography and Philosophy at the University of Kentucky. His research interests lie in theorising social life, and he is widely associated with a stream of thought called practice theory that is active today in a range of social disciplines, including geography, sociology, organisational studies, education, anthropology, international relations, and history. He has co-edited two volumes on practice theory: *The Practice Turn in Contemporary Theory* (2001) and *The Nexus of Practices* (2017). In addition, he is author of numerous articles on such social topics as flat ontology, social space, learning, large social phenomena, art, social change, materiality, governance, and discourses, as well as many essays on human action and on the philosophies of Wittgenstein and Heidegger.

Lídia Cunha Soares is an assistant professor at Adventist Institute of Paraná (Brazil) and a member of the Research Group in Learning and Knowledge

Studies (NAC-UFPB). She has a Master in Management from the Federal University of Paraíba. She was awarded best paper at the Brazilian Academy of Tourism (2014). Her research interests are gastronomy studies, practice-based studies, and organisational learning.

Anette Svingstedt is a senior lecturer at the Department of Service Management and Service Studies, Lund University. She is a marketing scholar interested in service encounters, sustainability and the digitalisation of retailing. Her research into these topics has been published in the *Journal of Retail and Consumer Services*, the *Journal of Service and Quality Management*, the *Scandinavian Journal of Hospitality and Tourism*, and other outlets.

Alexandra Witte is currently a doctoral candidate and teaching assistant in the School of Events, Tourism and Hospitality Management at Leeds Beckett University. Following the completion of an undergraduate degree in Sinology and a Master's degree in Tourism and Hospitality Management, she is now close to completing her PhD research in which she seeks to develop a theoretical understanding of the diversity of walking practices and experiences of domestic and international tourists on the Ancient Tea Horse Road in Southwest China. Her main research interests include cross-cultural issues in tourism, tourism in China, outdoor tourism, tourism mobilities and ethnography in tourism.

Foreword

Theodore R. Schatzki

Contemporary theories of practice have proved their mettle in diverse social disciplines. This stream of thought has long displayed theoretical diversification, which has only broadened since the turn of the millennium through a proliferation of so-called praxeologies and practice-based approaches. Today this diversification is also matched by a steadily expanding bounty of empirical studies that illuminate both familiar and obscure corners of social life.

It is no surprise that this family of theories is proving useful in studying tourism. The ontologies promulgated in theories of practice, like those informing broad social theories of any kind, claim to cover many social phenomena, even social phenomena in general. Tourism, consequently, falls within its gamut. What's more, tourism, like any complex social phenomenon, boasts a variety of practices and material arrangements that vary across space and evolve over time. A small number of practice-theoretical studies of tourism have already illuminated aspects of this sweep of practices and arrangements.

The present book, the first anthology to adopt a practice theoretical approach to tourism, extends these existing studies toward new horizons. Collectively, its chapters reveal that, because the practices and arrangements involved in tourism form bundles and larger constellations, aspects and dimensions of tourism that have been taken up separately in fact connect. In drawing, moreover, on the theoretical diversity of practice theory while reflecting about and employing a wealth of methods to study practices, it evinces and astutely realises some of the promise of this general approach to social life. Needless to say, the chapters also make a large contribution to illuminating tourism by increasing knowledge of the nexuses of practices and arrangements that compose it. The chapters illuminate both the "consumption" and "production" sides of these nexuses, examining such phenomena as walking, running, slow traveling, and both food and nature tourism, as well as cooking, destination governance, and the distribution of goods and services. In studying these and more, the volume furthers the multidisciplinarity character and dissemination of theories of practices, while also showing how practice theoretical concepts can be usefully linked with those of adjacent approaches such as activity theory, actor-network theory, rhythmanalysis, and anthropology.

In all, this splendid collection draws on all the theoretical, methodological, and disciplinary richness of practice theory to illuminate a social phenomenon with which readers are likely to be personally familiar. Enjoy!

1 Practices in and of tourism

Carina Ren, Laura James and Henrik Halkier

Introduction

The aim of the book is to critically engage with practice theories as a promising way to conceptualise and research tourism, and also to explore how the study of tourism could contribute to wider debates about practice. Practice theories point to the ways in which different institutions, actors and materials are continually connected, held together, recreated and reshuffled to enable what we know as tourism. Practice theorists avoid the privileging of structure or agency by taking practices as the primary unit of analysis and this approach offers a means to bridge themes and fields which have usually been addressed separately within tourism research: consumption and production, travel and the everyday, technology and the social, the public and private spheres of society.

In this volume, we bring together research on a broad range of sub-fields within tourism studies to examine more closely how practice theories are shedding new light on the ways in which tourism is enacted in specific contexts, how tourism is 'learnt', often together with other social practices, and how change, learning and innovation take place through these ongoing activities. The diverse academic backgrounds of the contributing authors reflect the fact that tourism is a multi-disciplinary field of research. We hope that the current volume will encourage interest in using theories of practice to research tourism from a range of different perspectives.

Practice theories – a brief introduction

Reviews of the 'practice' literature frequently note that there is no such thing as an integrated or unified practice theory but instead a set of distinct traditions which may be loosely grouped together as 'praxiological' (see Nicolini, 2012; Reckwitz, 2002; Schatzki et al., 2001). Whether inspired by attempts to resolve the structure-agency dualism, as in the work of Giddens (1984) and Bourdieu (2013) or the efforts of Wittgenstein and Heidegger to identify the site of the social in philosophy, these approaches commonly emphasise that even the most durable features of social and economic life – classes, institutions and organisations – should be considered as 'ongoing routinised and recurrent accomplishment[s]' (Nicolini, 2012:3). This gives rise to the notion of practices, conceived as sets of interconnected 'doings and sayings', as defined by Reckwitz (2002: 249):

> A 'practice' is a routinised type of behaviour which consists of several elements, interconnected to one another: forms of bodily activities, forms of mental activities, 'things' and their use, a background knowledge in the form of understanding, know-how, states of emotions and motivational knowledge.

According to Schatzki (2002), practices can be divided into *dispersed* practices which relate to singular and common social (inter)actions (greeting, texting, etc.) and *integrative* practices which are 'complex entities joining multiple actions, projects, ends, and emotions' (p. 88). Integrative practices are characterised by being 'bundled', are often specialised and relate to particular social groups, such as researchers conferencing. 'Bundle of activities' (Schatzki, 2002: 71) can be analysed in order to grasp how (inter)actions are integrated in a practice and how practices relate to one another to form complexes (Nicolini, 2012; Shove et al., 2012).

Practice theories adopt a 'flat' ontology where the social is conceptualised as inhabiting one level, that of practices. In exploring the 'plenum' (Schatzki, 2016) rather than specific social strata, traditional sociological categories such as micro and macro, actor and structure, lose their analytical importance and meaning. Often, what we could term as 'plenary' explorations trace the 'life of practices' (Shove et al. 2012), offering close, often historical descriptions of social phenomena. As this volume also exemplifies, practice theories lend themselves well to the study of everyday and seemingly mundane activities, or to what Nicolini terms 'zooming in' (2012). However, 'zooming out' to study networks of practices, or a 'practice-arrangement bundle' (Schatzki, 2016), also enables the analysis of more extensive social phenomena, for instance the interlinking between different practices (see Lamers and van der Duim, 2016). Through the iterative movement between zooming in, to closely describe specific practices, and zooming out to explore interconnections and bundling between several practices, practice theories tie together the various routines, activities, discourses, materials and practices of the social.

In all of its eclecticism, the current volume does not contribute to the solidifying of *a* practice theory, nor it is motivated by a wish to sanction specific concepts, epistemologies or philosophies of science. Rather, it offers a selection of analytical tools and empirical examples, which we hope will inspire others to explore practice-based approaches to tourism. We acknowledge the philosophical differences and traditions informing the different strands of practice theories but support Nicolini's (2012) suggestion to draw pragmatically on different approaches to make sense of the nexus of practices in which we live our lives.

This combination of approaches is apparent in many of the contributions to this volume. Chapters 6 and 9 both use Nicolini's tactics of zooming in and out to explore practices, the latter chapter also exploring in more depth Schatzki's (2002) rules, materials and teleo-affective structures. Chapters 4, 7 and 9 draw inspiration from the conceptual framework of Shove, Pantzar and Watson (2012), in which social practices are made up of three central elements: materials, competences and meanings. Chapter 2 draws on the concepts of recruitment, career and defection from Shove and Pantzar (2007). Chapter 10 uses the Communities of Practice approach (Lave and Wenger, 1991; Wenger, 1998) to analyse learning in tourism, while Chapter 3 draws on Reckwitz's work as a way to engage anew with the practice of walking. Chapter 5 draws on Henri Lefebvre and his concept of rhythmanalysis (Lefebvre 1984, 2004) to disclose responsible or environmentally sensitive practices in nature tourism.

Theories of practice in tourism

Practice theories have exercised considerable influence across the social sciences, in particular within research fields such as organisational studies (Schatzki, 2005; see also Feldman and Orlikowski, 2011) and consumption studies (Warde, 2005). In recent years tourism research inspired by practice theories has gained in prominence, although it is still a relatively small body of work (Rantala, 2010; Valtonen and Veijola, 2011; Cohen et al. 2011; Bertella, 2012; Rantala et al., 2011; James and Halkier, 2016; Bispo 2016; Lamers et al., 2017). Within tourism studies the concept of practice has been used to explore tourism as a cultural practice, often focusing on individual practices of tourism as consumption (Crouch, 2004; Minca, 2007; Rantala, 2010). In this sense the notion of practice as a marker of social distinction (Bourdieu, 1984) has been influential. Other researchers, such as Bertella (2012), have used the concept of 'communities of practice' to explore processes of learning and innovation in tourism industries. Valtonen and Veijola (2011: 182) argue that a practice-based approach allows an analysis of 'the complex and collective human and non-human materialities and arrangements' that are involved in tourism. Practice-oriented studies have explored a variety of tourism-related activities such as practices of sleeping (Valtonen and Veijola, 2011), air-travel (Cohen et al., 2011), wilderness guiding (Rantala et al., 2011) and polar expedition cruising (Lamers et al., 2017; Lamers and Pashkevich, 2018). Recently the role of practices in the production, as well as consumption, of tourist experiences has been explored (James and Halkier, 2016).

As argued by Jonas Larsen (Chapter 4 in this book), the slow uptake of practice-based approaches in tourism studies is perhaps not surprising as practice theories are concerned with routinised activities, and tourism was long conceptualised as the very opposite of routines (see Larsen 2008), an exotic escape from the humdrum of ordinary life dominated by work and family. However, as tourism researchers – and practitioners – are becoming increasingly aware, everyday life and tourism often and progressively overlap and intertwine. One reason to apply practice theories in the study of tourism is therefore their ability to illuminate the connections between the everyday and tourism through the creation and adaptation of the routines. As many of the chapters in this book demonstrate, tourism is a composite phenomenon that includes connections, relationships and 'doing and sayings' (Nicolini, 2012) that might be conventionally defined as outside of tourism 'proper'.

An analysis of these connections reveals the ways in which tourism is enacted in combination with many other 'non-touristic' practices. As is also shown in Chapter 5, where Rantala adds nature as a relevant component to the analysis of nature holidays, practice theories incorporate material objects, technologies and infrastructures as important and co-constitutive in social life. This understanding aligns in some respects with actor-network theory inspired tourism studies (see Van der Duim et al., 2012) and its symmetrical approach to humans and non-humans broadens our understanding of what constitutes tourism and who is involved in its making.

A third reason for practice theories being particularly promising for the study of tourism is their ability to illuminate processes of change. In the article *Learning to be a Tourist*, Orvar Löfgren (1994), for example, explores the 'becoming' of the tourist as a process of learning and relearning. In his historical analysis of a Swedish seaside resort, Löfgren shows how different kinds of holiday life and outlooks are produced in shifting social and historical conditions, thus conceptualising tourism as a situated cultural competence and practice. This points towards mutual practice-based learning being a crucial link between aspects of tourism – for example, consumption and production of experiences – that have been treated separately in much of the existing literature.

A situated approach challenges traditional models of learning and the creation of tourism-related knowledge. In Chapter 6, for example, we see how restaurant cooking is learnt not only through schooling or text books, but through the body and the senses. As illustrated in Chapter 11, where the concept of Community of Practice is used to explore learning processes in tourism, that learning is always collective, context-dependent and ongoing. While existing approaches in for example marketing and political science often polarise differences between different ways of encouraging development of tourist destinations, Chapter 7 demonstrates the links as well as the fragilities in the destination development practice bundle.

Lastly, but strongly connected to the previous point, research inspired by practice theories such as that of Shove and collaborators (Shove and Pantzar, 2005) have been central to the development of new tools to understand innovation in tourism. As illustrated by Chapters 8 and 9 in this book, innovation is not a straightforward rationalist endeavour, nor one driven by singular entrepreneurs. It is a meticulous, iterative and taxing endeavour with a specific historical trajectory and it includes the bundling of many different practices and the careful composition of various materials, competences and meanings. By displaying links – or the lack thereof – between related practices, a practice-based analysis of innovations such as the destination pass or Smart Tourism has the potential to inform policies on matters such as innovation, but also, as seen in Chapters 2 and 7, sustainability and destination governance.

Overview of the book

In the following, we introduce and shortly describe the individual contributions to the book, which is divided into 11 chapters. This first chapter introduces practice theory as an approach to the study of tourism and sets the other chapters in context.

The next three chapters concern practices of movement in tourism. In Chapter 2, Christian Fuentes and Anette Svingstedt examine the concept of slow travel, so far a marginal and small-scale phenomenon in tourism. Using the concepts of *recruitment, career* and *defection*, the authors explore how 'carriers' of slow tourism become enlisted into slow tourism as a practice, how they develop in their slow travels and how they might, temporarily or permanently, defect from this particular practice. As argued by the authors, a practice approach enables us to explore sustainable travel behaviour beyond the choices of individual consumers, to see slow travel as a learning process and also to understand slow travel as closely related to – and challenged by – networks of hypermobility.

In Chapter 3, Kevin Hannam and Alexandra Witte explore an often taken for granted and 'individual' practice, namely walking. They first discuss the theorisation of practices of walking in tourism and leisure contexts and go on to develop the conceptualisation of walking as a specific social practice. Examining the complex historical relationships between walking and tourism, they draw on an example of emerging recreational and touristic walking in China to show how so-called 'donkey friends' make walking the centre point of their tourism practices. As the case shows, this social practice is enabled through the bundling of walking and internet practices through which a walking community is constructed. The authors conclude that theories of practice can help us understand how walking as a social practice is dependent on various cultural and historical environments and contexts. Their study shows how individuals and communities draw on specific configurations of recreational walking practices – such as hiking – in order to make sense of their engagement with different leisure and tourism environments.

In Chapter 4, Jonas Larsen uses a practice-based approach to analyse running and running events, which allows him to decentre the study of running away from individual runners and on to the things, events, experts and discourses that enable practices of running. His contribution draws on interviews with runners participating in the Berlin Marathon and Etape Bornholm. Larsen asks how running can be understood as a differentiated practice. He is interested in what makes running so attractive to so many practitioners and how practices of running connect with practices of tourism. As his study shows, practice theory illuminates the ways in which everyday running practices are connected with occasional running events elsewhere.

Outi Rantala has long researched how tourists experience nature (Rantala, 2010; Rantala et al., 2011). In Chapter 5, she uses a rhythmanalytical examination of familiar tourism practices to explore how these are linked to the emergence of environmental sensitiveness. Like Fuentes and Svingsted, Hannam and Witte, and Larsen (Chapters 2, 3 and 4), she is interested in how tourists develop the skills and sensitivity for specific ways of living in the world, as they learn to 'practice' in a particular space and situation as part of their holidaying. In her contribution, Rantala also extends the suggestion that tourism only exists because other 'non-touristic' actors perform certain roles in their natural lives. Highlighting the role of non-human actors, she draws attention to the dynamics between mobile performative humans and the more-than-human world.

In Chapter 6, Marcelo de Souza Bispo, Lídia Cunha Soares and Erica Dayane Chaves Cavalcante explore cooking as practice through a study conducted in two Brazilian restaurant kitchens specialised in regional cuisine. Drawing on Strati's concept of organisational aesthetics, the authors show how the senses and aesthetic judgement are decisive for 'the doing' of cooking as a social practice in tourism and hospitality. Cooking is enabled through sensible knowledge as an outcome of hands, eyes, ears, smell, palate and aesthetic judgement performing together.

In Chapter 7, Henrik James and Laura Halkier use Shove et al.'s (2012) conceptualisation of practices as bundles of materials, competences and meanings to explore the evolution of tourism development practices in coastal tourism destinations in Denmark. Their chapter shows that variation in the combination of these practice elements helps to explain shifts in the dynamics of tourism development in different destinations. They also argue that the iterative accomplishment of practice creates path dependent trajectories, which can make it difficult to change tourism policy practices.

Chapters 8 and 9 deploy practice theories as a way to shed new light on technological innovations in tourism. In Chapter 8, Timo Derriks, René van der Duim and Karin Peters offer a genealogical account of a destination card as a technological innovation. Making use of insights from practice theory, the authors examine the 'bundling of practices' of the Zeelandpas card in the Netherlands, conceptualising this as a practice-material arrangement. By historically following the destination card actors and their actions, the authors identified four different periods in the bundling of practices. During these four periods, the development of the destination card combined, connected and reshuffled practices of destination branding, conducting market research and facilitating public transportation. The case illustrates that the bundling of practices with different meanings, clear end goals and intentions, or, as termed by Schatzki (2005), a common teleo-affective structure, is a far from smooth endeavour. It requires the development of practical and general understandings and clear rules. The case illustrates how the study of techno-logical innovation can benefit by connecting its practices to other areas of the social.

Similar conclusions can be drawn from Chapter 9, in which Carina Ren, Morten Krogh Petersen and Tanja Nielsen present ongoing attempts to foster Smart Tourism at a regional level in Denmark. While Smart Tourism is often described as a smooth digital evolution, going from 'less' to 'more' Smart, the authors make use of the work of Elizabeth Shove and collaborators to show how Smart Tourism practices are often also about other things. Drawing on fieldwork with tourism practitioners, they describe how Smart Tourism is a socio-technical phenomenon in which seemingly mundane and 'non-digital' issues are central. As the authors show, the development of Smart Tourism must necessarily be linked and integrated into everyday organisational prac-tices. A practice approach helps shed light on why the full potential of this new phenomenon has been difficult to realise even though the idea of Smart Tourism is embraced by almost all of the stakeholders in the area.

Chapter 10 explicitly addresses how learning takes place in tourism amongst various practitioners. Using the Communities of Practice (CoP) fra-mework, authors Giovanna Bertella, Cristina Santini and Alessio Cavicchi draw on a case of student-practitioner collaboration to better understand, describe and discuss learning in tourism. Combining CoP with the concept of location-based learning (LBL) they investigate how a learning destination emerges through collaboration between individuals and organisations from the tourism, civic and education sectors. As the authors show, the CoP fra-mework is helpful in both designing the event as well as evaluating it, thus drawing attention to how tending to practice can offer insights on how to improve current ways of managing, developing, teaching about and engaging into tourism.

In Chapter 11 we reflect on the openings and opportunities for practice-based approaches in tourism studies. It is our hope that the collection of chapters in this book will create a solid starting point for researchers and students who wish to learn about and try out practice theories in the field of tourism studies. We wish you all the best on your journey!

References

Bargeman, B., Richards, G. and Govers, E. (2016). Volunteer tourism impacts in Ghana: a practice approach. *Current Issues in Tourism*, 1–16.

Bertella, G. (2012). *A study about knowledge and learning in small-scale tourism in rural and peripheral areas*. Tromsø: University of Tromsø, Department of Sociology, Political Science and Community Planning.

Bispo, M. de S. (2016). Tourism as practice. *Annals of Tourism Research*, 61, 170–179.

Bourdieu, P. (1984). *Distinction: A Social Critique of the Judgement of Taste.* Cam- 33 bridge, MA: Harvard University Press.

Bourdieu, P. (2013). *Distinction. A social critique of judgement of taste.* London: Routledge.

Cohen, S. A., Higham, J. E. and Cavaliere, C. T. (2011). Binge flying: behavioural addiction and climate change. *Annals of Tourism Research*, 38(3), 1070–1089.

Crouch, D. (2004). Tourist practices and performances. In A. Lew, M. Hall and A. Williams (eds), *Companion of Tourism Geography.* Oxford: Blackwell.

Feldman, M. S. and Orlikowski, W. J. (2011). Theorizing practice and practicing theory. *Organization Science*, 22(5), 1240–1253.

Giddens, A. (1984). *The constitution of society: outline of the theory of structuration.* Berkeley: University of California Press.

James, L. and Halkier, H. (2016). Regional development platforms and related variety: Exploring the changing practices of food tourism in North Jutland, Denmark. *European Urban and Regional Studies*, 23(4), 831–847.

Lamers, M. and Pashkevich, A. (2018). Short-circuiting cruise tourism practices along the Russian Barents Sea coast? The case of Arkhangelsk. *Current Issues in Tourism*, 21(4), 440–454.

Lamers, M. and van der Duim, R. (2016). Connecting practices: conservation tourism partnerships in Kenya. In G. Spaargaren, D. Weenink and M. Lamers (eds), *Practice theory and research. Exploring the dynamics of social life.* London: Routledge.

Lamers, M., van der Duim, R. and Spaargaren, G. (2017). The relevance of practice theories for tourism research. *Annals of Tourism Research*, 62, 54–63.

Larsen, J. (2008). De-exoticizing tourist travel: everyday life and sociality on the move. *Leisure Studies*, 27(1), 21–34.

Lave, J. and Wenger, E. (1991). *Situated learning: legitimate peripheral participation.* Cambridge: Cambridge University Press.

Lefebvre, H. (1984). *Everyday life in the modern world.* New Brunswick: Transaction Publishers.

Lefebvre, H. (2004). *Rhythmanalysis. Space, time and everyday life.* London: Continuum.

Löfgren, O. (1994). Learning to be a tourist. *Ethnologia Scandinavica*, 24, 102–125.

Minca, C. (2007). The tourist landscape paradox. *Social and Cultural Geography*, 8, 433–453.

Nicolini, D. (2012). *Practice theory, work, and organization: an introduction.* Oxford: Oxford University Press.

Rantala, O. (2010). Tourist practices in the forest. *Annals of Tourism Research*, 37(1), 249–264.

Rantala, O., Valtonen, A. and Markuksela, V. (2011). Materializing tourist weather: ethnography on weather-wise wilderness guiding practices. *Journal of Material Culture*, 16(3), 285–300.

Reckwitz, A. (2002). Toward a theory of social practices: a development in culturalist theorizing. *European Journal of Social Theory*, 5(2), 243–263.

Schatzki, T. R. (2002). *The site of the social. A philosophical account of the constitution of social life and change.* Philadelphia: Penn State University Press.

Schatzki, T. R. (2005). Peripheral vision: the sites of organizations. *Organization Studies*, 26(3), 465–484.

Schatzki, T. R. (2016). Practice theory as flat ontology. In G. Spaargaren, D. Weenink and M. Lamers (eds), *Practice theory and research. Exploring the dynamics of social life* (pp. 28–42). London: Routledge.

Schatzki, T. R., Knorr-Cetina, K. and Savigny, E. V. (eds) (2001). *The practice turn in contemporary theory*. London: Routledge.

Shove, E. and Pantzar, M. (2005). Consumers, producers and practices: understanding the invention and reinvention of Nordic walking. *Journal of Consumer Culture*, 5(1), 43–64.

Shove, E. and Pantzar, M. (2007). Recruitment and reproduction: the careers of digital photography and floorball. *Human Affairs*, 17(2), 154–167.

Shove, E., Pantzar, M. and Watson, M. (2012). *The dynamics of social practice: everyday life and how it changes*. London: Sage.

Spaargaren, G., Lamers, M. and Weenink, D. (2016). Introduction: using practice theory to research social life. In G. Spaargaren, D. Weenink and M. Lamers (eds), *Practice theory and research. Exploring the dynamics of social life* (pp. 3–27). London: Routledge.

Valtonen, A. and Veijola, S. (2011). Sleep in tourism. *Annals of Tourism Research*, 38 (1), 175–192.

Van der Duim, R., Ren, C. and Jóhannesson, G. T. (eds) (2012). *Actor-network theory and tourism: ordering, materiality and multiplicity*. London: Routledge.

Warde, A. (2005). Consumption and theories of practice. *Journal of Consumer Culture*, 5(2), 131–153.

Wenger, E. (1998). *Communities of practice. Learning, meaning, and identity*. Cambridge, MA: Cambridge University Press.

2 The practice of slow travel

Understanding practitioners' recruitment, career and defection

Christian Fuentes and Anette Svingstedt

Introduction

Contemporary tourism practices have multiple and important negative effects on the environment, such as the overexploitation of natural resources and waste production (Verbeek and Mommaas, 2008). However, none of these is as important as the mobility component. Transportation accounts for as much as 90% of the environmental impact of tourism (Gössling, 2000). Many trips are also made by air. In the EU, more than half of outbound tourist trips (53.8%) are by air.[1] The general trend towards long-haul trips for shorter periods of time and the increase in air travel that has ensued are devastating for the environment (Verbeek and Mommaas, 2008).

Slow travel – a form of travel that rejects transportation by air and car in favour of slower and often more sustainable forms of travel – has developed as a way of addressing the many sustainability problems associated with contemporary tourism practices (Dickinson et al., 2011; Dickinson and Lumsdon, 2010). Slow travel is often characterised as a form of low carbon consumption that puts an emphasis on the travel experience, making travel a major part of the tourism experience rather than just a means of reaching a destination (Dickinson et al., 2011). Inspired by the slow food movement (see, e.g., Bommel and Spicer, 2011; Sassatelli and Davolio, 2010), slow travel is also a way of challenging mainstream tourism consumption. It is, at least in some cases, a way of politicising unsustainable forms of travel and engaging in a form of sustainable tourism (Dickinson and Lumsdon, 2010).

However, while the promoters of slow travel put much faith in this alternative tourism practice, it remains a marginal phenomenon. How can this be changed? How can the practice of slow travel spread? Or is it, despite the efforts of its proponents, bound to remain a small-scale phenomenon?

In this chapter, we try to answer these questions by drawing on a set of ethnographic interviews with slow travellers and by making use of the Practice Theory concepts of *recruitment, career* and *defection* (Shove and Pantzar, 2007). More specifically, our aim in this chapter is to explore how new 'carriers' are enlisted into the practice of slow travel, how these develop as practitioners over time and what (if anything) makes them defect from this practice (temporarily or permanently) as a means of understanding how slow travel, as a practice entity, is reproduced and spread.

Our analysis is based on a combination of ethnographic interviews, marketing and information material, and secondary data. We have conducted four interviews with self-identified slow travellers, read travel blogs on slow travelling, and collected and analysed marketing and information material on slow travel from a range of on- and off-line sources (webpages, travel guides, brochures). These materials are used in combination to produce a tentative analysis of the broader discourse of slow travel and how this emerging practice is performed and develops.

We do not intend to offer an exhaustive analysis of slow travel as a practice. What we present in this chapter is very much an exploratory exercise. Practice theory has only recently been acknowledged as a potentially fruitful framework for understanding tourism (Lamers et al., 2017; Bispo, 2016). Our primary ambition is to contribute to this emerging discussion by examining and evaluating the usefulness of the practice theory approach, and in particular the concepts of recruitment, career and defection, when analysing sustainable tourism practices such as slow travel. Additionally, this chapter can be read as an illustration and to some extent development of these concepts of recruitment, career and defection.

The rest of the chapter is arranged in three sections. We begin by developing our practice theory approach and by discussing and contextualising the concepts of recruitment, career and defection. Then follows the main part of the chapter – an analysis of slow travel – in which we take a closer look at slow travellers' recruitment, career and defection. The chapter ends with a discussion of the specific emergence and dynamics of the practice of slow travel and the fruitfulness of using practice theory to analyse the emergence and spread of alternative tourism practices.

Recruitment, career and defection in practice theory

In this chapter, we treat slow travel as a practice. That is, we argue that slow travel can be understood as a way of travelling that consists of a specific set of doings and sayings and involves a specific configuration of materials, competencies and meanings (Shove et al., 2012; Shove and Pantzar, 2005). Slow travel is a tourism practice (Lamers et al. 2017), but it is also a specific type of mobility practice (Hui, 2012). However, our objective is not mainly showing that slow travel is a practice or exploring the specific set of meanings, competencies and materials involved in stabilising and reproducing this tourism practice, although this is certainly an interesting and important task. Our goal here is to explore how this practice can be expanded and developed by examining how slow travellers are recruited, how their careers and practitioners evolve and if, how and why they will defect from this practice. This leads us to focus on three somewhat underdeveloped practice theory concepts – recruitment, career and defection (Shove and Pantzar, 2007) – and to also take into account the importance of time, a dimension of social practices that is often mentioned but seldom made part of the analysis (Shove et al., 2009).

For a practice to develop and survive, it has to *recruit* practitioners (Shove and Pantzar, 2007). That is, a practice has to capture and retain the interest of practitioners. This is equally true for novel sustainability practices, e.g. slow travel, as it is for mundane and established practices, e.g. brushing your teeth or playing soccer. Without these crucial carriers of practice, the practice cannot be performed and will consequently die out. There is, then, a dynamic relationship between practices and practitioners (Shove and Pantzar, 2007). One could say that practices and practitioners co-produce each other. Practices capture practitioners. However, practices are in turn defined by participation. This links with the well-known distinction between practice-as-entity and practice-as-performance introduced by Schatzki (2001). As Shove and Pantzar point out 'practices exist as sets of norms, conventions, ways of doings, know-how and requisite material'; as such, they exist as entities that 'potential participants can join or withdraw from' (Shove and Pantzar, 2007: 155). However, for these entities to exist, they have to be performed repeatedly, the links between these elements have to be remade on a continual basis. Agency and structure influence each other in reciprocal ways (Lamers et al., 2017).

This relationship is not, of course, static; practitioners and practices co-evolve. Being part of a practice changes a practitioner. This is well known across the social sciences and has been discussed extensively within consumption studies. As scholars such as Bourdieu (1984) and Giddens (1997), to take two of the better-known examples, have so convincingly shown, partaking in certain (consumption) practices changes how you perceive yourself, but also how you are perceived by others.

Beyond identity construction, the participants in a practice also develop as practitioners. One can speak of having a *career* as a practitioner in which one typically goes from novice to full-fledged competent practitioner. For example, the practice of climbing is learned over time and, as practitioners engage in this practice, they develop their skillsets. But they can also change their interest. Careers, one could argue, are not one-dimensional linear processes. There are various possible trajectories, routes that practitioners can take as they engage in and become part of a specific practice.

Practitioners also perform a practice differently (Warde 2005). This has been shown in studies of digital photography (Shove et al., 2007), floorball (Shove and Pantzar, 2007), shopping (Fuentes, 2014; Fuentes and Svingstedt, 2017) and expeditions cruises (Lamers et al. 2017), to name just a few examples. This difference can be related to the careers of practitioners. As practitioners accumulate competence, individually and collectively, they change as practitioners, eventually performing the practice differently (Shove and Pantzar, 2007). This is the other side of the coin. As practitioners develop, accumulate competence and develop skills, the practice can change. For example, in the case of floorball discussed by Shove and Pantzar (2007), the professionalisation of that sport was greatly linked to the development of key practitioners who sought to become more skilful as players.

These differences can be linked to the practitioner's particular background or disposition, i.e. linked to what these carriers of practices take with them as they become recruited into a practice. As a result, practices potentially change as a result of the development of active practitioners, but they can also change as new recruits, with different backgrounds, experiences and interests, become engaged in the practice. The same can be said about *defection*. The defection of certain practitioners means that a practice potentially changes as these carriers and their specific sets of backgrounds, dispositions and competencies are no longer active in the reproduction of the practice.

The fact that practitioners perform practices differently can also lead to the co-existence of different version of the same practice, either in the same or in different locations. Shove and Pantzar (2007), for example, show how floorball exists simultaneously as a stable, professionalised and institutionalised practice in Scandinavia and as a fragile and provisional practice in parts of the UK where it is has recently been introduced. Here, different practitioners in different locations perform the same practice – playing floorball – in radically different ways. These differences are at least in part related to the recruitment, career and defection of the practitioners involved. Recruitment, career and defection are thus all involved in defining the contours of a practice, and these parallel processes are undoubtedly linked to changes in how practices are reproduced (or not).

Crucial to understanding the reproduction and spread of slow travel is the issue of time. As the discussion above has already indicated, time is key to practices in general and to slow travel in particular. From a practice theory perspective, tourism practices, like all practices, are carried out at specific times and in parts of certain temporal structures. Seasonal cycles (both natural and commercial) are, for example, crucial to the tourism industry. Tourism practices, however, are also involved in the performance of multiple other temporalities. Tourism practices are often performed in order to break with certain temporal routines, but also have, paradoxically, their own routines. Paraphrasing Shove and colleagues (2009), tourism, broadly defined as a bundle of various practices, constitutes the field of social life in which temporal texture is configured and reproduced. Simply put, tourism practices not only happen in time, they also produce time, time experiences and temporal texture. As we will see below, in the case of slow travel, the production of specific temporality is key to both the practice and the tourism experience.

To conclude, to understand the processes and mechanisms involved in the reproduction and potential expansion of the practice of slow travel, we must examine how and why practitioners are attracted to this practice, how they perform it and how it performs them, and if and how these practitioners abandon the practice. Furthermore, in doing this, we must be sensitive to the multiple elements involved in the practice of slow travel and its specific spatial-temporal texture. The following analysis is an initial tentative attempt to accomplish this.

The emergence and performance of slow travel

In what follows, we examine how and under what circumstances practitioners are recruited into the practice of slow travel, how the careers of slow travellers develop, as well as if, and under what conditions, defections from the practice occur. Before embarking on this discussion, we will examine how the practice of slow travel is represented in the media. This offers us an introduction to how the practice of slow travel is commonly framed in the discourse before delving into the specific performances of the practice.

Representations of slow travel: scripts for a new mobility practice

Multiple representations of the practice of slow travel can be found on travel sites and in tourism guides and lifestyle magazines. Although these media frame slow travel in slightly different ways, there is still a surprising degree of homogeneity in the representations. The image that emerges through these accounts is one of slow travel as a new and complex type of tourism practice. While slow travel, as we mentioned in the introduction, is often framed as a sustainable mode of travel, it is also often described as much more than that. Slow travel is often framed as an antidote to 'tourist burnout'. It is seen as a way of counteracting the fast-paced travel that has emerged in contemporary society. In accounts of slow travel, sustainability, a respect for local destinations and a more relaxed and contemplative mode of travelling and experiencing destinations is interwoven:

> Slow travel is not so much a particular mode of transportation as it is a mindset. Rather than attempting to squeeze as many sights or cities as possible into each trip, the slow traveler takes the time to explore each destination thoroughly and to experience the local culture.[2]

Many of these representations, to be found in news articles or travel magazines, are clearly intended to be used as manuals for slow travel. They describe slow travel, explaining the meanings attached to this practice and also giving practical tips on how to 'go slow'. The ideal slow travel experience often includes taking a slow form of transportation – e.g. train, bicycle, boat or just walking – to your destination. It also involves a specific way of feeling or experiencing your travels. As a proper slow traveller, you have to enjoy the *experience of travelling*, actually making it a major part of your tourism experience and not merely a way of reaching your destination:

> The journey becomes a moment to relax, rather than it being a stressful interlude between home and destination. Of course slow travel is much more than just that. It is a whole way of looking at the world. Slow

travellers explore communities along the way, dawdle and pause as the mood takes them and check out spots recommended by the locals. Slow travel is downbeat, eco-friendly and above all fun.[3]

As this quote illustrates, slow travel is much more than just taking a slow mode of transportation. It is, in the words of its advocates, a 'mindset', a 'state of mind' or 'a whole way of looking at the world'. Slow travel, as it is depicted in these media, involves performing a specific set of activities and feeling certain things during the process. Drawing on the vocabulary of Practice Theory, it can be depicted as a routinised set of 'doings and sayings' guided and shaped by a specific teleoaffective structure, that is 'a range of normativised and hierarchically ordered ends, projects and tasks, to varying degrees allied with normativised emotions and even moods' (Schatzki, 2002: 80). In these representations, it becomes very clear that a slow traveller does not hurry from destination to destination, instead spending longer periods of time in one place, taking his/her time, and getting to know the local culture. This often involves connecting with people (taking the time to get to know the locals takes centre stage in many accounts of slow travel) and engaging in slow activities such as slow eating (ideally with locals and using local ingredients), enjoying art and/or just taking part in local communal life. What is important here is taking one's time, escaping the hectic life, adopting another pace and connecting with the local culture. The assumption here is that local culture is the same as slow culture, the 'other' is constructed here as a slower and more genuine local. This assumption echoes early anthropological analyses of 'the primitive', as a slow 'other' (Shove et al., 2009), albeit ascribed with more positive connotations in this context. The fact that multiple temporalities co-exist in communities and societies (Shove et al., 2009) is ignored here as the tourist's life at home is characterised as fast-paced and the local culture or community being visited is presented as slow.

As the above discussion shows, there are multiple representations of slow travel in circulation. These representations frame slow travel in similar ways and are designed to function as scripts for the practice. These representations are not, then, mere descriptions, but also attempts at stabilising this emergent practice. They are intended to promote the practice of slow travel and to function as a manual that potential practitioners can use when performing this specific form of mobility practice.

Tourism practices, like other practices, involve specific knowledge and know-how (Bispo, 2016). In addition, tourism practices, like other practices, also have to have a meaning or a purpose; there needs to be a reason for their performance (Lamers et al., 2017). The slow travel scripts discussed above are attempts at circulating these resources. They offer potential practitioners an image of how this practice is performed and they also ascribe certain meanings to it. More specifically, these representations of slow travel are devised to recruit new practitioners and to allow them to develop their practice careers. One can then ask: do these representations in circulation recruit slow travellers and do slow travellers follow these scripts?

The recruitment of slow travellers

Although not always familiar with the term slow travel, our informants all engaged in a 'slow' form of travel anyway. Some time ago, they had shifted their mode of travel in search of an alternative and more sustainable travel practice in which planes and cars were avoided in favour of slower forms of transportation such as going by bike, train, boat or on foot. It thus became clear that slow travel, to our informants, was a more sustainable form of travel. While the practice of slow travel was only occasionally primarily framed as a sustainability practice in the media representations in circulation, for our informants, it was primarily a more *sustainable* form of travel.

How, then, were these slow travellers recruited? When asked about how they got involved in slow travel, our informants responded in various ways. For the most part, it was clear that enrolment into the practice was not primarily motivated by the quest for a different type of slow-paced experience (although this was often the result of participating in the practice), but by an interest in finding more sustainable methods of travel. For some, enrolment into the practice of slow travel happened as far back as during childhood; they had been brought up with slow travel as their family norm:

> It was my mum who was extremely interested in a sustainable lifestyle. So we had no car most of the time when I was small … all our journeys were by train. And that this was an argument. Nope, we're not having a car. We're going by train as it's much better for the environment. And our holidays, then we went by train. And a bit later, there were biking holidays. And in that way, I'd probably say that there was a lot of that stuff that I grew up with … Yes, that was really what I had drummed into me. I feel that it's probably right to think like that. That's probably why I myself wouldn't want to book a flight. I've never flown with my family, with my mum for instance. We've never sat on a plane together.
>
> (Matilda)

Here, we see how both train travel and biking are framed as examples of slow travel. Also, a clear position against the car and air travel becomes important when positioning this practice.

In this and other cases, recruitment happens at an early age and the practitioners merely continue with this practice into adulthood. The motive underlying the practice and the necessary competence are taught by a parent, or another adult, and intertwined with family making.

Recruitment can also result from participating in a specific event:

> In 2009, there was this climate conference in Copenhagen and there was a group of us, I mean it was us, just while studying in Lund at that time.

There was a group of us interested in climate issues. There was one of us in particular who'd previously been involved in environmental conferences earlier on. Before this climate conference in Copenhagen. So he got hold of us and said: Yes, let's do this. And he knew some more people, sort of. And that was the start, well I became a lot more involved in climate issues specifically right then and there ...

Then I got quite involved in climate issues and realised that flying pollutes quite a lot, you see it creates quite a lot of emissions. And as it's something which to some extent, I mean to a rather large extent, can be avoided when you travel.

(Jacob)

In this case recruitment into slow travel (avoiding air travel or opting for the train instead) happens as the result of participating in a climate conference. While the context of family is not important here, the social context is. Participating in the conference was a social group activity. In fact, he was recruited by a friend, a member of the group of friends: someone who was already knowledgeable in environmental issues and who also had contacts that he shared with the group. Participating in the conference became, in fact, the recruiting activity and involvement with slow travel followed on as a result of this.

There were also other instances of recruitment in which environmental issues were marginal:

And I have a very clear image there and it's 1982. When the wife's lad asked, at the age of 10, what we'd be doing on holiday. Then he said, quite happily, like a 10-year-old: Can't we go biking on our holiday. And then, as an adult, you get put on the spot and you say, well I suppose so. And that's why I feel that it's typical things like that. Health arguments or something, children or something else that push it as a kind of challenge. And I don't believe that it's about environmental arguments initially.

(Lars)

Although not important for the initial recruitment of this practitioner, environmental issues became important later on, as a result of engaging in slow travel. As we will discuss in the next section, the meanings attached to the practice of slow travel are not static, changing as practitioners' careers develop but also as the practice itself changes over time.

What we can conclude from these examples is that recruitment can happen in a variety of ways and is often intertwined with another practice or set of practices, e.g. family-making practices and conference participation. It is also clear that various motives can push consumers into becoming engaged in a practice. One cannot assume, therefore, that all the practitioners were recruited for the same reason. Nor can one assume, as we will discuss in more detail below, that the reasons for engaging remain the same over time.

The careers of slow travellers

How do the practitioners of slow travel develop over time and how do their careers change the way that the practice is reproduced? Talking to our informants, it was clear that they had different careers as slow travellers and that these careers were not necessarily linear. Over time, participation in the practice of slow travel leads to the accumulation of knowledge and the development of a new set of skills. Lars, for example, talks about finding new options and 'thinking outside the box':

> And then, once I'd reduced that, as I mentioned, after 2000–2001. I decided that it's wrong to fly and this also means, of course, that you look for other ways. You see, you start thinking outside the box.
>
> (Lars)

Informants learned about the various existing alternatives to flying or taking the car, they learned about how and where to travel when looking for a 'slower' experience, and they learned about the negative consequences of fast travel. Our informants acquired this knowledge by engaging in slow travel, but also through their involvement with other related practices:

> In between, I've been active in the climate movement and understood the consequences of flying very well. And known how much carbon dioxide it creates in terms of emissions and how many degrees are dangerous and lead to a tipping point. So I've still, maybe between the age of 25 and 30, been very active there and perhaps also for social, perhaps [in] my social context I was actually a person who knew the consequences of flying or travelling in some particular way and ... Which makes it difficult to compromise.
>
> (Matilda)

The career of a slow traveller practitioner, then, is not only determined by his/her engagement in slow travel practice. Engagement in other related practices can also feed into and develop him/her as a practitioner.

However, the careers of slow travellers not only involve knowledge accumulation. Becoming a slow traveller also means rethinking the selection of a destination. While many 'regular' travellers choose their destinations according to current trends, personal history or finances, slow travellers have to take distance into account. It becomes a matter of finding a feasible destination, one that can be reached by train, boat or bike. This means re-evaluating destinations according to proximity criteria:

> My preference is to choose to go somewhere that's not especially far away. And to try to find destinations that ... there are so many that you ... you see Europe is really large. So I primarily choose somewhere, if I'm going on

holiday, so I try to find somewhere close by. It's my initial starting point when choosing a destination.

(Jacob)

In the course of developing as a slow traveller, Jacob learns to revalue destinations that are close by. While most of his peers have moved towards finding increasingly far-away and exotic travel destinations as part of their careers as tourists and travellers, Jacob is moving in the opposite direction and rediscovering Europe, which is 'really large' and offers multiple potential travel destinations that do not require air travel.

In other cases, it is not destinations that are being re-evaluated but the mode of transportation:

I think taking the train is a very comfortable way of travelling. You sit down, you can look out the window. You can nod off. You can read a book. It's a very, how can I put it, it's a very relaxing way of travelling. It's not at all as stressful as flying, I feel. The experience I have when flying, you have to get to the airport and that takes a long time, most of the time it takes at least an hour to get there, then you have to be there an hour in advance, and then you have to wait there. Then you also have to check in and your luggage, then there's the security checks you have to go through. And doing that doesn't always feel terribly pleasant. Then, when you're inside the plane, you sit there feeling cramped. When you get there, it takes a long time to get to where you're going, and all that stuff. So compare that with the train, even if it takes slightly longer.

(Jacob)

Here, Jacob learns to re-evaluate a mode of transportation and to travel at a different pace. What constitutes an appropriate travel time is here re-negotiated. Just as with the destination, the 'realisation' that taking the train is preferable to fast-paced air travel (and other forms of speedy mobility) is something that has developed through prolonged engagement with the practice, through repeated performance.

Finally, we also find that developing as a practitioner of slow travel has a lot to do with developing the appropriate emotional approach. It is about developing the right 'state of mind'. It is, in other words, about internalising and reproducing the teleoaffective structure of the practice and being able to get into a specific mood, to be able to access and reproduce the 'range of normativised and hierarchically ordered ends, projects and tasks, to varying degrees allied with normativised emotions and even moods' (Schatzki 2002: 80) connected with the practice of slow travel. The slow travellers we talked to all reported this development. So, while many of them initially became involved in slow travel because of its sustainability dimension, they also developed a specific way of experiencing travel as a result of the repeated performance of the practice:

Things also differ slightly as regards what the experience is composed of. For example, it can be fun to go by train and not take a book with you and to wait and see who ends up beside you. And it's not so unusual in Germany that people are prepared to tell you a lot about where they're going and which grandchildren they'll be meeting on the train. So in that way, it can be interesting to choose a method of transporting yourself that is not so focused and has a lot of downtime. And the fact that this downtime can lead to interesting experiences, or when I undertook that extremely long journey from Sweden to Scotland by train and everything. So I had a lot of time in Amsterdam. So I'm sitting there in Amsterdam. But what do you do in Amsterdam? You sit down in some café, or pub, and take a look around you, but what's on the menu? Well, maybe you should check this out and then I discovered, oh look, there's a cat. Yes well, cats in the café. Not so common in Sweden to find cats there. But that's what they had there.

(Matilda)

Here, Matilda talks about enacting a version of slow travel that is very much in line with the media representation we reviewed above. Slow travel is framed here as a way of connecting with people and experiencing local culture. The slowness of the travel is argued to lead to unexpected and unusual experiences.

In summary, the informants discovered that slow travel offered them new experiences. They valued the social interactions that occurred while traveling by train, bike, canoe or boat. They started interacting both with their travel companions and with strangers. These slow travellers experienced new things that, they argued, would not have happened if they had been travelling by plane or car, modes which are characterised by a different 'temporal texture' (Shove et al. 2009). Unexpected things happened during slow travel and this was highly appreciated: a small concert at a guesthouse, reading aloud on a canoe trip and chatting with a diplomat from Nigeria. Our informants compared their experiences with ordinary ways of being a tourist, e.g. travelling by plane, going to museums and seeing the sights, concluding that slow travel gives rise to more unexpected events.

In performing these activities, they also develop as slow travel practitioners. Drawing on our interviews, we argue that the career of a slow traveller involves three interrelated processes: i.e. the accumulation of knowledge, the re-evaluation of destinations and transportation modes, and the development of a specific way of feeling, what you could call a slow travel mood. Consequently, even though becoming a competent slow traveller means developing knowledge of the effects of air travel, of how to book trains when travelling across Europe or of how to find reasonable long-term accommodation at a specific destination, it also involves learning to re-evaluate travel and developing a slow travel mood. This is something that happens as the practice of slow travel is performed; in fact, this kind of knowledge, competence and emotion can only be developed in practice.

Temporary defection among slow travellers

The informants in our sample are all actively involved in slow travel. Nevertheless, they do not always take the slow route to a destination. We call these *temporary defections*: instances where our informants, who are otherwise committed to slow travel, feel they have to abandon this mode of travel. These temporary defections seem to be brought about by situations that our informants perceive to be unavoidable:

> Privately, I have also rejected flying, but I've actually had to give in on some occasions. On one occasion, we went to Thailand. Ok, are we going there by train? Not possible, is it? We've flown to that kind of destination, of course.
>
> (Harald)

Here, a family vacation to a destination popular with Swedes – Thailand – is the reason for this temporary defection. Compromises have to be made when family vacations are planned, informants argue. In other cases, it is a work scenario that prompts the defection:

> You see, there's a certain limit, at least for me, in any case now that I've started working. You don't really have as much time to do things. I've been living in London for the past 2 years and when I've gone to visit my parents, I've flown home. As I've experienced how long it takes, it takes a bit too long, kind of thing, to go all the way to Uppsala from London.
>
> (Jacob)

Here, we see that Jacob, an otherwise avid slow traveller, makes an exception for visiting his parents. His work scenario means that he lives far away from his family, but also that his time is very limited. These conditions lead to him temporarily defecting from slow travel when making his annual visit to his parents in Uppsala. However, as the discussion continues, it becomes evident that there can also be other reasons that explain why Jacob defects from the practice of slow travel. He also makes exceptions when visiting destinations that have a particular meaning to him:

> Yes I know, in 2015 I went on holiday to Japan. And I'd been studying Japanese for 3 years and I hadn't been there since 2008. I'd wanted to go there again to see how things had changed, you see I'd been living in Japan for a year. So it has a special place in my heart somehow. And it has, despite the fact that it was something great, kind of thing, something I'd looked forward to, it was still sort of, well it takes a long time to get there and it was sort of something you really treat yourself to. But it's not something that I'd choose to do annually, or something that I, well it sort of is something, it's a special thing to do.
>
> (Jacob)

As these examples show, various circumstances can lead up to the (temporary) defection. In all these cases, our slow travel practitioners were re-recruited into practices of hypermobility (Hall, 2010). In this case air travel enabled these practitioners to perform desirable practices that could not be accomplished through slow travel. More specifically, air travel offered them a practical way of going on holiday with their families, of visiting parents or of travelling to meaningful locations. Although seemingly banal, this is important to keep in mind. It is safe to assume that very few people travel by plane because they like flying. Instead, air travel is a means to other ends, i.e. performing specific practices and pursuing specific life projects. This means that, if you aim to develop more sustainable and slower alternatives to hypermobility in general, and to flying in particular, you will have to reconfigure not just flying but also all the practices and life projects connected with flying, a daunting task for any actor.

Discussion and conclusions

As we stated in our introduction, we wanted to show the applicability and usefulness of a practice theory approach, and of the concepts of recruitment, career and defection, in trying to understand the emerging sustainable tourism practice of slow travel. Lamers et al. (2017) argue that practice theory is particularly useful in that it allows us to gain an understanding of novel tourism practices, innovative practices that can lead to more sustainable outcomes. In this chapter, we have tried to illustrate the usefulness of a practice theory approach while also paying particular attention to the temporal dimension when investigating emergent sustainable tourism practices like slow travel.

Understanding the reproduction of the practice of slow travel

What does this practice theory analysis show us? What we have offered is a tentative analysis of the alternative tourism practice of slow travel. Slow travel, as we have shown, is a complex practice that consists of a specific set of doings and sayings, draws on and reproduces a set of competencies, meanings and materials, and produces and is part of a specific spatial-temporal texture.

Our informants performed and reproduced slow travel as a sustainable alternative to mainstream hypermobile tourism. This analysis suggests that, although emergent and embryotic, the practice of slow travel has a distinct shape. It involved getting to a destination by train, boat, bike or on foot, and then spending some time there engaging with the locals. Slow travel was often enacted by informants as a more social form of travel which both produced and formed part of a particular temporal texture; you spent more time with your travelling companions or with people you met along the way. It was also positioned as a less planned form of travel, capable of producing unexpected experiences in a way that regular and highly planned hypermobile tourism cannot.

Accomplishing this form of tourism required a different set of competencies, but also the development of a specific way of feeling. As slow travellers develop as practitioners, they accumulate knowledge of alternative modes of transportation (train and boat routes, hiking and biking trails), destinations to visit (nature destinations or urban sites nearby) and the equipment needed to perform this alternative tourism practice (e.g. a book and sleeping bag when taking night trains across Europe).

Slow travel is performed in contrast to what is perceived as mainstream tourism: fast-paced, highly planned and frenzied sightseeing trips to faraway destinations to which tourists travel by plane or car. In contrast to mainstream tourism, slow travel follows a different temporal logic and involves a different set of doings and sayings. It also requires a different set of competencies, and the cultivation of a specific way of feeling.

How, then, does this specific tourism practice expand and develop? What stands in its way and threatens its existence? The material collected suggests that new slow traveller practitioners are recruited in different ways and during different points in their lives. That is, recruitment into slow travel can happen in multiple ways. While some are socialised into slow travel from an early age, others are recruited later on in life, for example by participating in a specific event or through family members. Key to the recruitment of our informants was the sustainability dimension of slow travel. Recruitment can happen in a variety of ways and is often intertwined with another practice or set of practices, e.g. family-making practices and conference participation. Various motives can push consumers into becoming engaged in a practice, but not all practitioners are recruited for the same reason.

In addition, the reasons for engaging in a practice are not static, instead changing over time. The meaning of a practice is constantly evolving, both as a result of practitioners developing careers but also because the practice itself is in continuous motion (on the changing nature of everyday practices see for example, Shove et al., 2012). In this case, it was clear that the meanings consumer ascribed to slow travel changed over time, and as consumers engaged in the practice. While sustainability issues initially motivated our informants into taking up this practice, the actual performance of the practice generated new meanings, with practitioners developing a distinct way of doing and feeling while travelling. In this sustainable consumption practice, as in so many others, being and feeling good are interlinked (Fuentes, 2015; Soper, 2007), thus creating a powerful mixture. For our informants, slow travel often began as an altruistic form of ethical consumption, in order to address the environmental problems associated with air travel. However, assisted perhaps by the circulating representations of slow travel, it developed over time to *also* become a pleasurable tourism practice.

This also illustrates, to some extent, the dynamic relationship between practitioners, their performance of practices and the practice as an entity. The trajectories that slow travel takes are, at least in part, 'ready made by past experience and partly shaped by the integrative efforts' of eco-travellers

(Shove and Pantzar, 2007: 158). By framing and enacting slow travel as a *sustainable* tourism practice, and not merely as a different kind of travel experience, our informants are not only reproducing but are also reconfiguring slow travel as a practice entity. However, it also becomes clear that, as slow travellers perform the practice (repeatedly), they are also being produced by the practice's teleoaffective structure. They learn to understand, experience and feel slow travel in a practice-specific way.

The apparent stability of slow travel does not mean that the practice of slow travel is immune to defections. Although committed to this form of travel, slow travellers are not entirely loyal. Slow practitioners do defect, albeit only temporarily in our sample. The practice of slow travel exists in a dialectical relationship with established practices of hypermobility and tourism. It has emerged as an alternative to these, and thus depends on this antagonistic positioning in order to become meaningful; however, it is also under constant threat from these practices. In our sample, it was clear that when practitioners did defect from slow travel, it was because of the attraction of hypermobility. More specifically, air travel enabled practitioners to perform other desirable practices and to accomplish other projects – e.g. going on a family holiday to Thailand, visiting parents or going 'back' to a particularly meaningful destination already visited.

In experimenting with the practice of slow travel, these practitioners are also defining new pathways, opening up possibilities as regards to how travel can be done. It is challenging, however, as the interviews show, to carve out a new way of performing tourism in a landscape that is clearly designed and organised for hypermobility.

On the dispersion of the practice of slow travel

Our analysis, although tentative, provides some novel insights into how slow travel can be promoted as a sustainable tourism practice. Firstly, rather than merely explaining participation in slow travel as a matter of having the right attitudes or values, we explore the array of circumstances and mechanisms involved in enlisting consumers into these practices. This means that information campaigns aimed at informing sustainably minded tourists about slow travel or changing the attitudes of non-sustainable tourists should not be the sole focus. Recruitment can happen in multiple ways, and slow travellers can be recruited for various reasons. There is therefore no reason to restrict efforts to information campaigns. Instead, actors interested in the promotion of slow tourism should work towards identifying various events and practices where slow travel can be appropriately promoted. Examples can include conferences, family events and more traditional arenas such as travel sites and catalogues. The results also indicate that actors interested in promoting slow travel should work towards framing this alternative form of tourism in multiple ways. It can, for example, be promoted as a sustainability practice and a form of ethical consumption, but also as an alternative type of experience.

This analysis also points to the importance of a supporting socio-material infrastructure. Supporting the practice of slow travel are representations of slow travel and mobility infrastructures – e.g. railway and boat routes and trekking trails. While information can form an important piece of the puzzle, it cannot be the sole focus of policy or marketing campaigns that promote slow travel. Tourism practices – such as slow travel – are complex entities. Like other everyday practices, they exist in a nexus of practices and are supported by multiple technologies, conventions and discourses (Hand et al., 2005; Shove et al., 2012). Therefore, policies and marketing efforts designed to change travel behaviour by focusing on a single aspect – e.g. information – are likely to fail (for a similar argument see Lamers et al., 2017; Sahakian and Wilhite, 2014). Policy should also direct its attention elsewhere and examine, for example, the infrastructures enabling different types of mobilities.

Furthermore, this analysis also suggests that the promotion of slow travel is linked to the discouraging of hypermobility. As long as hypermobile practices remain widespread, they will pose an impediment and a threat to slow travel and other alternative forms of tourism. Because of this, it is important to work towards the reduction of hypermobility if the aim is to promote slow travel. This can encompass problematising hypermobility and working towards dismantling the vast socio-technical infrastructure that enables these forms of travel. De-marketing campaigns, legislation and taxation aimed at reducing the prominence of hypermobility and unsustainable tourism can all be important measures. Of course, reducing hypermobility can be both controversial and difficult. It essentially entails changing the temporal texture of everyday life – a difficult task to say the least.

Contributing to the emergence of practice approaches in tourism

To conclude, we contend that this analysis contributes to tourism research in two ways. Firstly, it is a contribution to the emerging field of practice-based tourism research. As is made clear in the introduction to this anthology, practice theory approaches have been scarce in the field of tourism studies (Bispo, 2016; Lamers et al., 2017). While practice theory has gained popularity in neighbouring fields, e.g. consumption studies (Shove and Pantzar, 2005; Warde, 2005; Röpke, 2009), organisation studies (Corvellec, 2010; Corradi et al., 2010; Miettinen et al., 2009) and marketing (Schau et al., 2009; Fuentes, 2015; Skålén and Hackley, 2011), the use of practice theory in tourism research has remained limited. This is surprising given the strong sociological tradition within tourism studies and its close connection with management studies where practice theory has attracted considerable attention. It is also surprising given the inroads made into tourism studies by similar and connected theoretical frameworks, most notably performativity, mobility (Sheller and Urry, 2006; Hall, 2005) and actor-network theory (Franklin, 2004; Valkonen, 2010).

Practice theory, it has been argued, can contribute to the study of tourism by allowing in-depth analysis of tourism consumption, enabling the understanding of change in tourism and bringing to the fore the embeddedness of tourism practices within broader complexes of practices (Lamers et al., 2017). In this chapter, we have tried to realise some of the potential of practice theory by offering some insights into how the practice of slow travel is performed and how it reproduces as practitioners are recruited, develop their practice careers and also (temporarily) defect from the practice. We have argued that slow travel, like other tourism practices, is to be understood as a dynamic practice, which is not static but changes over time. Taking temporality into account is crucial when it comes to understanding the dynamic nature of tourism practices and understanding how tourism practices are reproduced and expand.

Secondly, our tentative analysis of the practice of slow travel is also intended to be a contribution to the field of sustainable tourism. It has been argued that even though the (un)sustainability of tourism mobility is a well-researched area, it has also had a tendency to focus either on structural technological/economic issues or actors' attitudes (Verbeek and Mommaas, 2008). Largely missing from this body of work are analyses of 'holiday practices where individual and structural characteristics come together in context-specific ways' (Verbeek and Mommaas, 2008: 634).

Our approach and analysis can be viewed as an alternative to these two established research approaches. Although practice theory analysis considers the role that technological and economic structure play in the emergence and establishment of social practices, it does not focus solely on these issues. On the other hand, taking a practice theory approach also means moving beyond individuals and their attitudes and making social practices the unit of analysis instead. More specifically, the analysis conducted here indicates that engagement in a sustainable tourism practice, in this case slow travel, is not necessarily the result of consumers having a ready-made attitude, or set of values, which they then express by partaking in the practice. Rather, many are recruited into the practice first and then develop the meanings appropriate to that practice through repeated participation. The meanings of sustainable tourism practices are thus emergent and changing.

Notes

1 http://ec.europa.eu/eurostat/statistics-explained/index.php/Tourism_statistics_-_cha racteristics_of_tourism_trips#Air_travel_main_means_of_transport_for_over_half_ of_all_outbound_trips
2 www.independenttraveler.com/travel-tips/none/the-art-of-slow-travel
3 www.slowtraveleurope.eu

References

Bispo, M. d. S. (2016). Tourism as practice. *Annals of Tourism Research*, 61, 170–179.
Bommel, K. v. and Spicer, A. (2011). Hail the snail: hegemonic struggles in the slow food movement. *Organization Studies*, 32:12, 1717–1744.
Bourdieu, P. (1984). *Distinction – A Social Critique of the Judgement of Taste*. Cambridge, Massachusetts: Harvard University Press.

Corradi, G., Gherardi, S. and Verzelloni, L. (2010). Through the practice lens: where is the bandwagon of practice-based studies heading? *Management Learning*, 41:3, 265–283.

Corvellec, H. (2010). Organizational risk as it derives from what managers value: a practice-based approach. *Journal of Contingencies and Crisis Management*, 18:3, 145–154.

Dickinson, J. and Lumsdon, L. (2010). *Slow Travel and Tourism*. London – Washington, DC: Earthscan.

Dickinson, J. E., Lumsdon, L. M. and Robbins, D. (2011). Slow travel: issues for tourism and climate change. *Journal of Sustainable Tourism*, 19:3, 281–300.

Franklin, A. (2004). Tourism as an ordering. *Tourist Studies*, 4:3, 277–301.

Fuentes, C. (2014). Managing green complexities: consumers' strategies and techniques for greener shopping. *International Journal of Consumer Studies*, 38:5, 485–492.

Fuentes, C. (2015). How green marketing works: practices, materialities and images. *Scandinavian Journal of Management*, 31:2, 192–205.

Fuentes, C. and Svingstedt, A. (2017). Mobile phones and the practice of shopping: a study of how young adults use smartphones to shop. *Journal of Retailing and Consumer Services*, 38:3, 137–146.

Giddens, A. (1997). *Modernitet och självidentitet – Självet och samhället i den senmoderna epoken*. Göteborg: Daidalos.

Gössling, S. (2000). Sustainable tourism development in developing countries: some aspects of energy use. *Journal of Sustainable Tourism*, 8:5, 410–425.

Hall, C. M. (2005). Reconsidering the geography of tourism and contemporary mobility. *Geographical Research*, 43:2, 125–139.

Hall, C. M. (2010). Crisis events in tourism: subjects of crisis in tourism. *Current Issues In Tourism*, 13:5, 401–417.

Hand, M., Shove, E. and Southerton, D. (2005). Explaining showering: a discussion of the material, conventional and temporal dimension of practice. *Social Research Online*, 10:2.

Hui, A. (2012). Things in motion, things in practices: how mobile practice networks facilitate the travel and use of leisure objects. *Journal of Consumer Culture*, 12:2, 195–2015.

Lamers, M., Duim, R. v. d. and Spaargaren, G. (2017). The relevance of practice theories for tourism research. *Annals of Tourism Research*, 62, 54–63.

Miettinen, R., Samra-Fredricks, D. and Yanew, D. (2009). Re-turn to practice: an introductory essay. *Organization Studies*, 30:12, 1309–1327.

Röpke, I. (2009). Theories of practice – new inspiration for ecological economic studies on consumption. *Ecological Economics*, 68, 2490–2497.

Sahakian, M. and Wilhite, H. (2014). Making practice theory practicable: towards more sustainable forms of consumption. *Journal of Consumer Culture*, 14:1, 25–44.

Sassatelli, R. and Davolio, F. (2010). Consumption, pleasure and politics: slow food and the politico-aesthetic problematizations of food. *Journal of Consumer Culture*, 10:2, 202–232.

Schatzki, T. R. (2002). *The Site of the Social: A Philosophical Account of the Constitution of Social Life and Change*. Philadelphia: The Pennsylvania State University Press.

Schatzki, T. R., Cetina, K. K. and Savigny, E. v. (2001). *The Practice Turn in Contemporary Theory*. London and New York: Routledge.

Schau, H. J., Muñiz, A. M. and Arnould, E. J. (2009). How brand community practices create value. *Journal of Marketing*, 73:5, 30–51.

Sheller, M. and Urry, J. (2006). The new mobilities paradigm. *Environment and Planning A*, 38:2, 207–226.

Shove, E. and Pantzar, M. (2005). Consumers, producers and practices – understanding the invention and reinvention of Nordic walking. *Journal of Consumer Culture*, 5:1, 43–64.

Shove, E. and Pantzar, M. (2007). Recruitment and reproduction: the careers of digital photography and floorball. *Human Affairs*, 17:2, 154–167.

Shove, E., Pantzar, M. and Watson, M. (2012). *The Dynamics of Social Practice: Everyday Life and How It Changes*. Los Angeles – London – New Delhi: Sage.

Shove, E., Trentmann, F. and Wilk, R. (2009). *Time, Consumption and Everyday Life: Practice, Materiality and Culture*. Oxford – New York: Berg.

Shove, E., Watson, M., Hand, M. and Ingram, J. (2007). *The Design of Everyday Life*. Oxford – New York: Berg.

Skålén, P. and Hackley, C. (2011). Marketing-as-practice. Introduction to the special issue. *Scandinavian Journal of Management*, 27:2, 189–195.

Soper, K. (2007). Re-thinking the 'Good Life' – the citizenship dimension of consumer disaffection with consumerism. *Journal of Consumer Culture*, 7:2, 205–229.

Valkonen, J. (2010). Acting in nature: service events and agency in wilderness guiding. *Tourist Studies*, 9:2, 164–180.

Verbeek, D. and Mommaas, H. (2008). Transitions to sustainable tourism mobility: the social practices approach. *Journal of Sustainable Tourism*, 16:6, 629–644.

Warde, A. (2005). Consumption and theories of practice. *Journal of Consumer Culture*, 5:2, 131–153.

3 Theorising practices of walking in tourism

Kevin Hannam and Alexandra Witte

Introduction

Walking is an everyday, largely taken-for-granted individual practice that is undertaken by able-bodied people: we get out of bed and we walk. We walk around the home, we go outside and we encounter other people who may also be walking: "Not only, then, do we walk because we are social beings, we are also social beings because we walk" (Ingold and Vergunst 2008, 2). These encounters lead us to consider that we may walk with others who we may or may not know and that practices of walking become sociable and, indeed, habitual: walking to work or walking for leisure with friends or people we do not know. In this sense walking becomes routinised but also something we can change in different contexts. A change in the weather may mean we walk less and use alternative means of transport instead. If it is dark and late at night we may also walk less if we feel afraid and are not in a social group, although walking late at night on an Edinburgh ghost tour could be quite sociable if occasionally scary.

Walking may also be imbued with restrictions of a physical, social, cultural and political nature. For example, in different countries there may be constraints on where and when a person can walk such as curfews on walking at night. Seemingly public spaces, including beaches, may in fact be private, thus subject to the owner's discretion who may and who may not walk these spaces. At times particular social discourses may restrict parts of the population in their walking practices. We may for example talk about gendered spaces in which frequently women are seen as the more vulnerable targets and thus can feel restricted in their choices of when and where to walk. In turn walking can be a form of contesting existing power relationships – it can become the medium for social protest, as illustrated for example by 'Take back the Night' walks in protest of sexual violence (see Kretschmer and Barber, 2016). Walking as a form of non-violent protest has also frequently been invoked as a form of political intervention in colonial struggles as well as contemporary geopolitics. Indeed, more recently, walking became utilised as a geopolitical practice when the migrants and asylum seekers left Keleti railway station in Hungary in 2016 and walked along motorways in attempt to reach Germany (Hannam, 2017).

Although de Certeau (1984) showed walking as a potentially emancipatory project, this reflects a degree of romanticism about the everyday walker. Instead, walking is subject to many constraints and interventions – from other forms of technology, transport and, indeed, frequently other people (Middleton, 2011). In tourism we can point to the job of the tour guide (Hall and Smith, 2013), who is himself the directed (e.g. by employers, place, tourists' preferences) and director of movement, literally guiding tourists' walking in and through places in the co-production of scripted performances (Widtfeldt Meged, 2010; Diekmann and Hannam, 2012).

This chapter discusses the theorisation of practices of walking in tourism and leisure contexts. We begin by examining the theorisation of practices in the context of the mobilities turn in social science (Adey et al., 2013) and further develop the conceptualisation of walking as a specific social practice. We go on to examine the complex relationships between walking and tourism using an example from China. We conclude that practice theories can help us understand not just how people walk but how walking as a social practice may also lead to changes in how different cultures engage with various environments and contexts.

Theorising practices

Practice theories have been developed to avoid the structure-agency dualism that has been much discussed in contemporary social science (Giddens, 1984; Warde, 2014). The concept of practice has been foregrounded by mobilities researchers in terms of the ways in which we can understand the relations between the mobile structures of societies and individuals on the move through the different frictions of various environments (Cresswell, 2013). Much of this contemporary work has been developed within what has become known as the mobilities paradigm or turn within social science (Sheller and Urry, 2004; Hannam et al., 2006) but also within studies of consumer culture (Warde, 2014). In the latter context, Alan Warde (2005, 131) discusses the need to examine: 'the way wants emanate from practices, of the processes whereby practices emerge, develop and change, of the consequences of extensive personal involvements in many practices, and of the manner of recruitment to practices'.

He argues that we need to distinguish between practice and practices, citing Reckwitz (2002, 249):

> Practice (Praxis) in the singular represents merely an emphatic term to describe the whole of human action (in contrast to 'theory' and mere thinking). 'Practices' in the sense of the theory of social practices, however, is something else. A 'practice' (Praktik) is a routinised type of behaviour which consists of several elements, interconnected to one another: forms of bodily activities, forms of mental activities, 'things' and their use, a background knowledge in the form of understanding, know-how, states of emotion and motivational knowledge.

Hence we are interested in this context in the latter – routines of behaviour, bodily activities, habits, emotions and what has been termed 'lay' or everyday knowledge (Crouch and Desforges, 2003).

We are also, however, interested in the connections between what people may say and what they actually do, thus the interplay between discourses and practices, and the power and knowledge fields beneath them. The concept of performativity is significant here as it involves theorising language and movement (Hannam and Knox, 2010). Performativity is an attempt to develop "a more embodied way of rethinking the relationships between determining social structures and personal agency" (Nash, 2000, 654). It is about "practices, mundane everyday practices, that shape the conduct of human beings toward others and themselves at particular sites" and seeks to appreciate the ways in which ordinary people develop "the skills and knowledges they get from being embodied beings" (Thrift, 1997, 126–127). Drawing upon Thrift's work, Nash, meanwhile, argues that the notion of performativity:

> is concerned with practices through which we become 'subjects' decentred, affective, but embodied, relational, expressive and involved with others and objects in a world continually in process ... The emphasis is on practices that cannot adequately be spoken of, that words cannot capture, that texts cannot convey – on forms of experience and movement that are not only or never cognitive.
>
> (Nash, 2000, 655)

A crucial component of conceptualising performativity is attending to the agency of other people, non-human beings, materialities and mobilities. With the performative turn, attention to embodiment as well as agency expands inquiries to include relations of power between the actors involved. The notion of performativity is thus concerned with the ways in which people know the world without necessarily knowing it. As Peter Adey (2009, 149) notes:

> [t]his is an approach which is not limited to representational thinking and feeling, but a different sort of thinking-feeling altogether. It is a recognition that everyday mobilities such as walking or dancing involve various combinations of thought, action, feeling and articulation.

Whilst one specific practice involves many combinations of thoughts, actions and emotions, we also need to understand how specific practices of movement are themselves combined or 'bundled' together in complex, interdependent, integrated and systematic ways in the organisation of daily life. People combine different practices such as driving, walking and cycling depending upon their locations and activities such as being at home, at work or in the playground. Moreover, these practices are frequently shared socially either physically or virtually. Watson (2012, 491) has argued that "a practice approach to understanding personal mobility has clear resonances with insights from the activity-based approach to travel demand analysis". Travel demand analysis shows how people have to negotiate time and space in order to manage their days. Thus, walking as a personal form of mobility involves various time-space rhythms, which are fundamentally embodied cultural dispositions that are continually being re-performed. As we shall see below, walking may even be timetabled with specific durations, tempos, paces, steps and routes but is always negotiated in and through specific terrains, landscapes and environments leading to improvisations in walking practices and performances (Edensor, 2013).

Theorising touristic walking practices

Walking is a bodily pursuit that involves taking steps in an environment which become unconsciously produced and regular, i.e. rhythmic. In Bourdieu's (1977) concept of habitus cultural dispositions are acquired through unconscious bodily practices, "like a train bringing along its own rails" (Bourdieu, 1977, 79). Bourdieu's habitus, however, tends to underplay the potential of individuals as reflective, thinking and emotional actors who may change their practices.

Merleau-Ponty (1962) theorised the embodiment of human practices as an existential pre-objective relationship between the body and the world surrounding it (Williams and Brendelow, 1998). His understanding of the body is that of a body-subject that grounds our awareness of self and action within it. As Carman (1999, 208) states in his critical analysis of Merleau-Ponty's work: "we understand ourselves not as having but as being bodies." The body in Merleau-Ponty's perspective is more than simply a bearer of sensations and a means for the reproduction of culture and instead "our general means of having a world" (Carman, 1999, 214), one that is constantly integrating new experiences of being in the world.

Within what he calls "body schema" we are owners of a set of skills that anticipate and adapt to our surroundings even before we form thoughts or apply known concepts consciously or unconsciously. These skill sets or body schemata are "not a product but a condition for cognition". As Merleau-Ponty (1962, 70) points out his body "is my point of view on the world" and because the body, from this vantage point, is seen to work towards tasks, it has to be dynamic and adaptable (see also Crang, 2001).

Contemporary researchers from a mobilities perspective argue that our moving bodies are exploring and experiencing the world dynamically on multiple levels through movements and thus dynamically unfolding in performances of the moving body as representative and generative, reflexive and habitual (Edensor, 2008, 2013). Walking as a form of human practice in movement must then be seen as more than habitual but as a quintessentially social practice that carries with it the potential for reflexivity. As Ingold and Vergunst (2008, 2) argue:

Amidst the clamour of calls to understand the body as an existential ground for the production of cultural form, rather than only as a source of physical and metaphorical means for its expression ... we tend to forget that the body itself is grounded in movement.

Ingold and Vergunst conceptualise human body movement and not just the body at the heart of social action as a productive causal power that is grounded in corporeal materiality connecting us to the physical and cultural world. Thus: "[w]alking is not just what a body does, it is what a body is" (Ingold and Vergunst, 2008, 2).

Where social theory previously seemed to be focused on a more or less static body, contemporary researchers understand the body as a moving agent that is exploring, performing and experiencing a spatially and culturally organised world of meanings (Edensor, 2008; Farnell, 2012; see also Rantala as well as Larsen, Chapter 4 this volume). Human action utilises and generates a "variety of forms of embodied knowledge" that are "systemised in various ways and to various degrees involving cultural convention as well as creative performativity" (Farnell, 2012, 9). Hence we also need to pay attention to the historical and social framing of specific walking practices such as hiking and their representations through artists, writers and the media.

Walking, in both urban and rural settings, is thus practised in various contexts and conditioned by social expectations and cultural imaginaries as well as through many forms of regulations. It is "suffused with contending notions of how and where we walk, ideals and conventions" (Edensor, 2010, 69). These regulations come in the form of actual physical structures, e.g. fences barring the walker from walking through a field or private sites, in the form of external rhythms that incur adaptation of the body's own rhythms of movement, in the form of the lived social and cultural experiences that train the body to perform to particular conventions, or in the form of internalised social identities that are signalled and reformed through bodily movement. One may think about attempts at managing the walking experiences of tourists in national parks through waymarking and signs that warn or inform, thus implying "good" ways of walking. These formalised styles of walking communicate social, cultural and subjective meanings through rhythms and performances of walking (Edensor, 2000), bodily connecting the individual to social and cultural frameworks.

While there is no denying the existence of walking configurations and stylised practices that may be habitual and unconscious, the moving, walking body is at the same time beset by affect (Wylie, 2005). Walking in landscapes is not just a mechanical and smooth passing through (Edensor, 2013). Especially when it comes to long-distance walks, corporeal experiences of the body such as fatigue, muscle strain or blisters can at times heighten the awareness of one's own body as it walks. The natural setting can be such that it necessitates adaptation of walking performances that are new and thus felt on a more conscious level (Edensor, 2000). As Wylie (2005) describes, walking is a step-by-step engagement with one's surrounding bringing the walker often into close sensory contact with the affordances of place. It thus carries with it the potential for disruption, drawing an intense awareness and reflection about the way in which we move within our environment:

> Indeed, we might consider the stages and successive rhythms of a long walk where initial embarkation may feature sprightly gait, later on suc- ceeded by a more regular 'getting into one's rhythm' and culminate in exhaustion, sore feet and wobbly legs, inducing periods of rest before doggedly plodding ahead to journey's end. Moreover, terrain forces the body to intermittently leap, climb, and balance as streams and muddy patches are negotiated.
>
> (Edensor, 2010, 73)

When we walk, we walk to a certain rhythm, we adapt to the circumstances i. e. the affordances of place, objects and other people around us that we must negotiate and that at times interrupt and force to improvise (Edensor, 2010). Walking engages the haptic sense through the feet feeling and navigating the ground using the landscape as a "foothold" (Wylie, 2005, 239). The walker is in constant contact with the ground and the environment enfolding them through visual, tactile and sonorous sensing as well as the movement of the body itself, creating specific ways of walking and thus gazing at the sur- rounding landscape with their whole body (Wylie, 2005).

However, as Ingold and Vergunst (2008) pose, walking is a practice that moves beyond relations to purely external conditions and lets us experience a "world-in-formation" resonating with others' movements, thus rooting walk- ing in the social as well. People from different ethnic, social and economic backgrounds may develop different sensuous and embodied walking practices. Hiking and walking in nature is a well-established recreational and touristic practice in many Western countries such as Norway, Germany, USA or the UK with many cultural variants (Lorimer and Lund, 2003; Humberstone and Pedersen, 2001; Svarstad, 2010; Menzel et al., 2012; Ween and Abram, 2012). In the case study we present below, we discuss the development of touristic hiking practices in China in order to provide a nuanced example of how such walking practices may change over time leading to new valorisations of the environment as it is walked through.

Touristic walking practices in China

In many Western societies, walking and particularly hiking through nature has been a central part of historical and contemporary artistic responses to and interventions within the landscape since at least the eighteenth century (Gros, 2014). In the UK in the nineteenth century, romantic artists' portrayals of nature as a realm of the solitary and the spiritual became challenged by the presence of other leisure and tourism walkers such as the ramblers

(Macnaghten and Urry, 1998). The irony of this was that the practices and artistic productions of many Romantic writers and poets themselves became key inscriptions of new meanings of 'sublime' landscape and were distilled into the guide books of the emergent tourism industry (Urry, 1990). In this sense, we can see the emergence of one particular strand of Romantic practice – that of travel in sublime nature – being appropriated and transformed through cultural emulation and nascent consumer capitalism into a popular activity in the form of nature-based hiking tourism (Wallace, 1993).

Conversely, the consumption of nature in China in the nineteenth and twentieth centuries largely de-emphasised walking as a mode of engagement with nature (Li et al., 2017). Nature was largely seen as an instrument for human use rather than an aesthetic in its own right (Harris, 2006). Li et al. (2017) argue that walking in the Chinese context was largely seen as a goal-directed activity engaged in by the old and poor of health, rather than as a recreational choice. However, more recent research on the development of recreational and touristic walking in China has shown the contemporary emergence of a particular type of domestic Chinese tourist and recreationist, the so-called 'donkey friend', who makes walking the centre point of their tourism practices.

The Chinese donkey friend community can be seen as a product of increasing diversification in tourism and the widespread use of social media and online forums to connect with likeminded walkers (Chen and Weiler, 2014; Jocelyn and Sigley, 2014). Crucially, here we find that *internet practices* allow Chinese walking tourists to learn about *walking practices* (Witte and Hannam, 2017). In the Chinese online recreational walking sites, we find both similarities to and differences from its Western counterparts. On the one hand, the online Chinese donkey friend community is more oriented towards social togetherness and in-group hierarchies in their recreational walking practices than their Western counterparts (Chen and Weiler, 2014; Luo et al., 2014). This is exemplified in the use of specific terms for walkers of different skill levels within online walking communities. Such terms are earned through set challenges or the completion of a certain number of hikes affording the status of a particular animal such as a "mountain goat" or an "eagle" (Witte and Hannam, 2017). Status, in this case, is an accumulation of cultural capital through the completion of a series of structured walking practices.

The donkey friend community has been found to incorporate practices that draw upon Western Romanticised hiking practices, emphasising quests for nature and wilderness, as well as self-transformation through challenge (Jocelyn and Sigley, 2014). The emphasis on challenge, or, as Edensor calls it, a self-conceptualisation of recreational walking practices as "idealised Spartan Endeavours" (Edensor, 2000, 93), were also visible within an ongoing research project on walking tourism on the Ancient Tea Horse Road in southwestern China (Witte, 2018):

> In this case, self-identified 'donkey friends' frequently emphasised their practical experiences of challenge and physical hardship as central to

their touristic and recreational walking: Some donkey friends are really hardcore. They go hike up really wild mountains, really high ascents. That sounds really cool. I think at some point I want to do more mountain climbing too.

(Qiu, Yubeng-Ninong Trail, August 2016)

Here Qiu is emphasising that in order to add status to such practices they need to become more dangerous, difficult or 'hardcore'. Thus the difficulty of the walking practice confers cultural capital. Another respondent, Song, reflected on the possibility of doing long-distance hikes:

So, one of my friends, he is also part of our donkey group, he goes on long-distance hikes! He has been doing this kind of thing for years. I can learn a lot from him.

(Song, Yubeng-Ninong Trail, August 2016)

Here we see an understanding of walking practices emerging in China that resonates with the notion of walking as a practice that needs to be learnt.

This research also found that the very term 'donkey friend' appeared to serve as an active delineation of their individual touristic walking practices from 'normal' Chinese tourists, who were seen as group 'sightseers' who used technology to gain access to the mountains, as the following quotation from fieldwork suggested:

I think most [Chinese] tourists just go to famous mountains and just look at the views from the top. They take a cable car up and that's it. I've done that a few times when I'm with others but on my own, I would walk. I always feel otherwise it's just like sightseeing. It does not mean as much really. And sometimes actually the way is much more interesting than the views from the top.

(Xianmin, Xidang-Yubeng Trail, August 2016)

I think hiking is in the mountains. If it's just a field it's more like taking a stroll. There are many mountains in China. I've been to Emeishan, Huashan, Taishan and so on. I enjoyed the views from the top. But there were always so many people. Too many, I think. So, I prefer wild mountains without ticket barriers and cable cars and so on.

(Meiling, Shibao Mountain, July 2016)

These respondents emphasised that their walking practices became more meaningful when they were done on their own as individuals rather than as part of a social group. While being apparently inspired by Western understandings of walking practices such individuals also challenge the dominant Chinese discourse of nature that is traditionally anthropocentric, imperfect without human intervention and engaged primarily in a visual way e.g. by gazing at nature from a cable car (Harris, 2006; Li, 2008). Instead, similar to the Western hiking tradition, they draw upon a romanticisation of nature in seeking out embodied experiences of wilderness destinations 'off the beaten map':

> We do a lot of adventurous stuff. Go to places that are not really tourist places. Really unmanaged.
>
> (Dewei, Yubeng-Ninong Trail, August 2016)

Nevertheless, they also noted the need to incorporate technologies of walking into their practices of 'wild hiking':

> We really want to go to the Gaoligongshan Reserve because it's very remote. Tourists don't really go there but for me that would be a dream. When you just hike for several days without any official path to follow. Where you need to know how to read a map and use GPS and take your equipment with you. That is wild hiking.
>
> (Jiake, Nujiang Valley, August 2016)

Social media technologies are utilised to connect with each other and technologies, such as GPS, are used to enhance the engagement with wilderness. More significantly the symbolism of such specialised objects enable competent practice to be shown, demonstrated and learnt (see also Larsen, Chapter 4 this volume).

Chinese hiking communities challenge traditional Chinese attitudes towards nature as well as social conventions of community formation and hierarchies by showing little concern for the usual social ties such as family, work, geography or ethnicity which normally define their identities. Instead, they have increasingly developed a sense of 'individuality' within the overall online community identity that is based upon their individual practices of walking. Walking for leisure and tourism and the online clubs dedicated to these practices are a relatively new phenomenon in China. However, as Chinese tourism continues to develop, Chinese walking practices seem likely to continue to draw on existing Western discourses such as the anti-urban, especially those that valorise the physical and mental challenges of hiking, while also incorporating adaptations of traditional Chinese discourses which valorise particular forms of nature.

Conclusions

This chapter has discussed the theorisation of practices of walking in tourism and leisure contexts. Theorising walking practices in the context of the mobilities turn in social science emphasises both the embodied sense of walking as well as the social sense of walking in different environments.

Understanding walking as practice also opens up the possibility to understand how individuals and communities use specific configurations of recreational walking practices – such as hiking – in order to make sense of their engagement with different leisure and tourism environments.

However, examining walking as practice may also have significant policy and planning impacts as it reveals how such practices may also change in the context of different environments. Significantly for the development of more sustainable forms of tourism, Warde (2005, 140) has argued that: "The principal implication of a theory of practice is that the sources of changed behaviour lie in the development of practices themselves. The concept of practice inherently combines a capacity to account for both reproduction and innovation". Indeed, innovation has been shown through empirical studies of the transformation of specific Nordic walking practices (Pantzar and Shove, 2010).

In the Chinese case discussed above, walking as a recreational and touristic practice offers insights into the ongoing dynamics of the Chinese social and cultural context, drawing upon and adapting Western Romantic narratives of recreational hiking in nature whilst retaining more traditional Chinese perspectives on particular natural landscapes. Crucially, walking practices are learnt and, in the Chinese case, they are learnt through internet practices in online communities. Thus we see the combination of reproduction and innovation that Warde (2005, 2014) alludes to in that the sources of changes of behaviour lie in the practices themselves – in this case the combination or bundling of internet and walking practices.

References

Adey, P. (2009). *Mobility*. London: Routledge.

Adey, P., Bissell, D., Hannam, K., Merriman, P. and Sheller, M. (eds) (2013). *The Routledge Handbook of Mobilities*. London: Routledge.

Bourdieu, P. (1977). *Outline of a Theory of Practice*. Cambridge: Press Syndicate.

Carman, T. (1999). The body in Husserl and Merleau-Ponty. *Philosophical Topics*, 27 (2), 205–226.

Chen, H. and Weiler, B. (2014). Chinese Donkey Friends in Tibet: evidence from the cyberspace community. *Journal of China Tourism Research*, 10(4), 1–33.

Crang, M. (2001). Rhythms of the city: temporalized space and motion. In J. May and N. Thrift (eds), *Timespace: Geographies of Temporality*. London: Routledge, pp. 187–207.

Cresswell, T. (2013). Frictions. In P. Adey, D. Bissell, K. Hannam, P. Merriman and M. Sheller (eds), *The Routledge Handbook of Mobilities*. London: Routledge.

Crouch, D. and Desforges, L. (2003). The sensuous in the tourist encounter. *Tourist Studies*, 3(1), 5–22.

de Certeau, M. (1984). *The Practice of Everyday Life*. Berkeley: University of California Press.

Diekmann, A. and Hannam, K. (2012). Touristic mobilities in India's slum spaces. *Annals of Tourism Research*, 39(3), 1316–1336.

Edensor, T. (2000). Walking in the British countryside: reflexivity, embodied practices and ways to escape. *Body & Society*, 6(3–4), 81–106.

Edensor, T. (2008). Walking through ruins. In T. Ingold and J. Vergunst (eds), *Ways of Walking: Ethnography and Practice on Foot*. Aldershot: Ashgate.

Edensor, T. (2010). Walking in rhythms: place, regulation, style and the flow of experience. *Visual Studies*, 25(1), 69–79.

Edensor, T. (2013). Rhythm and arrhythmia. In P. Adey, D. Bissell, K. Hannam, P. Merriman and M. Sheller (eds), *The Routledge Handbook of Mobilities*. London: Routledge.

Farnell, B. (2012). *Dynamic Embodiment for Social Theory*. London: Routledge.

Giddens, A. (1984). *The Constitution of Society*. Cambridge: Polity.

Gros, F. (2014). *A Philosophy of Walking*. London: Verso.

Hall, T. and Smith, R. J. (2013). Stop and go: a field study of pedestrian practice, immobility and urban outreach work *Mobilities*, 8(2), 272–292.

Hannam, K. (2017). Tourism, mobilities and the geopolitics of erasure. In D. Hall (ed.), *Tourism and Geopolitics: Issues and Concepts from Central and Eastern Europe*. Wallingford: CABI, pp. 345–353.

Hannam, K. and Knox, D. (2010). *Understanding Tourism*. London: Sage.

Hannam, K., Sheller, M., and Urry, J. (2006). Editorial: Mobilities, immobilities and moorings. *Mobilities*, 1(1), 1–32.

Harris, P. (2006). Environmental perspectives and behavior in China. *Environment and Behavior*, 38(1), 5–21.

Humberstone, B. and Pedersen, K. (2001). Gender, class and outdoor traditions in the UK and Norway. *Sport, Education and Society*, 6(1), 23–33.

Ingold, T. and Vergunst, J. (eds) (2008). *Ways of Walking: Ethnography and Practice on Foot*. Aldershot: Ashgate.

Jocelyn, E. and Sigley, G. (2014). Walking the Ancient Tea Horse Road: the rise of the outdoors and China's first long distance branded hiking trail. *Journal of Tourism Consumption and Practice*, 6(1), 1–27.

Kretschmer, K. and Barber, K. (2016). Men at the march: feminist movement boundaries and men's participation in Take Back The Night and Slutwalk. *Mobilization: An International Quarterly*, 21(3), 283–300.

Li, F. (2008). Culture as a major determinant in tourism development of China. *Current Issues in Tourism*, 11(6), 492–513.

Li, P., Bin, Z. and Ryan, C. (2017). Hiking in China: a fuzzy model of satisfaction. *Tourism Management Perspectives*, 22, 90–97.

Lorimer, H. and Lund, K. (2003). Performing facts: finding a way over Scotland's mountains. *The Sociological Review*, 51(2), 130–144.

Luo, X., Huang, S. and Brown, G. (2014). Backpacking in China: a netnographic analysis of donkey friends' travel behaviour. *Journal of China Tourism Research*, 11(1), 1–18.

Macnaghten, P. and Urry, J. (1998). *Contested Natures*. London: Routledge.

Menzel, A., Dreyer, A. and Ratz, J. (2012). Trekking tourism as a special form of hiking tourism-classification and product design of tour operators in the German-speaking market. *Journal of Tourism*, 8(2), 23–46.

Merleau-Ponty, M. (1962). *Phenomenology of Perception*. Translated by C. Smith. London: Routledge & Kegan Paul.

Middleton, J. (2011). Walking in the city: the geographies of everyday pedestrian practices. *Geography Compass*, 5(2), 90–105.

Nash, C. (2000). Performativity in practice: some recent work in cultural geography. *Progress in Human Geography*, 24(4), 653–664.

Pantzar, M. and Shove, E. (2010). Understanding innovation in practice: a discussion of the production and re-production of Nordic Walking. *Technology Analysis & Strategic Management*, 22(4), 447–461.

Reckwitz, A. (2002). Toward a theory of social practices: a development in culturalist theorizing. *European Journal of Social Theory*, 5(2), 243–263.

Sheller, M. and Urry, J. (eds) (2004). *Tourism Mobilities: Places to Play, Places in Play*. London: Routledge.

Svarstad, H. (2010). Why hiking? Rationality and reflexivity within three categories of meaning construction. *Journal of Leisure Research*, 42(1), 91–110.

Thrift, N. (1997). The still point. In S. Pile and M. Keith (eds), *Geographies of Resistance*. London: Routledge, pp. 124–151.

Urry, J. (1990). *The Tourist Gaze: Leisure and Travel in Contemporary Societies*. London: Sage.

Wallace, A. (1993). *Walking, Literature and English Culture*. Oxford: Clarendon Press.

Warde, A. (2005). Consumption and theories of practice. *Journal of Consumer Culture*, 5(2), 131–153.

Warde, A. (2014). After taste: culture, consumption and theories of practice. *Journal of Consumer Culture*, 14(3), 279–303.

Watson, M. (2012). How theories of practice can inform transition to a decarbonised transport system. *Journal of Transport Geography*, 24, 488–496.

Ween, G. and Abram, S. (2012). The Norwegian Trekking Association: trekking as constituting the nation. *Landscape Research*, 37(2), 155–171.

Widtfeldt Meged, J. (2010). *The Guided Tour – A Co-produced Tourism Performance*. PhD Thesis. Roskilde University, Denmark.

Williams, S. J. and Brendelow, G. (1998). *The Lived Body: Sociological Themes, Embodied Issues*. London: Routledge.

Witte, A. (2018). *Walking Performances and Experiences on China's Ancient Tea Horse Road*. Unpublished doctoral thesis, Leeds Beckett University, Leeds, forthcoming.

Witte, A. and Hannam, K. (2017). A netnography of China's emerging hiking communities. In C. M. Hall, N. Shoval, and Y. Ram (eds), *The Routledge International Handbook of Walking*. London: Routledge.

Wylie, J. (2005). A single day's walking: narrating self and landscape on the South West Coast Path. *Transactions of the Institute of British Geographers*, 30(2), 234–247.

4 Running and tourism

A practice approach

Jonas Larsen

Introduction

Jogging is now *the* most popular form of sport in many Western societies (Cook, Shaw and Simpson, 2016; Latham, 2015). For instance, while a mere 2 per cent of adult Danes was running regularly in 1970s, the figure is now 35 per cent (Laub, 2011; Forsberg, 2012, 2014). In addition to such everyday running, there are many organised races at weekends. There are for instance almost 5,000 marathons around the world, and many of them attract huge numbers of international non-elite runners (and their supporting families) (Scheerder, Breedveld and Borgers, 2015). Half marathons and marathons are no longer considered extreme or the domain of the super-fit (although most joggers do not participate in races, let alone marathons); they attract very different types of people, of different ages, with different bodies and running biographies (Nettleton and Hardy, 2006; Scheerder, Breedweld and Borgers, 2015). This also indicates that running tied into leisure travel and running events has become part of the international staging of places for tourism consumption (McGehee, Yoon and Cárdenas, 2003; Shipway and Jones, 2007; Sheehan, 2006; Wicker, Hallmann and Zhang, 2012). It seems that more and more tourists are lacing up their running shoes and gazing upon the world while 'on the run' (Larsen, 2018b). Yet not much work has explored connections between tourism and running.

I will discuss how practice theory (in the work of leading contemporary practice scholars Andreas Reckwitz, Allan Warde, Elisabeth Shove and Sarah Pink) can help us to connect running and tourism and explain how, and why, what we might term 'running tourism' has boomed over the last two decades. It is perhaps no surprise that practice theory has not been much debated and employed by tourism scholars (but see Lamers, van der Duim and Spaargaren, 2017) given that practice theories are concerned with routinised activities, and tourism was long conceptualised as the very opposite of routines (Larsen, 2008). I will instead argue that practice theory and tourism studies can enrich each other, as everyday practices and tourism practices increasingly overlap. Tourism is no longer antithetical to routines and everyday life, as many seminal tourism texts argued, while everyday life is not as a-mobile and localised as assumed by much practice theory. Tourism scholars can move practice theory forward by discussing how modern everyday life is also performed on the move and away from home.

My focus will be on developing a practice approach to running and running events. So, my research question is three-fold: first, how can we understand running as a differentiated practice? Second, why does running now attract so many practitioners? Thirdly, how do practices of running connect with practices of tourism? I draw together marathons and tourism by discussing the literature on sport/running tourism and by briefly discussing my ongoing tourism research on the two running events: the Berlin Marathon and Etape Bornholm (for full accounts of this research, see Edensor and Larsen, 2017; Larsen, 2018c). At both races, I conducted short individual interviews and group interviews with runners (often in the company of their non-participating, non-sporty family). The interviews included questions about how and if they connect running and tourist practices and how often they travel in order to run. I interviewed an equal number of women and men (roughly) as well as causal and serious runners. Overall, I have conducted 44 (mostly group) interviews. Given my interest in practices and not individual runners, the focus in the interviews was on how running 'attracted', and made sense to, the interviewees, how they learned the practice, and how and where they perform it. However, I begin with discussing relevant practice theories and empirical studies of mobile practices by practice theorists.

Practice theories

Despite their differences, practice theories have certain common features. They are concerned with social practices, and they are, in the words of Reckwitz, defined as 'routines' and 'sets of routinised bodily performances'. These comprise several elements such as 'forms of bodily activities, forms of mental activities, "things" and their use, a background knowledge in the form of understanding, know-how, states of emotion and motivational knowledge' (Reckwitz, 2002: 249). So, practices comprise much more than bodily doings. They also include mental activities such as meanings, classifications and ideas, things such as technologies, tangible physical entities and infrastructures, know-how in the form of shared knowledge, technique and competences, states of emotions in the form of success or failure, and motivational knowledge in the form of aspirations and goals (see also Shove, Pantzar and Watson, 2012: 14). These 'elements' are related and we need to understand how they influence each other when we investigate the trajectory of a specific practice (Larsen, 2017, 2018a).

According to this multifaceted definition, running practices involve more than just running a given distance: this brute movement would make little sense, or be desirable or possible, without a shared language, discourses and meanings about the desirability and emotions of running; programmes about how to train and avoid injuries; aspirations to get fitter and run faster; and specialised objects such as running shoes, GPS watches and heart monitors. The latter illustrates how consumption and specific objects are necessary components of many practices as they carry specific symbolic meanings to experienced practitioners and *enable* agencies, competences and actions (Warde, 2005; Shove, Pantzar and Watson, 2012: 9). This explains why practice scholars are primarily concerned with the material affordances of consumer objects and not their symbolic words (the latter approach long dominated consumer studies; Warde, 2005). As Reckwitz (2002: 253) argues: 'Carrying out a practice very often means using particular things in a certain way. It might sound trivial to stress that in order to play football we need a ball and goals as indispensable "resources"'.

However, Reckwitz overlooks that a ball and goals are not enough on their own if there is not a suitable place for playing the game. While Reckwitz would probably stress that shoes and watches are essential for running, we also have to add specific events (races) and places such as tracks, parks, paths, pavements and the occasional closing-off of streets. This reflects that places are more or less absent in sociological accounts of practices (according to Larsen, 2018a). They are curiously de-spatialised as there is little direct discussion of how practices are emplaced and how routinised activities tend to take place at specific locations. We need to think of ways in which to include the material environment more actively into practice theory, as practices are placed in, and may depend upon, specific places, and we develop routines in familial places (see Simonsen, 2007; Pink, 2012). Here we can find inspiration in Pink's work on the sensoriality and affordances of sport environments that comprise 'geological forms, the weather, human socialities, material objects, buildings, animals, and much more' (Pink, 2011: 348). Practices are embedded in 'social, material and technological' environments 'charged with energy, emotion, shifting with the weather, and contingent on the activity of non-human organisms too' (Pink, 2012: 23). This approach enables a material understanding of running as 'a place-event with a complex ecology' of diverse things, corporeal bodies, places and environments (Larsen, 2018a: 45).

Pink also outlines how bodies modify when people develop sporting habits:

> Thus, we might start thinking of the body as part of a total environment, and recognise that the body provides us not simply with embodied knowing and skills that we use to act on or in that environment, but that the body itself is simultaneously physically transformed as part of this process.
>
> (Pink, 2011: 347)

This modification can involve weight loss and injuries, as well as musculature development. This resonates with Reckwitz's idea that 'a social practice is the product of training the body in a certain way: when we learn a practice, we learn to be bodies in a certain way'. This means that 'a practice can be understood as the regular, skillful "performance" of (human) bodies' (Reckwitz 2002: 251). Bodies are thus not static. People normally need to train in order to learn to perform a specific practice in a skilful manner. This focus on training and bodily change infers that potential practitioners do not yet have the required corporeal and mental competences to carry out a specific practice. But it also infers that such skills and aspirations can be learned if the social practice is both well established and attractive (for more detail, see Larsen, 2018a).

Practice theories are not concerned with routines and activities of single individuals, nor are they concerned with structures. Consummate with Giddens' (1984) structuration theory they see human agency and structures as recursively related. They stress the recursive nature of such an amalgam of 'elements' and are interested in explaining how they form an 'entity' that enable specific routinised practices that have enduring existence across individual moments of activity, performed by many, more or less knowledgeable and capable, actors. Practice theorists argue that such elements need to be performed to be reproduced and to become normalised.

This is why practice theorists distinguish between 'practice-as-entity' and 'practice-as-performance' (Schatzki, 2001; Shove, Pantzar and Watson, 2012: 7; Warde, 2005: 133). The former frames how it is possible to do, learn, or speak about, a particular practice (Shove, Pantzar and Watson, 2012: 7). 'Elements' are enacted by attracting practitioners that 'feature as the *carriers* or hosts of a practice' (Shove, Pantzar and Watson, 2012: 7). Practitioners are captured by practices and their skills and motivations are moulded by the elements rather than their individual preferences. So:

> in practice theory, agents are body/minds who 'carry' and 'carry out' social practices. Thus, the social world is first and foremost populated by diverse social practices which are carried by agents. Agents, so to speak, 'consist in' the performance of practices to norms: They understand the world and themselves, and use know-how and motivational knowledge, according to the particular practice.
>
> (Reckwitz, 2002: 249)

Yet practices need to be filled out and reproduced through repetitive doings, which is called 'practice-as-performance' (Shove, Pantzar and Watson, 2012: 7). To return to the example of football: this sport is constituted through participation and it will only exist as long as people play the game. While performances such as football are scripted by rules and established ways of playing, they are not performed by passive and preformed practitioners and there are always possibilities for improvisation and novelty. Practitioners are *co*-producers of practices-as-entities (Pantzar and Shove, 2010; Shove and Pantzar, 2007: 155, 448; Larsen, 2017, 2018a). Practices change as and when they are performed differently, attract newcomers or lose regulars. As Warde writes:

> Social practices do not present uniform planes upon which agents participate in identical ways but are instead internally differentiated on many dimensions. Considered simply, from the point of view of the individual person, the performance of driving will depend on past experience, technological knowledge, learning, opportunities, available resources, previous encouragement by others … From the point of view of practice as a whole, we can think of a dedicated and specialised domain comprising many different competencies and capabilities.
>
> (Warde, 2005: 136)

Practice theories explore the trajectories of old and emerging practices: how they evolve and rise in popularity, endure or change over time (Larsen, 2017). This can be done by analysing: first, how elements and the connections between them change due to innovation, policy, political movement, societal trend or consumer preference (Shove, Pantzar and Watson, 2012: 12); second, how practices – 'as vampire like entities'– (Shove and Pantzar, 2007: 166) – recruit and deflect particular practitioners over time; third, what is involved in participation and how requirements has changed over time (Shove and Pantzar, 2007: 15); and fourth, how relations between related practices as practices 'compete with each other for recruits and carriers' (Shove, Pantzar and Watson, 2012: 87) and yet are 'bundled with' with other practices. Practices attract practitioners from competing practices and by making alliances with other practices. I now give three ethnographic examples of how practice theorists go about exploring the trajectories of mobile practices (floorball, Nordic walking and commuting cycling) that are somewhat related with, and hence competing with, practices of running.

Shove and Pantzar (2007) have explored the emergence and changes of practices of floorball (indoor hockey) and Nordic walking (leisurely walking with a stick) in Finland and the UK. Across the two studies, they demonstrate how a given sport can change due to new rules, particular ways of playing and sets of meanings and aspirations. They particularly discuss how new competitive and sporty approaches to leisurely floorball caused conflict and divide between practitioners in the UK. New practitioners entered the scene and changed the practice from within. This alienated some seasoned practitioners who insisted on playing the game in the usual style while others defected from the practice altogether. This illustrates that different practices of floorball (or any other activity) may exist simultaneously and that innovation is an on-going process. Practices are differentiated and a given practice can be performed in different ways (sometimes against the script and design).

In their studies of Nordic walking, Shove and Pantzar (2005) give equal weight to the walking stick industry and the practitioners, as they argue that both parties are involved in giving meaning and shape to the constitutive elements of this emerging practice. The key challenge faced by Nordic walking was that walking sticks were associated with the frail and the disabled, not with fit and healthy people enjoying a walk in nature. Such associations had to be broken. Shove and Pantzar show how the industry and practitioners worked hard to change that perception. At the same time, Nordic walking flourished by being 'bundled with' practices of leisurely walking, new state-sponsored discourses about the health benefits of outdoor exercise (such as jogging), an infrastructure of walking paths, and so on. Both studies show that such practices are contagious in the sense that practitioners recruit each other, which is important in relation to the key argument within practice theory that practices always depend upon attracting new practitioners

My recent research has employed practice theory in examinations of bicycle mobilities in pro-cycling Copenhagen (Larsen, 2017, 2018a). It explores why, and how, cycling in Copenhagen attracts so many everyday bike practitioners, seen from a combined planning and everyday commuting perspective. I argue that the municipality recruits everyday cyclists through the heterogeneous engineering of building bike infrastructures and promoting pro-cycling meanings (discourses and aspirations) that bundle commuting and cycling. Cyclists are emplaced in a pro-cycling environment that makes cycling perfectly normal and possible for the many and not just the hardened, competent few (as in many car-dominated societies). At the same time, I show that Copenhageners reproduce cycling practices as a form of convenient transport (rather than leisure) through specific meanings and styles of cycling that are integrated into their wider ecology of everyday practices. Copenhageners cycle if it is quick, do-able, comfortable and practical in comparison to motorised competitors.

Practices of running

Informed by practice theory, I now discus the different materials (including environments), meanings and competences that organise and systematise (different) marathon running practices. Consummate with practice theory, I am not concerned with *individual* runners and their supposedly individual experiences. Their bodies, motives or doings are not seen as personal attributes but rather as 'elements and qualities of practices in which the single individual participates' (Reckwitz, 2002: 7). Individual running practices are seen within a wider societal context. I thus de-centre studies of running away from individual runners and on to the things, events, experts and discourses that enable pleasurable *practices* of running. I ask how and why different (aspiring) runners learn, and perform, this practice, and how we can understand the constitutive roles of doctors and running experts, discourses of health and slim bodies, sports equipment and environments in this process. What sort of discourses and practices are running bundled with? How do people become devoted carriers of the practice and what meanings, knowledge, aspirations and bodily transformations are associated with being a runner? At the same time, I explore how marathon running attracts certain groups of people and repels others.

Running is, of course, not something new, as humans are built to move rapidly on foot and transport their body, at speed and over significant distances. Humans are born with the ability (competence) to run and they develop this competence through practising it. However, while running is much faster than the rival practice of walking, it is nevertheless not as attractive because it is a more physically demanding way of transporting oneself. Modern people walk. Running is reserved for those rare moments when we are escaping danger or running late, or more often when people are engaged in sport activities such as playing football. Throughout the 20th century, running was associated with serious sport and the practice only attracted a small crowd of serious and usually young physically competent devotees, almost exclusively male practitioners, of which most joined clubs and followed strict regimes of daily training and fiercely competitive races where you ran to win (Bale, 2004; Bryant, 2006; Scheerder, Breedveld and Borgers, 2015). Running, competition and sport were closely bundled.

These meanings changed slowly in the 1970s with the emergence of the fitness and jogging movement in the US, and later in Europe, inventing a new practice of running that was suitable for increasingly sedentary and overweight men and women habituated to motorised travel, desk jobs and energy-rich diets (Agger, 2011; Latham, 2015; Qviström, 2017). 'Jogging' was invented 'to counter the systematic diminution of necessary corporeal effort occurring throughout the urban environment – whether that be through the substitution of the automobile for walking, lifts and escalators for stairs, or television for more physically demanding pastimes' (Latham, 2015: 104). Americans were caught in an ecology of practices that made them ill, overweight and inactive. The jogging movement cut the ties with sport and competition by inventing new meanings and understandings of appropriate materials and competences. It renamed 'running' as 'jogging' and bundled it with emerging health discourses, green urban spaces and casual leisure (rather than sporty) clothing. Running became associated with (urban) well-being and health in a sedentary, overweight and accelerated society. Jogging also bundled with aesthetic discourses of the body (often exemplified in lifestyle magazines) that promoted running as a route to a slim, attractive beach-ready body (Abbas, 2004). The meanings and competences of running was desportified and hence democratised through training programmes that were do-able for less fit and portly middle-aged bodies that lacked time to get involved in organised forms of collective, community-based sports. Jogging made sense to time-squeezed professionals because running is based on the body's established – yet largely neglected – competences, and showed how these can be easily and quickly improved. By adhering to training programmes, people were told that they would quickly develop the required habits, capabilities and aspirations to become a jogger – and without running into injuries in that process (Latham, 2015).

However, in the early days, joggers were stigmatised, insulted and called names (Scheerder, Breedveld and Borgers, 2015). Over the years, however, practices of running became casual and acceptable and the practice attracted many new – more or less loyal – practitioners, especially women, middle-aged and older bodies. The prevalence of running shoes and trainers (or 'sneakers' in the USA) as everyday shoes meant that many would-be joggers were already equipped. The low entrance barrier to jogging also concerned the environment, with joggers being instructed to use their immediate neighbourhoods and local parks for running (Latham, 2015). This illustrates how the rise of running practices has not been supported by urban infrastructures designed especially for runners (but see Qviström, 2017), which is in contrast to cycling where bike lanes play a key part in popularising cycling (Larsen, 2017). Nonetheless, running can attract many practitioners because the required 'materials' (shoes and pavements/paths) are easily available. This makes the practice cheap and time effective, as people do not waste time travelling to some specific sports venue where they might be dependent upon other peoples' presence and commitment. While jogging was scripted as a locally emplaced and individualised practice, it did create a loosely bounded community of practice where skilled practitioners empowered novices and joggers recruited each other. Moreover, jogging itself became a differentiated practice. Some practitioners became highly engaged and devoted and they began to participate in road races for joggers and competitive road races as they slowly began to embrace joggers, which eventually came to dominate such races.

The New York Marathon was the first marathon designed to cater for, and indeed 'eventify', the 'jogging boom' (Bryant, 2006: 9). Prior to this event, marathons were serious, small-scale events for elite runners and participants who often had to finish within three hours. For the first couple of years (1972–75), the race consisted of repeated loops of Central Park, but the marathon craze took off in 1976 when the course covered all five boroughs of New York City. Streets were closed off to traffic, and musicians and cheering spectators made the marathon atmospheric and fun to participate in. Over the years, as the number of participants rose dramatically at the New York Marathon, and many other urban marathons around the world, joggers inspired each other to take on this daunting challenge and step up the training, often for half a year or so, if not longer (Scheerder, Breedveld and Borgers, 2015).

The average marathon runner is now older and slower, and women now account for around 40 per cent of the participants. Many slower marathon runners are novice runners, have limited competences, somewhat out-of-shape bodies and little sport ambitions (Axelsen and Robinson, 2009: 243; Scheerder, Breedveld and Borgers, 2015). This change suggests that marathons revolve less around running fast and winning, and more on participation and completion. The aspirations of this new generation of marathon practitioner are to challenge themselves, complete this daunting distance and simply participate in this urban carnival (Goodsell, Harris and Bailey, 2013; Ogles and Masters, 2003; Rupprecht and Matkin, 2012).

Marathons can never rely on regulars alone, but need to entice many new practitioners each year. Many consider a marathon an once-in-a-lifetime experience and return to casual jogging after they had achieved this ambition. Thus, the increase in marathon running has happened despite the fact that many abandon marathon running after a brief flirtation, often because the training is too demanding, time consuming or they run into a serious injury. Yet some joggers become 'regulars'; they transform themselves into runners that train seriously and participate in marathons (and other races) in order to improve their 'personal best' and be highly placed in their age or gender division (for studies of such 'serious runners', see Green and Jones, 2005; Hockey and Allen-Collinson, 2015; Smith, S., 1998; Smith, G., 2002).

All this suggests that running is not a uniform practice as people have different competences and perform it with more or less regularity, at different speeds, and for different reasons. Smith (1998) makes a simple but useful distinction between joggers, runners and athletics, while others distinguish between casual (e.g. joggers) and serious (e.g. runners and athletics) runners. At the same time, as just described, we need to acknowledge that practitioners may move from one category to another. However, we should not assume (contrary to many studies) that most joggers develop running careers where they become more committed and competent over the years. Research indicates that many 'joggers' do not adhere to any programmes and have very irregular running routines. They force themselves to run because of the perceived health effects and not because they enjoy it, and they do not identify themselves much with the practice or let alone participate in runs. In addition, they usually run alone (Cook, Shaw and Simpson, 2016; Hitchings and Latham, 2017). However, for others, the practice of jogging and running involves participating in running events such as marathons and, as I will now discuss, such events are often designed to bundled with tourism, and they generate much travel and tourism.

Running and tourism

The bundles between tourism and running practices are evident with organised runs. Many of these have become events that are designed to, and indeed do, attract runners from near and far (McGehee, Yoon and Cardenas, 2003; Lisle, 2016; Shipway and Jones, 2008). So how do marathons attract so many (different) runners, and why are runners willing to invest significant time and money in travelling to, and staying overnight, in another place? Based upon a literature review, and a summary of my fieldwork at the Berlin Marathon and Etape Bornholm, I will argue that race organisers (often athletics clubs) through spatial design, marketing and branding, on the one hand, and participants, on the other, bundle running practices and tourism practices in unique ways. I therefore employ a *co*-production perspective, where attention is given to the sayings and doings of runners, as much as event managers and physical designs. While travel and sightseeing is seldom the main attraction of running a race, it is nonetheless a crucial element of the practice. Runners, we may say, travel a lot because the practice of participating in events require it. This reflects more broadly that 'practices, rather than individual desires, we might say, create wants' (Warde, 2005: 137)

Berlin Marathon

A local running club organised the first Berlin Marathon in 1974. The event was designed for serious runners and athletics and as few as 286 runners (men) participated. Over the next decades, Berlin was one of the marathons that were successful in attracting (serious) joggers and simultaneously establishing itself as one of the world's fastest and most competitive marathons. Berlin Marathon is today one of the most iconic and popular annual road marathons in Europe. The actual race is made up of a medley of different running practices and bodies of different shapes (although most are relatively slim) and abilities, both young and old, of both sexes. It attracts some of the world's best elite runners, 40,000 recreational runners and joggers (80,000 people apply a year in advance) from 141 countries and an estimated million spectators.[1] The running club – now under the name of SCC EVENTS – employs more than 40 and they arrange a dozen of running events in Berlin throughout the running season. Berlin Marathon is one of world's most prestigious 'must-do' marathons in part because it is part of the famous World Major Marathon Series (together with Boston, New York, Chicago, London and Tokyo). It therefore holds a particular meaning for seasoned marathon runners. In terms of 'materials', it is famous for being extremely flat and fast (the current world record was set here) and it is therefore known as a perfect environment for chasing a new a 'personal best' or trying a marathon for the first time. The route is also renowned for the sights and the carnival atmosphere, which makes it attractive to tourists. The organisers write:

> The BMW BERLIN-MARATHON offers one of the most attractive courses at the 42.195k distance. Not only is the course in Germany's capital flat and ideal for setting personal bests, but it is also extremely attractive for tourists. A sightseeing tour could not have more spots in its program. The loop course is great for spectators following the race. Live music – ranging in style from classical to jazz to samba – lines the course.[2]

The marathon starts in Tiergarten and symbolically ends at the Brandenburg Gate. It takes runners, spectators and viewers on a tour of the city's most iconic tourist sites, such as: Regierungsviertel (the Government Quarter) with the spectacular Reichstag; Kurfürstendamm Boulevard; NeueNationalgalerie; Berliner Philharmonie; Potsdamerplatz; the two cathedrals on Gendarmenmarkt

Square; Unter den Linden boulevard; the iconic Karl Marx Strasse and multi-cultural and hip Kreutzberg.[3] Moreover, the race organisers design and orchestrate a vivacious visual and sonic atmosphere by hiring bands that play along the route and distributing 'clapping devices' to spectators. Techno, samba, brass, heavy rock blend with clapping, vocal exhortations and whistling. Such races are much more than just running events and runners and spectators are 'emplaced' in an eventful environment. This unique route and atmosphere provides this marathon with a unique 'sense of place' that enables participants to develop a 'topophilia' for the event and city (for more detail, see Edensor and Larsen, 2017).

Most of my interviewees – all living outside Germany – acknowledged that marathon running include a touristic element (beyond travel) and that the 'emplacement' matters; it is important that the race takes place in an exciting city and the racecourse is scenic and atmospheric, as with the Berlin Marathon. This was particularly the case for 'joggers'. Yet even serious competitive runners told me that they looked forward to experiencing Berlin as a scenic and noisy, carnivalesque backdrop. An extraordinary practice as marathon running somehow requires an equally extraordinary scene as this make the painful experience of endurance running more bearable, even eventful. Running a marathon in a nondescript environment with no atmosphere does not make sense. Streets brimming with cheering spectators and vocal support motivate and carry forward tired runners. Their motivation is to enjoy this iconic marathon *and* the running experience. They can do so because the racecourse displaces pedestrians, playing children and car-drivers that normally demand cautious attention from runners (Cook, Shaw and Simpson, 2016; Ettema, 2016; Gimlin, 2010). Now they can go with the flow and practise the tourist gaze (Larsen, 2018b). Indeed, running a marathon is an extraordinary event that requires substantial training over relatively long period of time to make the body race-ready, to build up the required mental and physical competences to run this daunting distance (in a good time). Much of this training is somewhat uneventful: it is repetitive, lonesome and takes place locally (for more detail, see Edensor and Larsen, 2017).

Many of those interviewed at the Berlin Marathon had participated in several marathons that involved domestic and international travel and overnight stays. These interviewees have developed what is known as 'event travel careers' in the sport tourism and leisure literature (Getz and Andersson, 2010; Getz and McConnell, 2011; Shipway and Jones, 2007). The overseas interviewees appreciated that Berlin is one of Europe's most famous cities and that Berlin Marathon is one of the world's most prestigious marathons. Many novices and slower runners expressed a burning desire to experience the city *and* the marathon, while seasoned runners were on a mission to complete a conspicuous marathon biography by finishing all six majors. This reflects that marathon running is a professional middle-class sport that attracts those with a substantial income and mobile lifestyle (Nettleton, 2013). Runners are willing to travel to marathons that take place in exciting cities, with fast and scenic routes, and hundreds of thousands of vocal supporters throughout the course. While most refrain from certain typical tourist practices before the race, many – especially novices – told me that they stay an extra night to have time for sightseeing and other urban tourism practices after the race. I have shown how tourist travel plays a significant supporting role for running practices at Berlin Marathon. The next section makes the argument that running shares the main role with tourism practices at Etape Bornholm.

Etape Bornholm

Etape Bornholm is a five-day touristy running event on the Danish island of Bornholm. It is also open for children and they run shorter distances and only for three days. It is organised by a local non-profit athletic club that also organises other sports events on the island. Compared to the Berlin Marathon, it is also a much smaller running event as the maximum capacity is 2,300 runners. The race is designed to attract tourists from Copenhagen and Copenhageners make up 70 per cent of the participants. As the race takes places over five days, the race director accentuates that they need to sell the prospect of a good holiday (for the whole family), which requires that they bridge this event with family tourism They also brand the event as 'active tourism' and bundle it with suitable active tourism products on the destination (Chalip and McGuirty, 2004; Axelsen and Robinson, 2009). The race needs to align with other tourist practices as it lasts a whole week (allowing registration and travel) and takes place during the school summer break. The stages take place in the evening, so that it does not conflict with other tourist practices on the island. This also means that Etape Bornholm is fully dependent upon the overall tourist desirability and competitiveness of Bornholm as a tourist destination; no tourist product is an island.[4] Etape Bornholm is, at the same time, promoted by the central tourism organisation on the island. Active tourism practices are the destination's fastest growing market and many new businesses sell experiences in relation to cycling, kayaking, hill walking, climbing and running. There is a growing recognition that more and more tourists experience the island through active, corporeal engagement (cycling, kayaking, hill walking, climbing and running)[5] and not merely through picturesque gazing (see Larsen, 2006, for an account of aesthetic making of Bornholm as tourist place of the tourist gaze).

Etape Bornholm is a very different marathon: the daunting 42 kilometres is divided into five races that take place over five consecutive days and in five different places, which makes it physically less demanding and therefore open to practitioners with limited running abilities and it does not require as much training. Compared with the Berlin Marathon, this was reflected in a greater variety of differently shaped bodies and less serious clothing. However, racing for five days on an often hilly and sandy terrain is challenging. The five racecourses deliberately include many of the island's distinctive tourist sights and landscapes. We may say that the route is designed to give a grand tour of the island's major tourism attractions. For instance, the second day is a beach-and-cliff race where runners literally run over sandcastles, while the fourth day is a hilly trail run that commences and ends at two famous sights. The final four hundred metres through extremely step hairpin bends are (in) famously demanding. Yet the atmosphere is equally breath-taking: loudly cheering locals and tourists line the narrow streets and there are painted names and messages of support on the tarmac.

My interviews and observations shows that Etape Bornholm attracts many participants that otherwise do not run much or travel to participate in races. Nonetheless, all of them had enrolled for the race before arrival and they would spend 3–4 hours (including transport) on the event every night for five days. Running as such was not the main thrill for them. They mainly participate because other family members participate and they like the fact that they could do something together as a couple or a family. They also praised the whole atmosphere of the race and the fact that they see and experience so much of the island. While most of them have trained a little, it was not regarded a necessity to be physically well prepared to enjoy this race. This illustrates that causal joggers and not only serious runners are potential tourism runners, at least if they are 'recruited' by their family members. Moreover, the majority of the interviewees were regulars. They returned regularly to this event because it affords a unique corporeal experience of Bornholm's varied and dramatic landscapes and has many vocal supporters and a convivial sociality amongst the runners.

It is a unique combination of this particular running event *and* the pleasures of the island as a tourist places that attract people to Etape Bornholm. This is also why the interviewees explained that the evening races should not take centre stage and rule out other tourist practices. Restitution between races was not an excuse from abstaining from energy-consuming tourist practices such as going for a long walk. Family conflicts occurred if the family holiday turned into a running holiday, even in those cases where most of the family actively participated. However, this did seldom happen as otherwise 'serious runners' should not be too serious with their running on a family holiday, and some of them merely use the race as a hard (and eventful) training week. While many said that this event was the main reason why they spend (parts of) their summer holiday here, there were few other places where they would spend so much time and money on running. In addition, people with a family connection to the island use this particular event to catch up with their dispersed family members (on family networking in tourism, see Larsen, Urry and Axhausen, 2007). Indeed, it may be said that the key to the success of Etape Bornholm is the knowledge amongst the organisers and the participants (especially the regulars) that the stage race plays a secondary role to the place as a tourism island and the specific tourism practices that are performed in the busy summer months (for more detail, see Larsen, 2018c).

Conclusion

Practice theory is yet to make a sustained impact on tourist studies where economic models and cultural theories about representation, discourses and gazing prevail. For instance, studies of sport tourism (Weed, 2009) have been preoccupied with the economic impact of big sporting events and not so much with how tourists experience them as spectators or participants. I have argued that practice theory can be useful in analysing practices of running, as well as connections between running and tourism. Practice theory is concerned with analysing the routinised and scripted nature of specific practices, how such practices attract and deflect practitioners, and how such practitioners learn to become competent performers that co-produce and re-innovate the practice through 'playing it out' in multiple ways. I have discussed how practice theory informed my research on running and marathons and helped me to discuss how localised everyday running links with occasional running events in other places. Practice theory can help us to understand how running and marathons suddenly captured so many practitioners' hearts and imaginations, and how tourist travel, tourism places and activities are bundled in this process.

I have shown how running events organised by running clubs – or what may be called civic entrepreneurs – attract many domestic and international tourists and generate many overnight stays. Major races do *not* take place in provincial cities or unknown out-of-the way locations, but in iconic tourism cities (such as London, Paris, New York, Tokyo and Berlin) and destinations (such as Bornholm) with appropriate infrastructures and attractive sights and landscapes. Running can become one of the ways in which people 'collect places' (Shipway and Jones, 2007: 380) through both individualised tourist travel as well as family practices. However, in contrast to literature that suggests that the interest in a specific race wears off once it has been 'completed-and-collected' (Shipway and Jones, 2007; Axelsen and Robinson, 2009), many of my interviewees had done the Berlin Marathon or Etape Bornholm several times. They had an affection for the race (and the city or the island) and participating in the race had become a tradition. They are not so much collecting as dwelling in those races. Moreover, the study of Etape Bornholm uniquely showed casual joggers can be attracted to running events if they are designed to cater for their needs and aspirations.

Now I briefly reflect upon what tourism studies might learn from such an approach, and what practice theory, in turn, might gain from engaging with tourism rather than just 'everyday life'. It is crucial that tourism not merely adopt and apply practice theory, but also develop it. First, practice theory (somewhat similar to performance theory, see Edensor, 2001; Urry and Larsen, 2011) allows tourist researchers to scrutinise tourism in relation to everyday practices (such as training) rather than seeing tourism as an isolated island. Practice theory and tourism studies can enrich each other as everyday practices and tourism practices increasingly overlap. Tourism scholars can move practice theory forward by discussing how modern everyday life is performed away from home and routinised everyday practices travel along with tourists and are enacted in a new spatial context. Second, practice theory can shed a new light on the historical trajectory of specific tourist practices and could explore how, say, photographing, gazing, strolling, sightseeing, sunbathing, wayfinding and eating foreign food emerge as distinct tourists' practices that came to attract many faithful practitioners over the years. A crucial part of such a history is analysing how tourists *learn* to carry out specific practices in a skilful and pleasurable manner, as tourism studies have largely ignored looking at how tourists learn to become competent tourists (but see Löfgren, 2002). Practice theory can help tourism studies to mitigate that shortcoming. Finally, this approach allows us to theorise the typical holiday as consisting of a variety of different practices and to challenge the idea that tourism is essentially about gazing or sightseeing or sunbathing or some other activity. Tourism is about performing everyday practices in a new spatial context and practising a new place in a (hopefully) stimulating way.

Notes

1 www.bmw-berlin-marathon.com
2 www.bmw-berlin-marathon.com/en/race-day/spectators.html
3 www.bmw-berlin-marathon.com/en/race-day/course.html
4 Interview with race director.
5 Interview with destination manager.

References

Abbas, A. (2004). The embodiment of class, gender and age through leisure: a realist analysis of long distance running. *Leisure Studies*, 23(2): 159–175.
Agger, B. (2011). *Body Problems: Running and Living Long in Fast-food Society.* London: Routledge.
Axelsen, M. and Robinson, R. N. (2009). Race around the world: Identifying a research agenda for the distance runner. *Annals of Leisure Research*, 12(2): 236–257.
Bale, J. (2004). *Running Cultures: Racing in Time and Space.* London: Psychology Press.
Bryant, J. (2006). *The London Marathon: The History of the Greatest Race on the Earth.* London: Arrow Books.
Chalip, L. and McGuirty, J. (2004). Bundling sport events with the host destination, *Journal of Sport & Tourism*, 9(3): 267–282.
Cook, S., Shaw, J. and Simpson, P. (2016). Jography: exploring meanings, experiences and spatialities of recreational road-running. *Mobilities*, 11(5): 744–769.
Edensor, T. (2001). Performing tourism, staging tourism. (Re) producing tourist space and practice. *Tourist Studies*, 1(1): 59–81.
Edensor, T. and Larsen, J. (2017). Rhythmanalysing Berlin Marathon: a drama of rhythms. *Environment and Planning A*. E-pub ahead of press.
Ettema, D. (2016). Runnable cities: how does the running environment influence perceived attractiveness, restorativeness, and running frequency? *Environment and Behavior*, 48(9): 1127–1147.
Forsberg, P. (2012). *Motionsløbere i Danmark – Portræt af danske motionsløbere.* København: Idrættens Analyseinstitut.
Forsberg, P. (2014). Segmentation of Danish runners. In J. Scheer-der, K. Breedveld and J. Borgers (eds), *Running across Europe – The Rise and Size of One of the Largest Sport Markets.* New York: Palgrave Macmillan.

Getz, D. and Andersson, T. D. (2010). The event-tourist career trajectory: a study of high-involvement amateur distance runners. *Scandinavian Journal of Hospitality and Tourism*, 10(4): 468–491.

Getz, D. and McConnell, A. (2011). Serious sport tourism and event travel careers. *Journal of Sport Management*, 25(4): 326–338.

Giddens, A. (1984). *The Constitution of Society: Outline of the Theory of Structuration*. California: University of California Press.

Gimlin, D. (2010). Uncivil attention and the public runner. *Sociology of Sport Journal*, 27(3): 268–284.

Goodsell, T. L., Harris, B. D. and Bailey, B. W. (2013). Family status and motivations to run: a qualitative study of marathon runners. *Leisure Sciences*, 35(4): 337–352.

Green, B. C. and Jones, I. (2005). Serious leisure, social identity and sport tourism. *Sport in Society*, 8(2), 164–181.

Hitchings, R. and Latham, A. (2017). How 'social' is recreational running? Findings from a qualitative study in London and implications for public health promotion. *Health & Place*, 46 (July): 337–343.

Hockey, J. and Allen-Collinson, J. (2015). Digging in. In W. Bridel, P. Markula and J. Denison (eds), *Endurance Running: A Socio-Cultural Examination*. London: Routledge, pp. 227–242

Lamers, M., van der Duim, R. and Spaargaren, G. (2017). The relevance of practice theories for tourism research. *Annals of Tourism Research*, 62: 54–63.

Larsen, J. (2006). Picturing Bornholm: producing and consuming a tourist place through picturing practices. *Scandinavian Journal of Hospitality and Tourism*, 6(2): 75–94.

Larsen, J. (2008). De-exoticising tourist travel: everyday life and sociality on the move. *Leisure Studies*, 27(1): 21–34.

Larsen, J. (2017). The making of a pro-cycling city: social practices and bicycle mobilities. *Environment and Planning A*, 49(4): 876–892.

Larsen, J. (2018a). Commuting, exercise and sport: an ethnography of long-distance bike commuting. *Social & Cultural Geography*, 19(1): 39–58.

Larsen, J. (2018b). Running away, or with, the tourist gaze. In O. B. Jensen, M. Sheller and S. Kessellring (eds), *Mobilities, Complexity and Post-carbon Futures*. London: Routledge.

Larsen, J. (2018c). Running on sands castles: rhythmanalyzing a touristy running event. Manuscript in preparation.

Larsen, J., Urry, J. and Axhausen, K. W. (2007). Networks and tourism: mobile social life. *Annals of Tourism Research*, 34(1): 244–262.

Latham, A. (2015). The history of a habit: jogging as a palliative to sedentariness in 1960s America. *Cultural Geographies*, 22(1): 103–126.

Laub, T. B. (2011). *Danskernes motions- og sportsvaner*. København: Idrættens Analyseinstitut.

Lisle, D. (2016). Exotic endurance: tourism, fitness and the Marathon des Sables. *Environment and Planning D: Society and Space*, 34(2): 263–281.

Löfgren, O. (2002). *On Holiday: A History of Vacationing*. California: University of California Press.

McGehee, N. G., Yoon, Y. and Cárdenas, D. (2003). Involvement and travel for recreational runners in North Carolina. *Journal of Sport Management*, 17(3): 305–324.

Nettleton, S. (2013). Cementing relations within a sporting field: fell running in the English Lake District and the acquisition of existential capital. *Cultural Sociology*, 7 (2): 196–210.

Nettleton, S. and Hardey, M. (2006). Running away with health: the urban marathon and the construction of 'charitable bodies'. *Health*, 10(4): 441–460.

Ogles, B. M. and Masters, K. S. (2003). A typology of marathon runners based on cluster analysis of motivations. *Journal of Sport Behavior*, 26(1): 69–81

Pantzar, M., Shove, E. (2010). Understanding innovation in practice: a discussion of the production and re-production of Nordic Walking. *Technology Analysis & Strategic Management*, 22: 447–461.

Pink, S. (2011). From embodiment to emplacement: re-thinking competing bodies, senses and spatialities. *Sport, Education and Society*, 16: 343–355.

Pink, S. (2012). *Situating Everyday Life: Practices and Places*. London: Sage.

Qviström, M. (2017). Competing geographies of recreational running: the case of the 'jogging wave' in Sweden in the late 1970s. *Health and Place*, 46: 351–357.

Reckwitz, A. (2002). Toward a theory of social practices: a development in culturalist theorising. *European Journal of Social Theory*, 5: 243–263.

Rupprecht, P. M. and Matkin, G. S. (2012). Finishing the race: exploring the meaning of marathons for women who run multiple races. *Journal of Leisure Research*, 44(3): 308–331.

Schatzki, T. (2001). *Social Practices*. Cambridge: Cambridge University Press.

Scheerder, J., Breedveld, K. and Borgers, J. (2015). Who is doing a run with the running boom? In J. Scheerder, K. Breedveld and J. Borgers (eds), *Running across Europe* (pp. 1–27). London: Palgrave Macmillan UK.

Sheehan, R. (2006). Running in place. *Tourist Studies*, 6(3): 245–265.

Shipway, R. and Jones, I. (2007). Running away from home: understanding visitor experiences and behaviour at sport tourism events. *International Journal of Tourism Research*, 9(5): 373–383.

Shipway, R. and Jones, I. (2008). The great suburban Everest: an 'insiders' perspective on experiences at the 2007 Flora London Marathon. *Journal of Sport & Tourism*, 13(1): 61–77.

Shove, E. and Pantzar, M. (2005). Consumers producers and practices understanding the invention and reinvention of Nordic walking. *Journal of Consumer Culture*, 5: 43–64.

Shove, E. and Pantzar, M. (2007). Recruitment and reproduction: the careers and carriers of digital photography and floorball. *Human Affairs*, 17: 154–167

Shove, E., Pantzar, M. and Watson, M. (2012). *The Dynamics of Social Practice: Everyday Life and How It Changes*. London: Sage.

Simonsen, K. (2007). Practice, spatiality and embodied emotions: an outline of a geography of practice. *Human Affairs*, 17(2): 168–181.

Smith, G. (2002). Racing against time? Aspects of the temporal organisation of the runner's world. *Symbolic Interaction*, 25: 343–362.

Smith, S. (1998). Athletes, runners, and joggers: participant-group dynamics in a sport of 'individuals'. *Sociology of Sport Journal*, 15(1): 174–192.

Urry, J. and Larsen, J. (2011). *The Tourist Gaze 3.0*. London: Sage.

Warde, A. (2005). Consumption and theories of practice. *Journal of Consumer Culture*, 5(2): 131–153.

Wicker, P., Hallmann, K. and Zhang, J. J. (2012). What is influencing consumer expenditure and intention to revisit? An investigation of marathon events. *Journal of Sport & Tourism*, 17(3): 165–182.

Weed, M. (2009). Progress in sports tourism research? A meta-review and exploration of futures. *Tourism Management*, 30(5): 615–628.

5 With the rhythm of nature

Reordering everyday life through holiday living

Outi Rantala

> I slip into my grandfather's old jacket and into my uncle's slippers. I reach for the water bucket and go get fresh water from the well. Once the coffee is on, I get the bilberries from the veranda, whip some vanilla sauce, set the table with our handed-down porcelain and decorate it with late summer flowers. I go out and wake up my mother – she is cuddled up under woollen blankets in the hammock. I then visit the tent at the other end of the garden and wake up my husband and kids. The afternoon coffee is set.
>
> (From second home field notes, 2015)

Through a practice perspective, tourism can be viewed as a set of possibilities for humans and non-humans to enact, (re)assemble and organise (de Souza Bispo, 2016). In this chapter, I am interested in analysing the possibilities that emerge from 'the material interactions of human corporeality and the more-than-human world' (Alaimo, 2010: 2; see also Kinnunen, 2016; Ulmer, 2017) during nature holidays. What kind of possibilities for environmental sensitiveness – for openness towards alternative ways of living in the world – emerge when we become tourists in natural settings and use 'marginal', simplified outdoor living tactics? The chapter deals with nature holidays that include overnight stays in nature either in a tent or in a simple sort of holiday home, that is, one which would have reduced facilities in comparison to tourists' everyday life (e.g. cabins that are heated with wood, which do not have electricity or have limited electricity, which often do not have running water, and have an outdoor toilet). When staying overnight in this sort of close-to-nature setting, both the embodied experience of the outdoors and the role of simplified outdoor living tactics become highlighted. Thus, one is able to observe the manifestation of the sensitivities that we develop when we spend time in nature.

Lamers, van der Duim and Spaargaren (2017) suggest that the application of practice theories within tourism studies has mostly concentrated on unpacking a specific social phenomenon, examining single practices and applying qualitative, participatory methods. De Souza Bispo (2016: 176), however, points out that 'to understand tourism as practice aims at offering a theoretical basis wherein tourism is seen from a broader perspective.' He

underlines that tourism only exists because other 'non-touristic' actors perform their roles in their natural lives; tourism requires tourists, locals and
tourism workers to perform their overlapping roles to build the tourism
practice. This idea can be broadened to involve non-human actors: Examining tourism through a practice perspective draws attention to the diverse
dynamics between mobile performative humans and the more-than-human
world. A practice perspective in this sense can be seen as in line with non-
representational research, which is concerned with relations, doings, events
and affects (Vannini, 2015).

Jóhannesson, Ren and van der Duim argue that tourism is very much
entangled with other ordering attempts – and 'as a mode of ordering (re)
arranges people, things, technologies, discourses and values in certain, rather
than other ways' (Franklin, 2004, 2012, cited in Jóhannesson, Ren and van
der Duim, 2015: 3). The examination of tourism orderings can be conducted
by applying already tested approaches to single practices or by applying
diverse lenses to explore the phenomenon at different levels, as Nicolini (2009)
suggests. Despite differences in applying practice theory, a common idea
shared by those applying the theory is that a practice perspective avoids dualistic approaches (e.g. humans/non-humans, nature/culture, body/mind),
recognises practices as units of analysis that allow a new understanding of a
social phenomenon and focuses on its diverse connections.

Discussing the ordering and disordering of a nature holiday contributes to
the 'aesthetic tradition' within practice theoretical approaches that concentrates on aesthetic or affective qualities of practices (de Souza Bispo, 2016;
Gherardi, 2017). To reach the affective quality of knowing, Henriques (2010),
for example, has developed a vibration model that recognises participants'
tacit, enacted and embodied ways of knowing in a dancehall setting. When
discussing the practice and affect approaches, Gherardi (2017) proposes the
empirical study of how affect is produced in mundane situated encounters.
Hence, the practice perspective aims at going beyond a representational
description and is concerned with linking the cognitive and the affective. It
directs attention towards how fewer things mediate the practices in ways that
one 'may or may not be consciously aware of' (Henriques, 2010). Within
practices, certain possibilities exist for enunciation (de Certeau, 1984) and
improvisation, but grasping how practices are improvised and being able to
address the intensity of the socio-material situatedness of practices is challenging. Recent studies have developed such conceptualisations as 'within
corporality' and 'sensory release' through exploring the presence of sleep and
wakefulness in the academic practices (Valtonen, Meriläinen, Laine and Salmela-Leppänen, 2017). Valtonen et al. (2017) see these conceptualisations as
possibilities to overcome the challenge of grasping the relational and situated
nature of practices and as ways to illustrate, for example, the inner rhythmi-
city of body and the gradual changes in the body's sensory attachment.

Gherardi (2017) suggests addressing the situatedness of practices through
making the affects and affective atmospheres visible and by being sensitive to

epistemological issues. Gherardi's suggestion can be linked to Ingold's (2011) ideas of becoming and being-in-the-world, which, put simply, is that there is a richness in our everyday environments and in how we improvise our encounters. According to Ingold, the improvisation lays in the ability to observe our (and other's) presence in the world and in the movement along a way of life. For Ingold the becoming is constructed along paths where 'lives are lived, skills developed, observations made and understandings grown' (Ingold, 2011: 12). The reference to path seeks to capture how humans and non-humans make their ways in the world – in relation to each other.

This relationship between surroundings and perceiver can be seen in the in-between dynamics of nature holidays practices, that is, 'the dynamics of bringing things into your presence' (Ingold, 2017). To this process, I apply Henri Lefebvre's rhythmanalytical tools to unveil certain responsible or environmentally sensitive practices. By sensitiveness, I refer to Höckert's idea of openness towards alternative ways of 'being, doing and knowing together' (Höckert, 2015: 5), which aims towards acknowledging diverse agencies and resembles Ingold's idea of bringing things (and here agencies) into presence. However, it is difficult to identify certain practices that would enhance the sustainability of nature-based tourism better than other practices. For example, it could be expected that carrying all the food needed for a five-day wild camping (e.g. camping in wilderness without marked trails) trip in a rucksack, cooking the food on a fire or portable stove and dealing with the waste produced without waste containers would provide a material basis for a nature tourist to carry out recycling practices in a somewhat routinised way in his or her everyday environment. But, in fact, contrary to this, the rhythmanalytical exploration showed that the situation is far more complex and dynamic. The social, embodied and materially mediated conditions for recycling in everyday environments differ from those in wild camping environments. Therefore, becoming 'a friend of nature' (Salonen, 2014) seems to require something besides trying to internalise and routinise the practice of recycling, to name one.

The rhythmanalytical examination has helped in identifying what it can mean when the rhythm of carrying familiar practices changes. For example, there might be new intensity in caring for the family (Rantala and Varley, no date) and the impact of the material environment on one's practices (and body) is reflected upon (Rantala and Valtonen, 2014), and one's attunement to everyday routines and relations changes (Rantala, 2015). This chapter goes deeper into these insights. I first briefly introduce recent applications of the rhythmanalytical approach and the empirical context of the chapter. Next, I explore the possibilities for environmental sensitiveness by analysing the practical concerns related to practising tourism in nature environments, the ways of doing otherwise and the intertwined rhythms of ordinary living. I end the chapter by discussing when an environmental practice becomes constructed as a holiday practice and how these holiday practices could be turned into objects of observation of everyday life and 'sustaining life' (Ingold, 2017).

Rhythms of nature, rhythms of everyday life

Lefebvre's *Rhythmanalysis* has been used to illustrate how normative rhythms (often linked to state and capitalist processes) interact with diverse counter rhythms, constructing dynamics of ordering and disordering (Edensor, 2010). In Lefebvre's (2004) rhythmanalysis, 'cyclical time' refers to the natural and cosmic rhythms to which humans have been exposed from the beginning of time until the development of modern civilisation. In modernity, this repetition continues but it is derived from technology, work and production (Gardiner, 2000: 87; Lefebvre, 1984: 6). According to Lefebvre, linear repetition may resemble cyclical rhythm but can never become an actual rhythm. Hence, the interferences between cyclical and linear time make an especially interesting observation point for the rhythmanalyst, which becomes evident in the contrast between clock time and lived time (Elden, 2004: x; Rantala and Valtonen, 2014).

Within the approach, the focus on measuring various intersecting rhythms, such as polyrhythmic, eurythmic, isorhythmic and arrhythmic beats, offers a tool for a researcher to overcome dualistic examination and description (Conlon, 2010). Polyrhythmia refers to the multiplicity of rhythms and to the uniqueness of particular rhythms, eurhythmia to how the rhythms unite with one another in everydayness; and arrhythmia to when they are discordant (Lefebvre, 2004: 16). Isorhythm refers to the harmony formed by the innumerable rhythms present in the body (Meyer, 2008: 150). The examination of these rhythms can be conducted either on the level of embodied experience of rhythms, by focusing on rhythms within a specific social practice, or by exploring the level of wider societal rhythms. Whatever the scale of analysis, what is important is the production of diverse understandings by considering representations in tandem with materiality and embodied experience (Hensley, 2010). In doing so, the rhythmanalytical approach can be in itself seen as an approach that avoids contradicting representational and non-representational approaches. Instead, it takes rhythm and the dynamics between time and space as the starting point. It focuses on the process of becoming (Edensor, 2010).

Lefebvre's description of rhythmanalysis has been criticised as partly failing to reach the actual embodied experience and the body's capacity to affect and be affected (Edensor, 2010: 5). In addition, Conlon (2010: 73) points out that Lefebvre in his analysis tends to describe the linear, institutional rhythms in ways that construct dualism between those and cyclical, resistant beats – even though his aim is to avoid such dualism. Despite its limitations, the approach does offer a loose framework that encourages the researcher to pay attention to the interplay between ordering and disordering qualities of practices.

Spinney (2010: 119) argues that the interplay between ordering and dis-ordering qualities should not be seen as resistance *per se*, but as different orientations towards material and immaterial affordances and as diverse engagements in the process of making do – or the process of becoming, as Ingold (2011) would call it. For example, by exploring how rhythms of cycling in London are structured through the different experiences of time, vulnerability and energy, Spinney (2010: 119) is able to explain 'inappropriate' rhythms as improvised and as a process of perceiving and possessing affor-dances other than those facilitated by the dominant ordering of the city (commuting). He underlines that the act of cycling in a city should not be seen merely as resistance towards the official ordering of space and time, but as illustrative of the existence of a broad range of rhythms – 'produced and experienced simultaneously' (Spinney, 2010: 119).

The rhythmanalytical approach has been applied in a similar manner to Spinney's interpretation by Vannini and Taggart (2015) in their context of Canadian off-grid homes. Vannini and Taggart illustrate how the off-grid home functions in synchrony with the textures of darkness, brought by weather, seasons and natural daily cycles of light. In their analysis, the affec-tive significance of the likelihood of running out of power and the importance of values such as efficiency are brought up by exploring the rhythms of everyday practices. The rhythms of practising off-grid life intertwine around an anticipation of weather. Vannini and Taggart link off-grid everyday living to an opportunistic way of synchronising energy production, consumption, everyday rhythms and rhythms of light and darkness.

In the current chapter, the figures of the opportunistic off-gridder and improvising city biker are applied to the case of the nature tourist, who stays overnight in nature. I especially pay attention to the improvisation generated by practical concerns and to the affective qualities of ordering and disorder-ing practices. I use examples drawn from empirical fieldwork conducted during 2012 and 2015 and from a writing competition related to second-home living, which was organised in 2004. The discussion of the rhythms of envir-onmental practices of a nature tourist takes place in the context of Finland and northern Norway and with experiences of Finnish nature tourists. It should be noted here that even though in larger cities in Finland one can live 'an urban life', the cities are largely embedded in natural environments, and, due to everyman's rights, there is good access to the nearby nature areas,[1] and participation in different outdoor recreation activities is common. For exam-ple, 96.1% of the Finnish population participated in outdoor recreation in 2010, the most common activities being walking, biking and second-home living (LUKE, 2010) and more than half of the Finnish population has access to a second home. However, there are several studies showing how the everyday embodied experience of environment changes when one does not need to work for heating (or air conditioning), light and dealing with waste (e. g. Hitchings, 2011; Willamo, 2005). I try to avoid constructing the 'nature tourist' through urban-rural polarisation, but aim to examine the dynamics of everyday practices in a holiday context, which is expected to have a different rhythm from the everyday context.

Improvising on a nature holiday

In Lefebvre's rhythmanalysis, the role of dynamics between cyclical and linear time is central, and this dynamic is very dominant in the ordering of daily holiday life in nature. The tempo of a nature holiday, especially when one spends overnight in nature, is constructed with the seasons and with the elemental influence of the weather at hand. The lack of alarm clocks, electric lights, indoor toilets and running water, and the reduced use of mobile devices mean that the patterns of activities and communications – or patterns of being still – are adjusted according to the cycles of nature. Everyday practices that have been carried out in a linear rhythm based on daily routines (e.g. work, school and day care) are re-rhythmed during a nature holiday little by little according to cyclical rhythms of light and darkness, bodily rhythms and weather. Nature tourists say that it takes some time to get into the rhythm of a nature holiday. Within a few days' time the body leaves the accustomed rhythm of everyday life and adjusts to the new holiday rhythm. Similarly, when coming back, nature tourists slowly readjust back to the everyday rhythm: 'We have a specific way – we start to open ourselves little by little to the world outside – when we turn on the radio, when we pick up the mobile phones' (Focus group interview, 2012).

Since the cyclical rhythms of nature, light and weather so strongly affect the carrying out of holiday practices, teasing out the environmental sensitiveness of the practices becomes obscured. At first glance, the nature tourist seems to be sensing the more-than-human agency through the whole body. To take a step further from the sensual embodied experience, one needs to focus in a more concrete way on how the nature tourist is oriented to the world while engaging in a nature holiday. What are the orderings according to which the nature tourist 'navigates' (Spinney, 2010) in nature? Nicolini (2009: 1403) suggests studying the practical concerns towards which practices are oriented in order to describe how the members experience the ordering capacity of practices. A closer look at the practices of nature tourists shows that even though the practices are carried out within the rhythm of nature, the practices are very much human-centred. Practices are oriented towards the embodied agency of the nature tourist or towards materialities that relate to the embodied being in nature.

> Suddenly the sun starts to really shine and the place warms up. The packing flows better with the sunshine, and when mosquitos do not fly into your mouth. The place feels nice again. The waterfall continues to rush; it provides us with fresh water to drink and to wash with – both dishes and ourselves.
>
> (Field notes 2015).

The nature tourist is concerned with keeping the body warm, keeping hunger and thirst away, and at the same time keeping life peaceful. He or she is concerned with keeping themselves, and their companions, safe. The nature tourist is also concerned about keeping things clean (not so much for the sake of cleanness but for safety). Without electricity and running water – or perhaps with the reduced equipment of a second home – the rhythm of a nature holiday intertwines around practices that are related to keeping warm, eating and sleeping – that is, practices related to being safe and alive. Much attention is paid to choosing the campsite, setting up camp or building and preparing the second home, making food with available equipment, warming up the cabin or attending to the sleeping bags and mattresses for keeping warm.

Without the rhythms of waged work and materialities of the everyday environment, the order of the nature holiday is constructed around the rhythm of the body and that of the environment, and the intense interaction – and often struggle – between these two. The interaction between body and environment is mediated through handling equipment and through specific skills related to that equipment. It is the cabin that 'grows old with you', the tent that forms 'my wonderful own home', and the rucksack, boots or skis that mediate the interaction. The cabin and the tent are discussed with care in the nature tourist's voice, and this illustrates the being and doing together – the process of becoming together. For instance, by carrying a tent along, by packing and unpacking it, by trying to make it dry, by falling asleep and waking up in the special light of the tent, the nature tourist makes her/his way in nature in relation to the tent.

Overall, the orderings according to which a nature tourist sets about engaging in the holiday are oriented towards human wellbeing. The cyclical rhythm of nature is strongly present and experienced nature tourists use this cyclical order to enhance their wellbeing. For example, having fewer lights on in the evening is not discussed in relation to use of natural resources, but in relation to getting into the rhythm of nature and 'achieving balance'. In a similar way, having fewer technologies and artefacts is explicitly connected to human wellbeing by discussing how having fewer things gives one a greater feeling of autonomy and freedom (instead of tending to things – finding, cleaning, repairing, organising).

The human-nature interaction thus seems to enhance human wellbeing by enabling the nature tourist to listen to the rhythms of one's body and how the rhythms are in balance – or often arrhythmic – with the surrounding environment. Nicolini (2009: 1403) suggests that practical concerns are never held tacitly but are customarily addressed verbally and discussed, for example, through the vocabulary of justifications. The justifications construct the shared understanding of what needs to be done (ibid.). One clear example of justifications is the idea of a slower life: the scarcity of equipment when one is engaged in simplified outdoor living tactics enables one to turn attention to the 'within corporeality' (Valtonen et al., 2017) instead of taking care of running everyday errands. Within corporeality refers to circadian (bodily rhythms of day and night) and social rhythms that are often set aside in – for example – the work environment, but which are brought to the fore in an outdoor living environment. Observing circadian and social rhythms in relation to how the use of equipment is justified illustrates what kind of role more-than-human agency is given.

There are examples that hint towards sensitive interaction with more-than-human agency in the context of what is seen as appropriate on a nature holiday and what is not. A group of Scouts told me – when I visited their snow caves in Spring 2012 – that they try to show to the younger ones that you can go camping without fancy equipment. The camp that the local Scouts organise in a gorge of a fell in western Lapland every spring is based on the idea of not having any other purpose than making the snow caves where the teenagers and the organisers sleep and 'hang around'. They make meals in small groups when they feel hungry, visit a nearby open hut to dry the wet equipment, slide down hills or ski off-piste at the fell. The participants do not buy new equipment for the winter conditions, but gather all kinds of 'at hand' equipment.

I still have a very vivid image from my visit to the gorge: different kinds of sleds, skis and snowshoes lying around, clothes hanging from trees, a variety of portable stoves on shelves made of snow (Figure 5.1). In April 2012, spring arrived late and there were no spots free of snow even on the sunny side of the gorge, so the Scouts constructed warm places to sit on from sledges or hung hammocks in trees. When comparing this image to the field notes I have of my own wild-camping trips and then to my colleague Peter Varley's field notes and to the data from second-home writings, the role of improvising with

Figure 5.1 Entrance and 'cooking corner' next to a snow cave.

available equipment gets stronger. First, especially in the case of wild camping, the nature tourist has to manage with the materialities that have been brought along or that are available in nature. Often something is missing or materials are used in creative ways, such as constructing shelves with snow, stones or branches. The ordering of a nature holiday becomes constructed in connection to scarce resources and the improvised use of available resources – through an opportunistic attitude towards the resources. Hence, environmental sensitivity here could mean readiness to interrupt one's own (learned) ways of 'being, doing and thinking' and being open (sensitive) towards different ways of being, doing and knowing with nature (Höckert, 2015).

Second, even though equipment bought for the very purpose of the nature holiday becomes very dear to the nature tourists – such as the tent as a wonderful own home – a lot of equipment has been originally bought for another purpose and is now being reused in the context of a nature holiday, for example, old film containers that are used to store spices or old baby towels that dry easily and are used in camping conditions even when the children grow up. In second homes, clothes and shoes are shared and old porcelain and furniture are cherished. Kinnunen (2016) describes our relationship to materialities that have no instrumental value to us – to things that refuse to be useful, and suggests that we should learn to co-exist with waste. With co-existing, she refers to both caring for things but also to the potential for emotional engagement with things that could be regarded as waste. In wild camping and at second homes not only useful items are cherished and their use improvised, but one also needs to improvise with many different kinds of (disgusting) waste produced during the holiday – and either reuse them, pack them out, burn them or bury them properly.

The agency of equipment is observed in the process of handling and valuing the equipment and hints towards sensitivity that could be constructed, as Ingold (2011) refers to it, 'along the paths'. Pink and Leder Mackley (2016) have also applied Ingold's idea of paths in their study of mundane improvisation, in which they describe everyday routines and routes in the pathways of movement. They see routines as moments of movement where interventions are already being made by the participants. Improvisations and interventions presuppose an ongoing process of knowing and being together with the more-than-human world. Improvisation along the path requires 'skilful handling' (Ingold, 2011) of the equipment and this skilfulness develops as we move along the path. When environmental sensitiveness is about being, doing and knowing together with the equipment of camping or 'thinking with' (Ulmer, 2017) the objects we do camping with, the importance of caring for these objects emanates. We develop care towards the non-human world through improvising with waste, rocks, fresh water, film containers and old baby towels. This way the change of rhythm on a nature holiday opens up possibilities for not only human wellbeing, but also for the wellbeing of the more-than-human world. This wellbeing derives from the mundane orientation towards caring (Kinnunen, 2017).

The ordering of a nature holiday becomes constructed through repetition of cyclical rhythms and bodily rhythms. Getting out of everyday linear rhythm, away from clock-time and everyday errands into the cyclical rhythm of nature is seen as beneficial (see also Varley and Semple, 2015). The ordering of a nature holiday does not exist without the everyday environment but in connection to it (Hall and Holdsworth, 2016; Larsen, 2008). Everyday life constructs the need for balancing it with, for example, spending the holiday outdoors and listening to the rhythms of one's own body brought up by the rhythms of nature. During nature holidays, the practical concerns deal with getting along with the things we have chosen to bring with us: with making sure, that these things keep us warm and content. The shared understanding of what needs to be done during nature holidays covers mundane care for equipment and improvisation with scarce resources. Hence, well-being of the more-than-human world is made possible when our practical concerns and care for the more-than-human world are made tangible. By focusing on simplified outdoor living, the manifestation of sensitivities towards nature and its agency can be teased out – such as the caring for things we have around us when there is a scarcity of things.

Disordering human-centred practices

One of the participants in the writing competition regarding second-home life[2] captures the 'sensory aesthetics' (Pink and Leder Mackley, 2016) related to conducting familiar everyday practices in a nature holiday context: the morning starts outside (in the wooden outdoor toilet) – not in the indoor toilet of the primary home. The sensory aesthetics of being outdoors is present in the descriptions of early mornings, late evenings, struggles with ever-changing weather, in the moments of being still, in the moments of being scared – in the soundscapes and lightscapes of the outdoors. These moments seem to construct a counterpart to the routinised, controlled and mechanical everyday life (Bauman, 1996: 42–45; Ehn and Löfgren, 2010: 80). It seems to be clear that the rhythm of nature provides an aesthetic dimension for conducting everyday practices – without the actual routines needing to be different from the everyday. The strong agency of nature makes the *could-be-otherwise-ness* (Germann Molz, 2014) visible. Conducting familiar everyday routines in the tempo of nature shows how contingent our social arrangements and material worlds are. These worlds afford security and confidence, but also constrain action and exploration because of their 'weight' (Rantala and Varley, no date).

The could-be-otherwise-ness is revealed, for example, in a moment of being thoroughly worried about one's family – for instance, when spending a night in the wilderness with small children, far away from all security networks (Rantala and Varley, no date). The could-be-otherwise-ness becomes obvious in the dearness of old furniture and clothing cherished at the second home – in the improvised and tacit ways of manipulating the consumer-centred culture (Henriques, 2010; Rantala, 2015). The could-be-otherwise-ness encompasses a privileged position of testing one's readiness to interrupt the learned ways of being, doing and thinking – but simultaneously preserving the right to return back to the everyday, which may burst with artefacts and possibilities. The could-be-otherwise-ness is exposed during the evenings at the camp – when one spends the evening skipping stones on the river with the kids, preparing dinner in a pouring rain, being irritated by mosquitoes or reading the map and imaging possible routes for the days to come. Having dinner with the family, you enjoy the settling of the night, the happiness of the kids, and the quiet atmosphere of the hut (Figure 5.2).

Figure 5.2 Dinner in an open hut.

Gherardi (2017) suggests that the search for post-epistemological possibilities to link the social and the natural, the mind and the body, and the cognitive and the affective come together when a practice approach and an affect approach are combined (Gherardi, 2017: 5). Furthermore, Gherardi (2017) refers to the in-betweenness that is in the core of relational epistemology. Similarly, Hensley (2010: 165) suggests (in the context of rumba) that in order to produce diverse understandings of rhythmic embodiment, we should ask if the notion of 'having rhythm' always relies on a body/mind and nature/culture division – or whether we could understand the process of *having* as a process of *becoming* with other people and through particular places. The possibilities for sensitiveness that are 'hidden' in a nature holiday lay in a rhythmic embodiment that derives from the process of becoming in connection to the outdoors where we camp and in connection with the people with whom we camp. This becoming does not mean that we would turn into responsible and environmentally sensitive persons during our nature holidays, but rather refers to the dynamic and continuous process of transformation that is intertwined with the material, situated world where we spend the holiday – a transformation that entails possibility for alternative ways of living. The process of becoming entails possibilities since it shows us the fragile could-be-otherwise-ness of our everyday living. Sometimes the otherwise-ness illustrates a change for the worse, sometimes for the better.

In a similar way, becoming is a theme in Hall and Holdsworth's (2016) analysis, where they show how holidays can be used to perform the everyday as it should be – either by consuming luxurious products or, as would be the case in a wild camping situation, by spending intensive time together as a family and by living in a healthy environment. Even though these utopian quality holidays would not always be achieved fully in practice, the value of a holiday is in that it provides a space for making disappointments visible and dealing with the frustrations of everyday life (Hall and Holdsworth, 2016: 296). In practice, the pictures from fieldwork do not show picturesque dinners (see Figure 5.2 in this chapter and Figure 1 in Hall and Holdsworth, 2016), but this does not diminish the importance of holiday practices in the process of becoming – and especially in opening new possibilities within the process. During a nature holiday we face – not avoid – both pleasant and unpleasant encounters in a very intensive and intimate way. This opens up the possibility for reflection and for reordering, for developing skills, but also for seeing ourselves as more sensitive persons.

Nature holiday practices seem to hold a strong essence of in-betweenness that emerges through a rhythmanalytical approach. For example, it is highlighted that it is not the clock-time but the differences in light and darkness that are followed, or the feelings of one's body, or the feelings of the company in connection to one's own feelings. The affective qualities, located between the body and mind and between nature and culture, define the process of becoming a nature tourist. Emphasis should be on the becoming. One is always becoming because the rhythm of being in nature is constructed in relation to the rhythm of the everyday and one does not exist without the other. (Unless being in nature IS your everyday life – but even in a story from the writing competition that was written by a farm owner who constructed a cabin at the far end of her farm, the rhythm of the farm differed from the rhythm of the second home.)

Even though the in-betweenness is constructed on holiday and in relation to everyday life, it should, perhaps, not be seen as resistance to everyday life in itself, but more as a re-purposing, which holds the capacity of becoming sensitive (see also Spinney, 2010). Living in the tempo of nature and in synchrony with the surrounding nature, one's body and companions are 'a way of learning to be sensitive to the "vibrant matter" of the lifeworld and the vitality of the things inhabiting the interface between animate and inanimate life' (Vannini and Taggart, 2015: 651 referring to Bennett, 2010). Vannini and Taggart (2015: 651) argue that if we wish to become more opportunistic and more efficient in energy consumption and production, we can no longer afford to ignore the cosmic and climatic rhythms of daylight and darkness. For them, the renewed attention to the rhythms of entanglements of society and nature might be one of the keys to the sustainable regeneration of everyday life – for sustaining life.

Höckert (2015) refers to the idea of 'welcoming the other' when she explores responsible ways of doing togetherness among ourselves. This idea of welcome calls for readiness to be interrupted as a spontaneous, individual subject (ibid.). The in-betweenness of the agencies and orderings can be captured with the idea of openness and welcoming the other and multiple others. In the rhythm of nature – in the aesthetic tempo – one needs to welcome one's body as it is, the conditions of the campground as they are and the companions with their failures, frailties and skills as they are and use everything that one has at hand in the situation of being in the wilderness (see also Rantala and Varley, no date). For example, an older second-home owner describes the process of growing old with her cabin: she tells that nowadays they – she and the cabin – recognise one another's 'creaks and detritions'. Other second-home owners describe in a similar manner how their second homes have worked as arenas of encounters between generations, between the family and surrounding nature and as an arena for people's life-journey. Clingerman (2017) calls this 'aesthetic attunement' or 'wholehearted engagement'. The wholehearted engagement with one's surroundings is not about picturesque moments described in the beginning of the chapter, but about the dynamic engagement that is included in these moments (either picturesque ones or ones that deal with struggle). The dynamic engagement with diverse cosmic, climatic and social rhythms means facing and welcoming alternative ways of being. Here, within the in-betweenness, there exists the possibility for disordering the human-centred orientation of nature holidays.

Intertwined rhythms of ordinary living

Nicolini (2009) highlights the importance of studying practices at multiple levels, from closely to at a distance, in connection to the associations and effects the practices hold. Here, it has been suggested that the sensory aesthetics of nature holiday practices hold a possibility to enhance environmental awareness in everyday life as well by making us aware of the things we are engaged with and by making our caring tangible. In addition, the connections between everyday and holiday practices have been pointed out: The ordering of a nature holiday exists in connection to everyday (Hall and Holdsworth, 2016; Larsen, 2008). Despite the mobile character of the contemporary life, it has been suggested that nature holidays construct a specific time and space within which the tacit routines of everyday life are somehow disrupted (Kinnunen, 2017). Hence, the simplified nature holiday tactics have been seen as a vantage point from which to study the possibilities for environmental sensitiveness. For example, the role of improvisation and the role of scarcity of things become highlighted when observing the practices that take place during overnight stays in nature.

In order to study how the encountering of the more-than-human agency in a nature holiday context travels to the sphere of everyday life, one should study the nature tourist in an everyday context. Are the aesthetics of a cyclical tempo present in everyday living? How do we nurture improvisation in the everyday? How do we allow for wholehearted engagement with our environment?

Law and Urry (2004) and Law and Joks (2016) suggest that we should not try to compromise and fit different realities together, but instead we should search for down-to-earth material practices that fit well together (see also Verran, 1998). Applying their idea, we can see the nature tourist and the everyday person as participants in different spheres of life – or in different realities, who in a practical manner bring rhythms and agencies with them from one sphere to another. At the same time, the very same materialities make the spheres different. For example, the portable stove, the knife with a reindeer bone and wooden handle, the warm sleeping bag and the spices in old film containers – all these important and dear objects are stored in the closet during everyday life, but they hold a strong agency during the nature holiday. However, the mundane orientation towards caring that is present in the simplified outdoor living tactics can also be transferred into the sphere of everyday life, instead storing it. For example, the attunement towards alternative ways of living in the world may be present in the way we face pleasant and unpleasant everyday encounters, in the way we care for the things and people in our everyday environments, or in our attitudes towards the climatic rhythms and in the ways of coping with these rhythms.

Vannini and Taggart (2015) are also concerned with intertwined rhythms of ordinary living and show how off-gridders challenge the speed, light and power assemblages of modernity by cultivating a slower rhythm and power self-sufficiency. Some of the off-gridders work in town but live in homes that are in a temporal space removed from the rhythms of the city. The off-gridders are able to see the value of their current slower domestic practices in relation to their previous lifestyles or to the lifestyles of their friends and relatives (see Vannini and Taggart, 2015: 646). In a similar fashion, the different temporal and material spaces construct different realities for the nature tourist at the primary home and at the second home or in the wilderness and their everyday environment, but the different arrangements do not exist in a vacuum. Instead, there is a continuous interplay and in-betweenness existing between the different realities and their rhythms. It is argued here that becoming a friend of nature – a person who perceives the nuances of more-than-human agency in nature – can take place through being able to articulate the values of a slower life or through having new rhythms in life (see also Salonen, 2014). These emerge with small details such as having fewer lights on in evening, improvising with existing things instead of buying new ones or moments of intimate care for things or people around us. The new rhythms are embodied during a nature holiday, but are carried in the body and in the equipment to the sphere of everyday life.

Conclusion

This chapter has discussed how the practices that take place in the sphere of nature tourism create certain orderings and possibilities for disordering in relation to being environmentally sensitive. Tourism has often been studied in isolation from everyday life, as a distinct phenomenon. Practice theoretical approaches aim to overcome various dualities – such as nature/culture, human/non-human and body/mind – emerging from this everyday disconnect. The practice theoretical approach helps the researcher to pay attention to the rhythms of different times and spaces and to study how these rhythms travel between the everyday and holiday life. Furthermore, the dualism is not a tangible object to be measured and categorised, but something that should be addressed by being sensitive to epistemological issues. Here, sensitiveness has been practised by paying attention – in the form of the aesthetic tradition within the practice theoretical approach – to how materialities, embodiments and representations are carried in diverse cyclical and linear rhythms and how those travel from everyday living to holiday life and back.

The discussion has taken place by illustrating the practice theory approach in the context of nature holidays. Practising nature-based tourism and everyday life in northern Finland and Norway differs from practising it in many other places: the easy access to relatively safe wilderness and to second-home living enables the rhythms of a nature holiday and the everyday to travel quite easily between these realities. Associating the Finnish nature tourist with Canadian off-gridders or with a city-biker from London shows that there are important lessons learned when studying rhythmic practices – which can be applied more widely. First, the environmental practices that take place on a nature holiday should not be understood as resistance to everyday life but as processes of becoming in connection to particular materialities, to other people and to particular places. The rhythms are intertwined in ordinary living. Second, even though everyday life and holiday life can be seen as different realities, formed by different spaces and times, the rhythms of these realities do travel in the form of embodied practices and sensitivities. The rhythms of the different realities are made tangible both customarily and tacitly. Third, even though the environmental practices are oriented towards human wellbeing, there are rhythms of entanglements of society and nature involved and included. These rhythms bring forth the more-than-human agency and make environmental sensitiveness possible.

As pointed out, the discussion has taken place in the context of Northern Europe – there are places in the world where gathering daily food from the forest, sleeping in a tent, coping with the changing rhythms of weather and seasons, dealing with waste and caring for the scarce things inherited are part of the everyday. This should not prevent us from asking – as Ingold (2011: 32, see also Pink and Leder Mackley, 2016) does: How do we 'design *for* improvisation'? How do we prepare to be unprepared (Höckert, 2015)? How could the rhythms that are lived in nature environments also be enabled in modern everyday life so that we are forced to improvise with the waste we produce and with the things and people we have around, and also forced to reflect on the consequences of our improvisation. There have been recent calls for research to pay attention to how we live through different existential realities, different rhythms and different sensory states (Valtonen et al., 2017) and to explore mundane encounters in polluted destinations, pollen-intensive regions and hygiene-less settings and services (Jensen Trandberg, 2016). These topics help us to examine possibilities for environmental sensitiveness further in new contexts.

Notes

1 In Europe, public right of access is most widely applied in the Nordic countries. The most important features of everyman's rights are that they give everyone the basic right to roam freely in the countryside, no matter who owns or occupies the land. Camping for a short period is also possible as well as picking berries and mushrooms (Finnish Ministry of Environment 2013).
2 The writing competition was organised through a magazine targeted at second-home owners who were asked to write about their holiday home and about their free time. Altogether 95 entries were received.

References

Alaimo, S. (2010). *Bodily Natures: Science, Environment, and the Material Self.* Bloomington, IN: Indiana University Press.
Bauman, Z. (1996). *Postmodernin Lumo.* Tampere: Vastapaino.
Bennett, J. (2010). *Vibrant Matter.* Durham, NC: Duke University Press.
Clingerman, F. (2017). Imagination and the Space of Politics. Paper presented at 2nd Peaceful Coexistence Colloquium – Reimagining Ethics and Politics of Space for the Anthropocene. 6–9 June 2017. Pyhä, Finland.
Conlon, D. (2010). Fascinatin' rhythm(s). Polyrhythmia and the syncopated echoes of the everyday. In T. Edensor (ed.), *Geographies of Rhythm. Nature, Place, Mobilities and Bodies.* Surrey: Ashgate, pp. 71–82.

de Certeau, M. (1984). *The Practice of Everyday Life*. Berkeley: University of California Press.

de Souza Bispo, M. (2016). Tourism as practice. *Annals of Tourism Research*, 61: 170–179.

Edensor, T. (2010). Introduction. Thinking about rhythm and space. In T. Edensor (ed.), *Geographies of Rhythm. Nature, Place, Mobilities and Bodies*. Surrey: Ashgate, pp. 1–18.

Ehn, B. and Löfgren, O. (2010). *The Secret World of Doing Nothing*. Berkeley: University of California Press.

Elden, S. (2004). Rhythmanalysis: an introduction. In H. Lefebvre, *Rhythmanalysis: Space, Time and Everyday Life*. London: GBR.

Finnish Ministry of Environment (2013). Everymans right in Finland. www.ym.fi/en-US/Latest_news/Publications/Brochures/Everymans_right(4484)

Franklin, A. (2004). Tourism as an ordering: towards a new ontology of tourism. *Tourist Studies*, 4(3): 277–301.

Franklin, A. (2012). The choreography of a mobile world: tourist orderings. In R. Van der Duim, C. Renand and G. T. Jóhannesson (eds), *Actor-Network Theory and Tourism: Ordering, Materiality and Multiplicity*. London and new York: Routledge, pp. 43–58.

Gardiner, M. (2000). *Critiques of Everyday Life*. London: Routledge.

Germann Molz, J. (2014). Camping in clearing. In S. Veijola, J. Germann Molz, O. Pyyhtinen, E. Höcker and A. Grit (eds), *Disruptive Tourism and Its Untidy Guests. Alternative Ontologies for Future Hospitalities*. Hampshire: Palgrave Macmillan, pp. 19–41.

Gherardi, S. (2017). One turn … and now another one: do the turn to practice and the turn to affect have something in common? *Management Learning*: 1–14.

Hall, S. M. and Holdsworth, C. (2016). Family practices, holiday and the everyday. *Mobilities*, 11(2): 284–302.

Hensley, S. (2010). Rumba and rhythmic 'natures' in Cuba. In T. Edensor (ed.), *Geographies of Rhythm. Nature, Place, Mobilities and Bodies*. Surrey: Ashgate, pp. 159–172.

Henriques, J. (2010). The vibrations of affect and their propagation on a night out on Kingston's dancehall scene. *Body & Society*, 16: 57–89.

Hitchings, R. (2011). Researching air-conditioning addiction and ways of puncturing practice: professional office workers and the decision to go outside . *Environment and Planning A*, 43(12): 2838–2856.

Höckert, E. (2015). *Ethics of Hospitality: Participatory Tourism Encounters in the Northern Highlands of Nicaragua*. Dissertation, Department of Social Sciences, University of Lapland. http://lauda.ulapland.fi/handle/10024/62200.

Ingold, T. (2011). *Being Alive. Essays on Movement, Knowledge and Description*. London: Routledge.

Ingold, T. (2017). Ways of telling. Lecture series Northern Cultural Studies. March 16, 2017. University of Lapland.

Jensen Trandberg, M. (2016). Hypersensitive tourists: the dark sides of the sensuous. *Annals of Tourism Research*, 57: 234–278.

Jóhannesson, G. T., Ren, C. and van der Duim, R. (2015). Tourism encounters, controversies and ontologies. In G. T. Jóhannesson, C. Ren and R. van der Duim (eds), *Tourism Encounters and Controversies. Ontological Politics of Tourism Development*. Surrey: Ashgate, pp. 1–20.

Kinnunen, V. (2016). Jakaisimmeko elämämme jätteen kanssa? Eettisen materialismin hahmottelua [Would we share our lives with waste? Sketching ethical materialism]. *Sosiologia*, 3: 310–317.

Kinnunen, V. (2017). Tavarat tiellä. Sosiologinen tutkimus esinesuhteista muutossa. [Things in and on the way. A sociological study on the relationship between people and things.] *Acta Universitatis Lapponiensis 362*. Rovaniemi: Lapland University Press.

Lamers, M., van der Duim, R. and Spaargaren, G. (2017). The relevance of practice theories for tourism research. *Annals of Tourism Research*, 62: 54–63.

Larsen, J. (2008). De-exoticizing tourist travel: everyday life and sociality on the move. *Leisure Studies*, 27(1): 21–34.

Law, J. and Joks, S. (2016). Luossa and Laks: salmon, science and LEK. *Anthropology of Knowledge*: 1–12.

Law, J. and Urry, J. (2004). Enacting the social. *Economy and Society*, 33(3): 390–410.

Lefebvre, H. (1984). *Everyday Life in the Modern World*. New Brunswick: Transaction Publishers.

Lefebvre, H. (2004). *Rhythmanalysis. Space, Time and Everyday Life*. London: Continuum.

LUKE (2010). Outdoor recreation statistics. Available at www.metla.fi/metinfo/monika ytto/lvvi/tilastot_2010/2010-taulukko-1.htm. Visited on 21 April 2017.

Meyer, K. (2008). Rhythms, streets, cities. In K. Goonewardena, S. Kipfer, R. Milgrom and C. Schmid (eds), *Space, Difference, Everyday Life. Reading Henri Lefebvre*. New York: Routledge, 147–160.

Nicolini, D. (2009). Zooming in and out: studying practices by switching theoretical lenses and trailing connections. *Organization Studies*, 30(12): 1391–1418.

Pink, S. and Leder Mackley, K. (2016). Moving, making and atmosphere: routines of home as sites for mundane improvisation. *Mobilities*, 11(2): 171–187.

Rantala, O. (2015). Lomakodin rytmittämä arki [Everyday rhythm at the second home]. *Sosiologia*, 2: 89–103.

Rantala, O. and Valtonen, A. (2014). A rhythmanalysis of touristic sleep in nature. *Annals of Tourism Research*, 42: 18–30.

Rantala, O. and Varley, P. (no date). Wild camping and the weight of tourism. Unpublished manuscript.

Salonen, T. (2009). Luonto, arvot ja matkailu. Ihmisen ongelma ja pohjoisen ihmisen kadotettu luonto [Nature, values and tourism. The problem of the human and the lost nature in the north]. In V. Tökkäri (ed.), *Valta, luonto ja ihminen. Symposiontekstejä, Lapin yliopiston menetelmätieteiden laitoksen raportteja, esseitä ja työpapereita 13, filosofia*. Rovaniemi: Lapland University Press, pp. 127–169.

Salonen, T. (2014). Luontokeskuksista luontoa tuntemaan [Getting out from the nature centres to experience the nature]. In J. Valkonen and T. Salonen (eds), *Reittejä luontosuhteeseen*. Rovaniemi: Lapland University Press, 37–64.

Spinney, J. (2010). Improvising rhythms. Re-reading urban time and space through everyday practices of cycling. In T. Edensor (ed.), *Geographies of Rhythm. Nature, Place, Mobilities and Bodies*, Surrey: Ashgate, pp. 113–128.

Ulmer, J. B. (2017). Posthumanism as research methodology: inquiry in the Anthropocene. *International Journal of Qualitative Studies in Education*, 30: 832–848.

Valtonen, A., Meriläinen, S., Laine, P.-M. and Salmela-Leppänen, T. (2017). The knowing body as a floating body. *Management Learning*, 48(5): 520–534.

Vannini, P. (2015). Non-representational ethnography: new ways of animating lifeworlds. *Cultural Geographies*, 22(2): 317–327.

Vannini, P. and Taggart, J. (2015). Solar energy, bad weather days, and the temporalities of slower homes. *Cultural Geographies*, 22(4): 637–657.

Varley, P. and Semple, T. (2015). Nordic slow adventure: explorations in time and nature. *Scandinavian Journal of Hospitality and Tourism*, 15(1–2): 73–90.

Verran, H. (1998). Re-imagining land ownership in Australia. *Postcolonial Studies*, 1 (2): 237–254.

Willamo, R. (2005). Kokonaisvaltainen lähestymistapa ympäristönsuojelutieteessä. Sisällön moniulotteisuus ympäristönsuojelijan haasteena [A holistic approach in nature conservation sciences]. *Environmentalica Fennica 23*. Helsinki: Helsinki University Press.

6 Cooking as practice

An aesthetic approach for tourism and hospitality

Marcelo de Souza Bispo, Lídia Cunha Soares and Erica Dayane Chaves Cavalcante

Introduction

Considering the tourism and hospitality fields, gastronomy expresses a "set of practices and knowledge related not only to the preparation but also the tasting of food, having as a tonic the pleasure and the sensorial and symbolic experiences involved in this process" (Gimenes, 2011, p. 20). That is, gastronomy is a social practice (Gomez and Bouty, 2011; Domaneschi, 2012; Bispo, 2016; Soares and Bispo, 2017), culturally constructed and reproduced. Despite going through a process of professionalisation, gastronomy has in its non-canonical practices many mysteries and charms. The search for knowledge of how diverse flavours are created, and the relationship between cooking and local culture, make gastronomy and regional food a motivation for the tourism market as well as the subject of academic research (Gomez and Bouty, 2011; Domaneschi, 2012; James and Halkier, 2014; Soares and Bispo, 2017). The search for theories that help to better understand gastronomy, as well as the complexity and dynamics of regional cuisine in the maintenance and promotion of culture (and, at the same time, a product and tourist attraction), opens space for an aesthetic organisational approach (Soares and Bispo, 2017). The study reported in this chapter is an attempt to fill this gap in order to contribute to the theorising of the practice of cooking and to broaden the horizons of knowledge on the practice of regional cooking as an integrated part of current trends in hospitality and tourism.

Organisational aesthetics is a theoretical approach that seeks to understand and apprehend – through the senses – how to build knowledge about something that has tacit and subjective content. For this reason, it was used to investigate the practice of cooking, especially in the regional cuisine of northeastern Brazil, which is full of history and at the same time, reproduces history and culture of the place where it is produced. Organisational aesthetics are produced through the senses and the aim is to understand how knowledge and activities of high tacit and subjective content contribute to the production of daily life – something in which cooking and gastronomy are a part and considered a social practice (Gomez and Bouty, 2011; Soares and Bispo, 2017).

One cannot speak of a typical food from the region of João Pessoa. However, one can speak of a food that has the flavour, the visual and the typical styles of preparation of the region, wherein the food is the result of a historical, social, geographic and economic process (James and Halkier, 2014). Through historical influences derived from Portuguese techniques and African cuisine, João Pessoa's tastes were created (Soares and Bispo, 2017). The region's food is represented by oceans, rivers, ponds and mangroves – fish, seafood (fish, crab stew, shrimp, garfish) – and the interior – "sertão" and "cariri" are two sub-regions of Paraiba's interior characterised by dry weather and a specific way of life (sun meat; green beans; *macaxeira, arrumadinho* and *maxixada* – specific dishes from Brazilian Northeast; yucca flour mush; corn products; etc.) (Leal, 2002).

In this chapter, we analyse cooking as a social practice in the light of Strati's organisational aesthetics at two regional food restaurants in João Pessoa/ Paraíba (Brazil). The study is part of a larger dissertation project that aims to analyse the learning process of cooking in taste formation in the light of social practices and organisational aesthetics. To reach this study's objective, qualitative research based on an aesthetic approach was carried out in two restaurants in João Pessoa specialising in regional cuisine, in keeping with the ontology and epistemology of the practices of cooking (Schatzki, 2001; Reckwitz, 2002; Miettinen, Samra-Fredericks and Yanow, 2009; Gherardi, 2009).

Drawing on a practice-based approach, it is possible to analyse and to understand the dynamic process of how restaurants' cooking practice develops and share cultural knowledge and its contribution to the tourism and hospitality fields. The aesthetic approach is considered by many authors (e.g., Strati, 2007a, 2007b; Gherardi, 2009) an important aspect of practice that is overlooked by many scholars. The key element of the aesthetic approach is the possibility to enlarge the understanding of tacit knowledge and embodied aspects of human senses and the role that artefacts and objects play in social life. For tourism (Bispo, 2016), the aesthetic lens is useful in understanding the interplay between human senses and tourist motivations considering human and non-human interaction. This chapter is structured in the following way: the introduction is followed by the presentation of gastronomy and organisational aesthetics through the lens of social practices. The methodological aspects of the study are explained after which the analysis is unfolded preceding the final considerations.

Gastronomy and organisational aesthetics

According to Tonini (2011, p. 135), gastronomy is the meeting of food with feeling: "It is the result of creativity (…) it is the union of necessity and pleasure (…) it provides the sense of belonging to a folk, their continuity and perpetuation of traditions, keeping alive part of an identity."

Gastronomy represents a form of social expression, which, when amplified by contemporary innovation, does not lose its sensitive, historical and contextual features from where it is produced originally. Thus, gastronomy can be better understood as a social practice (Soares and Bispo, 2017).

Gastronomy can be investigated using Strati's organisational aesthetic approach due to its perceptive and sensorial character, which promotes sensible knowledge and the use of perceptive faculties. By sensible knowledge, we follow Strati's (2007b, 2009) idea that it is the embodied knowledge produced by the human experience in the world through the senses. Sensible knowledge has a tacit feature, and we learn it in action, i.e., it is a knowing-in-practice process. Sensation "is not the mere capacity to 'receive' the sensible qualities of people and artefacts – their presence/absence, visibility/invisibility, materiality/ immateriality – but rather the capacity to enjoy them and understand them by experiencing them within ourselves" (Dufour-Kowalska, 1996, p. 161).

Gagliardi (2009) explains that the term "aesthetics" comes from the Greek *aisthànomai* – to perceive or to know through the senses. It refers to all sensory experiences and not just what is related to what is beautiful. Aesthetics raise sensible knowledge, tacit knowledge, an unconcerned and impulsive form of action, and a form of non-oral expression, shared by "feeling". According to Strati (1992, 2000, 2007a, 2007b, 2010, 2009), organisational aesthetics are expressed through the perception of the five senses – hearing, sight, touch, smell and palate – as well as the capacity to perform aesthetic judgement of what we experience. This judgement is expressed through what we do when we are in touch with the world through the body. We perceive things through our body and judge whether what we feel is "good", "bad", "beautiful", "ugly" etc. We use our collective social construction to perform aesthetic judgements.

According to Soares and Bispo (2014), organisational aesthetics and sensible knowledge allow for a good understanding of the phenomenon of gastronomy since they seek to understand tacit and sensorial knowledge, which is difficult to explain through the spoken language but possible to share through perceptive faculties (organ of the senses). The knowledge of gastronomic practice becomes possible through a socially shared "feel" and is described as "coherent" – theoretically called aesthetic judgement (Strati, 2007a). Aesthetic judgement is similar to a sixth sense with which it is possible to discern whether what has been perceived by the sense organs is pleasant or unpleasant, good or bad, whether it engages us or leaves us indifferent, and whether it attracts us or repulses us (Strati, 2007a). Analysing cooking as a practice through organisational aesthetics allows for an understanding of the relevance of the perceptive faculties in the process of cooking.

Regional cuisine expresses the everyday life and the culture of a society presenting its unique and contextual character. Regional cuisine can be understood as "a set of know-how that encompasses ingredients, culinary techniques and recipes that are arranged in a relatively coherent, geographically delimited and recognisable landscape" (Bahl, Gimenes and Nitsche, 2011, p. 2). Typical dishes are emblematic foods that are part of the regional cuisine and have the power to inherently represent a people. This is the case of *Churrasco* (barbecue) for the *Gaucho*, *Pão de queijo* (cheese bread) for the *Mineiro* and *Acarajé* (croquet) for the *Baiano* – all typical food from different regions of Brazil (Gimenes, 2009). Gastronomy involves the art of cooking (food preparation, cooking), eating well (dish presentation, pleasure provided by food, accompanying drink, service) and food culture (ingredients and technique) (Kivela and Crotts, 2006; Furtado, 2011).

Gastronomy carries symbolic and unique aspects of a people and these aspects are expressed in preparation, eating and food culture. Cooking a dish that can express uniqueness is possible through taste. Taste is a social construction drawing on contextual, unique and social features of everyday life where it is recognised. The words *saber* (to know) and *sabor* (taste) are related; the root of the two words is the same, the Latin term *sapere*, which means "to have taste". This indicates that the source of direct empirical knowledge is etymologically associated with the sense of taste (Carneiro, 2005, p. 73). Theoretically, the generation of taste occurs in cooking as a practice when cooks (practitioners) learn and know how to enjoy a specific flavour (Lane, 2014; Soares and Bispo, 2017).

Cooking is an activity with special features since it is a very practical activity and is often considered an art (Hegarty and O'Mahony, 2001; Lane, 2014). In a professional restaurant kitchen, there are at least three professionals who are directly involved in cooking, the chef, the cook and the kitchen assistant. The chef is the professional responsible for creating and executing meals and managing the kitchen. The cook is a professional with specific knowledge of culinary techniques (Meneses, 1997), and the kitchen assistant is the professional responsible for the pre-preparation (*mise en place*), hygiene, organisation and small food production.

According to Kivela and Crotts (2006), gastronomy is a multidisciplinary field because it counts on the collaboration of several fields of knowledge. Kivela and Crotts (2006) hold that in addition to pleasure, food is a sensorial experience since gastronomy is the art that allows the human being to use the five senses: sight, hearing, touch, smell and palate. Therefore, gastronomy has a high level of practical and aesthetic content in such a way that it is not possible to separate the "use of the senses", "cooking" and "everyday life". In other words, gastronomy is a social phenomenon, tangible through its utensils and dishes, but it is also intangible through its odours and sensations; it is a field of daily practice that has much to contribute if explored from the scientific and theoretical perspective of social practices and organisational aesthetics. To do so, gastronomy, while a scientific subject, demands adequate research strategies that can guarantee a deeper understanding of gastronomic studies from the aesthetic point of view.

Methodology

In this study qualitative research was carried out. We have chosen the aesthetic approach – or aesthetic style – of Strati (Strati and Montoux, 2002;

Strati, 2010, 2009). Strati (2009, 199) explains what is meant by "aesthetic style" by two steps:

> (a) chooses a topic, style, and object of analysis according to his/her taste and personal preferences for method and theory; (b) activates his/her sensory faculties and aesthetic judgment upon immersing him/herself in the texture of organisational actors as they act and interact.

In this way, multisensoriality (Strati, 2009; Jensen, Scarles and Cohen, 2015) was used in the collection of empirical data, activating all perceptual-sensorial faculties and aesthetic judgement in research. This research shares the ontology and epistemology of social practices (Schatzki, 2001; Reckwitz, 2002; Miettinen, Samra-Fredericks and Yanow, 2009; Bispo, 2015; Bispo, 2016). The key aspects of practice-based research, which drive the researcher to use qualitative technics, are: a) seeing practices as the unit of analysis of the research; b) exploring collective performances, e.g., the touristic or the organisational rather than the tourist or the organisation; c) going beyond descriptions of what people do, but identify and analyse meaning creation, identity formation and ways of organising. In sum, according to Bispo (2015, p. 316):

> [t]he first important thing in order to identify a practice is to assume that it is something that happens but not as a priori practice in the sense of theory testing. It means that to identify a practice it is necessary to observe it and understand its dynamics (process). This is the main goal of the researcher: to understand, describe, analyse and explain why things are the way they are through the practice lens.

In this research, the practice considered as unit of analysis was the "cooking practice". We drew on different techniques of empirical material gathering: participant observation (Flick, 2009), informal conversations, semi-structured interviews and imaginary participatory observation (Strati 2007a) – that is a technique wherein the researcher reflects about he/she feelings during the experience in the research field and use this as data. Observations were carried out in two regional food restaurants in João Pessoa-PB (identified as RI and RII): in RI from June 9th, 2014 until January 11th, 2015, and in RII from June 27th, 2014 until January 14th, 2015. A total of 46 visits were made: 26 in RI and 20 in RII, totalling 107 hours in the field. Observations were made in the kitchen of the restaurants where it was possible to observe the work performed and the development of the practice, as well as the cooks and kitchen assistants. Table 6.1 presents the characteristics of the actors who performed cooking as a practice.

The observations were guided through the zooming in and zooming out technique (Nicolini, 2009) which entails to stay close to the phenomenon for enough time to understand the cooking practice logic (zooming in) and

Table 6.1 Actors participating in research.

Fictitious name	Role	Restaurant time	Schooling	Professional cooking experience
Raissa	Cook	1 year 10 months	High school	No previous experience, started in the company as a general service assistant.
Mateus	Cook	3 months	Studying technology in gastronomy	13 years of experience
Artur	Cook	9 years	High school	19 years of experience
Daniela	Kitchen assistant	1 year	High school	No previous experience
Silvia	Kitchen assistant	8 months	High school	No previous experience
Flavia	Kitchen assistant	12 months	High school (unfinished)	6 years of experience
Sara	Kitchen assistant	9 months	High school (unfinished)	No previous experience
Amanda	Kitchen assistant	1 year 9 months	Middle school	4 years of experience
Luiz	Maître	4 years	–	–

Source: Authors.

keeping out in certain periods to reflect and "see" the organising way of cooking practice and its performativity (zooming out). During the observation process, we engaged in informal conversations about the cooking practice along with restaurants' staff, observed the interaction of the human actors, including clients and restaurants' professionals – using a diary for field notes or even the cell phone to take pictures and record some scenes. Also, we read official documents to be aware of the official rules, regulations and institutional conditions of the restaurants and compared them with daily activities. All these procedures were allowed by restaurants managers and other staff and followed the Brazilian's research ethics orientations.

We started carrying out observations in the two restaurants simultaneously In September 2014. At first, we did not have a practice in mind; we just tried to understand the logic of organising of the restaurants (zooming in) until the cooking practice emerged. After the chosen of "cooking as practice," we started to focus our attention on the kitchen doing field notes and informal conversations. The observations notes were registered in a field notebook and later transcribed with MS Word, totalling 42 pages. While the transcription was carried out, imaginary participatory observation proceeded. This occurred as follows: while reading, the speeches, smells, sight and what had been heard from the organisational atmosphere were remembered, and the data were gradually improved by imaginary participatory observation using pictures and videos besides the transcripts. We used to do group discussions (authors) to analyse the data. We proceeded with evocative interpretative analysis theorising the restaurants experience with our philosophical assumptions. The questions that remained after the first step of analysis we decided to taken into the field again and carry out some informal conversations. Analysis were again performed in an evocative and interpretive manner (Strati, 2007a, 2009) up to our decision that we were able to describe, interpret and explain our data.

Analysis: cooking as practice

After four months in the field observing social dynamics in the two restaurants studied, gastronomy emerged as a highly salient aspect. More specifically, regional Cuisine and how it is produced drew our attention due to its relevance in the production of local culture. We noticed that regional Cuisine is a way of cultural production through the learning of cooking as a practice. Thus, cooking was shown to be stronger in this context, and aspects of regional cooking became more pronounced in relation to other aspects of the restaurants such as management for instance.

The perceptive-sensorial faculties emerged as a key element for the understanding of the creation of regional cooking tastes. In this sense, we chose to demonstrate how perceptive-sensorial faculties individually support cooking as practice and the construction of a specific sensible knowledge of regional Cuisine cooking (Strati, 2007b). Although it is known that sensible knowledge is a personal issue, its social dimension is not ignored. Strati (2007b, p. 63) holds that "sensible knowledge highlights the diversity between one person and another, but also empathic openness towards the diverse Other generated by a specific and contingent point of view". The perception of each faculty results in sensible knowledge and is the result of a social and historical construction; the result of the experiences lived and learned by the organisational actor and shared by the practitioners while they use the faculty and produce the aesthetic judgement.

The following sections present how cooks and kitchen assistants know cooking as a practice through the hands, eyes, ears, smell, palate and what Strati (2007a) calls a kind of sixth sense – aesthetic judgement.

Cooking with the hands

Inside the kitchen, hands are constantly used to perform all sorts of activities. In this way, the use of touch is crucial. While people work in the kitchen, their hands are used to interpret, learn, know and act. While recognising the relevance of the technological revolution for the accomplishment of labor practices, tact is indispensable. It may seem quite natural to note the importance of touch. However, it has often been disregarded in traditional qualitative studies about work, and for this reason, we emphasise its importance from an organisational aesthetic analysis (Strati, 2007b).

As a way of illustrating hands' relevance, we use the examples of Sara and Artur's work. Sara puts one hand in the cheese deposit, fills it with cheese and puts it on top of the rice (Field notes, July, 2014). The hands are used as a form of measurement, a perceptive-sensory measure that is not scientific but sensible i.e., measure becomes a sort of "sensing-in-practice". Although all proteins are provided (based on the nutritional scientific recommendation of how to use them), most of other ingredients are placed based on perceptual faculties without having any other scientific parameter. The hand is used as a measuring instrument in the kitchen, which demonstrates the strength of touch in cooking as practice.

The hands are also used in place of other kitchen utensils, as can be seen from fragments of the observations: Artur picks up the seasoning with his hands, spreads it gently on the meat, almost massaging the meat (Field notes, July, 2014). Felipe uses his hand to support the food on the grill and flips the fish with the help of his hands (Field notes, August, 2014). It is also observed that, although there are spatulas, brushes and grippers, the use of the hands instead of these utensils is common. Moreover, the hands are used as a measure. To be a cook in the restaurants under study, it takes more than having a "good hand for" cooking which involves "knowing how to season" but having a hand that knows how activities are performed in cooking as practice (Field notes, July, 2014). In this way, there is a "know-how" to which the use of hands is indispensable. In cooking as a practice, knowledge with the hands is essential.

One example of how hands are used to measure and manipulate ingredients is the preparation of fried ball of codfish. The cook uses both hands and two spoons to do it (see Figure 6.1). This process is a typical example of learning-in-practice (Strati, 2007b; Gherardi, 2009) wherein a person learn how to do it following a senior practitioner.

Observing the picture is possible to notice that without using a scale the balls have similar sizes and weights. We weighed six balls from three different cooks, and the difference between them was around 5% what indicates how a knowledge based on the senses can organise a cooking practice.

Cooking with the eyes

The perceptive-sensory faculty of vision was used mainly as a measure in the cooking practice. When observing, the community of cooks do not use equipment to measure such as scales and thermometers while cooking – they use the eyes as well as the hands as instruments of measurement, as this is a simple expression of sensible knowledge. By watching one has learned to judge a certain amount of a certain ingredient for a particular food; by looking, one judges the "standard" size of a particular ingredient; through the gaze, one judges if the dish was prepared in the correct way.

In many moments during the immersion in the field, it was possible to strengthen this perception. As observed: Mateus made a *Rubacão* (rice and beans cooked together), when the meal was ready, he put the serving into the bowl. The observer (researcher) noted that the portion is larger than usual; it

Figure 6.1 Handling fried ball of codfish.
Source: Lídia Soares (2014)

went well beyond the usual amount the restaurant ordinarily makes. Everyone in the kitchen looks at the dish and Flavia shouts: "It's too full!" Mateus looks at Flavia and asks, "Is it too full?" Flávia replies "Yes!" A waiter looks and shouts: "It is well served". "But it cannot be, tomorrow the customer will come back and want another one of it, but this is wrong, it is out of the standard", says Flavia. Artur says, "Take it out of it". Mateus asks, "But should I undo the dish?" Artur replies, "Yes!" He approaches the plate already assembled, picks up a container and take out a certain amount of the dish. The dish was disassembled and replaced according to the restaurant's standard portion (Field notes, July, 2014).

The plate was not weighed at any moment nor compared to the technical sheet of the dish. The cook and kitchen assistant looked at the dishes, made the collective aesthetic judgement and stated that it was out of the restaurant standard. Sensible knowledge mediated the relationship along with aesthetic judgement, keeping something important for practice: the support of standards. The norms were reproduced and sustained through aesthetic judgement. These norms result from a collective construction of how is the "right" way to prepare the dish. These norms are based on the sensible knowledge that sustains the practice. This reference is the parameter to do aesthetics judgements of what is "right" or "wrong" (Gherardi, 2009; Strati, 2007b; Soares and Bispo, 2017).

Cooking with the ears

Drawing on organisational aesthetics, there is a direct difference between the eyes and the ears. The eyes can be closed and it is impossible to see behind one's back without turning around, but the ear cannot be closed or turned off and it works well even when one's back is turned; it is a faculty that cannot be turned off or omitted. In the kitchen, auditory perceptive faculty is used daily to interpret sounds; these include the whistle of the oven, the microwave, the noise of food being fried (grill, frying pan or machine) and the noise of the exhaust fan. The sounds of the kitchen also permeate the speeches of actors, including laughter and silence. The importance of the ears was emphasised by all practitioners of the two restaurants researched as a way of perceiving the cooking point of food by hearing. This is because, on the grill and in the casserole, the foods make characteristic sounds when they are ready. Ignoring this perception may mean changing the taste of food. This impression raises the use of the ear sensitively and requires a perceptive aesthetic judgement, a "trained" ear for cooking.

Sara had worked in the kitchen for a shorter time compared to the other assistants and only picks up the pots to serve. After listening to the rice boiling, she left what she was doing and begins to stir the pot (Field notes, July, 2014). Everyone was busy in the kitchen with other activities and Sara stopped setting the dish to stir the rice as she realised by the sound that it would be necessary to take that action. This demonstrates her aesthetic knowledge about cooking as a practice, which was able to activate her aesthetic judgement and act for the correct course of work (Strati, 2007a). The action performed by Sarah is not mediated by the mind, but by the previous bodily and social experience (Essén and Värlander, 2013). If someone who has never heard that sound enters the kitchen, they will not act as Sara did due to the lack of previous experience to support the action taken. It is the experience that helps to develop the sensible knowledge and the aesthetic judgement needed to guide the action.

Cooking with smell

During the observations of cooking as practice, it was possible to understand how odours are manifested. The following fragments reflect how the perceptive faculty of smell is used in the practice of cooking and its influence on the taste (Gherardi, 2009; Soares and Bispo, 2017) of both kitchen practitioners and consumers. The fragments show how odours are used to learn how to cook with regard to perishability. In addition, it is emphasised that in many moments the senses of smell and palate are used in a sequential form. Inside a kitchen, food is dated according to Sanitary Surveillance rules. Everything that is produced for daily use, or before being stored, is dated with an expiration date; perishability is treated with great rigor, as it can cause harm to the client (damage to health) and punishment to the restaurant (interdiction by the government). The expiration date is an aspect of scientific knowledge about the perishability of food. Even so, often the faculty of smell and taste are used as a judgemental way for decisions on the perishability of food.

As it was shown in the observations, Amanda said, "It's better to throw it away, I have smelled it, it's not good," (Field notes, July, 2014). On another occasion, Daniela calls Raissa and asks, "Is this okay?" "Smell it here to see if it's okay, because it's not expired, but I do not think it's good." Raissa looks at the rice, smells and says, "No, throw it out!" Then, Daniela dumps the rice in the trash. At another time, Daniela says "You can use it, this one is fine" (Field notes, September, 2014). Even when a food was within its period of validity (scientific knowledge), it was the smell that mediated the practice of work. In the example gave, it is possible to notice that Daniela and Raissa resorted their sensible knowledge activated by the smell to judge whether the food is good or not. Smell things is a relevant skill to perform cooking as practice. Things are thrown out even when they have not expired if the smell indicates that it is spoiled or the odour is doubtful. This judgement is based on a social and collective construction and disregards scientific knowledge since the sensitive has become "more precise" than the scientific (Strati, 2007a, 2009).

However, the smell is also a possibility to catch the attention of people prior to or during the consumption of the restaurant food. During our observations, a client once decided what she was going to eat just smelling the dish that was on the table next to hers. The waiter asked "Are you ready to order?" to which she answered, "Yes, I'd like the same dish that is smelling so good nearby!" (Field notes, August 2014). This example highlights that cooking is not just a "cook" practice, but also necessarily involves those that "sell" the dishes (waiter) and those who eat them (restaurant customers). A practice is a bundle of activities of many practitioners (Schatzki, 2001) and the non-human elements involved (Gherardi, 2009; Soares and Bispo, 2017).

Cooking with the palate

Although restaurant service is a complete experience (attendance, environment and food), food is the central element, materially produced and of great importance; it is also what characterises food's taste. The ultimate measure for evaluating food is the palate. The chef's palate has been educated to experience the flavours of regional cuisine. This experience comes from their cultural roots in their homes for those from Paraíba State. For those from other regions, the learning process to develop the regional Cuisine taste is through knowing-in-practice with other senior practitioners (Gherardi, 2009; Gomez and Bouty, 2011). The gustatory faculty is used to see if the food is at the correct cooking point, if the taste of the food is good, that is, with the characteristics – flavour and texture – adequate and if the taste of regional cuisine is presented. In this way, the gustatory faculty of cooks regulates the taste of food and tasting is an everyday activity in the kitchen. Based on taste, judgement is made and stated whether food is good or bad, whether it needs more salt, whether it has too little or too much seasoning. The palate works as a measuring instrument capable of judging a characteristic taste. This is because the cooks' palate has been trained and is sophisticated. It is linked to the shared aesthetic judgement (Fine, 1996; Strati, 2010) to experience and appreciate the characteristic flavours of regional food.

The pattern of an activity is institutionalised not only by evocative aesthetic knowledge but also by a more directed aesthetic judgement, as was observed in one occasion: while Felipe was preparing a sauce to be frozen, he tasted it and then called Raissa to taste it too. Raissa tasted the sauce and remained silent. Felipe then asked her to try the other sauce that was ready (produced previously and that is in the water-bath being used during that evening). Raissa tasted it and was silent. Felipe then asked "So what?" Raissa smiled and continued in silence (performing her aesthetic judgement). Felipe asked: Which one is better? She answered without saying a word, just looked and pointed her finger at the sauce that was already done in the water-bath (Field notes, August, 2014).

The gustatory faculty is not inherent in the mouth. Taste and texture are learned culturally and socially negotiated. Aesthetically expressing a taste is something complex; the description of a taste and the judgement of it as tasty are difficult to describe and explain. Taste is socially developed, considered and expressed metaphorically, and communicated by aesthetic expressions such as "good" or "not good". Expression of the aesthetic category does not refer to beauty. It is more related to the sublime, something difficult to explain and represent that practitioners only know is a certain way (Fine, 1996; Strati, 2007a).

Taste knowledge is still used for the analysis of regional cuisine. This cuisine is represented by a characteristic taste of the region since it contains ingredients, techniques and recipes from a region (Bahl, Gimenes and Nitsche, 2011). Some authors hold that food culture is not only based on culinary heritage but also on everyday innovations (Braga, 2004; James and Halkier, 2014). Although regional cuisine in many restaurants features regional dishes with traditional features and ingredients, innovative rereadings of dishes also take place. However, this aspect does not make dishes lose its local feature because it continues to express the food culture of the region.

The palates of cooks are loaded with aspects connected to the regional cuisine such as the ingredients, the way of cooking and the taste. The use of certain ingredients is linked to the food culture of the region. To demonstrate how regional ingredients interfere with cooking practices, let us consider how butter stands out as a regional element, sometimes used as an (industrialised) innovation or as a historical (bottled) ingredient.

In general, butter helps characterise Joao Pessoa's taste in cooking. Butter is constantly used either in its industrial form at restaurant I (RI) and bottled at restaurant II (RII). Butter is widely used in various recipes and is very central in the kitchen. Much butter is used from one day to another (Field notes, August, 2014); and often ten kilograms of butter can be finished very quickly. Butter is used in many different recipes and with many different ingredients, such as in the preparation of shrimp, rice, *farofa*, cheese mush, *macaxeira* mush and *macaxeira*.

In light of the above, it is understandable to state that butter is a relevant ingredient in the taste of food that is prepared in restaurants and socially perceived as tasty. On one occasion, while being observed, Amanda drew attention to it: "Look how delicious this butter is, I would eat all of it" ("All of it" refers to a bowl with about two kilos of *farofa*), says Amanda pointing with the chin. "Think ... It's way too good! See here [...] try a little bit" (Field notes, September, 2014).

Butter, whether produced industrially or handcrafted (bottle), is a good example of how the palate influence the practitioners in cooking as a practice. The main difference regards the specific taste that butter in the bottle has and it is not used in other different parts of the country outside the Brazilian Northeast. Although the butter in the bottle is only one ingredient, it makes a difference in the dish taste for those from the Northeast. It should be emphasised that the function of butter in the two restaurants differs. In RI, industrialised butter is used only in food; the only aesthetic senses that can possibly identify it are smell and taste. Even so, it is hard to specify how much this is possible since often an ingredient used in isolation has a distinctive flavour and texture, but when added in the recipe it turns into a harmony of flavours (Lunardelli, 2012).

In RII, butter is more than an ingredient; it is also a symbol of the regional food and taste. Beyond the dishes' composition, the butter in the bottle goes to the table as a kind of "garnish", an "extra" seasoning to add flavour to the food. It is used to make the meat look better so that it can be associated with an evocative component of the beauty category. It is thus appreciated by the senses of vision (directly and metaphorically), touch, smell and palate.

Indeed, the gustatory faculty of cooks interferes with the practice of cooking; the interpretation of taste is mediated by food culture when it is understood as tasty by cooks (Lane, 2014). The result of the aesthetic judgement about how food is made is taste itself, which also interferes with cooking as a practice. How cooking as practice is set expresses regional food culture and heritage. Cooking as practice produces the taste and this continues to interfere with cooking as practice. This perception is strengthened when one observes regional food being recognised as tasty based on an aesthetic judgement from a sensible knowledge shared. For Gherardi (2009) practice is always an expression of refining performances and the "taste" is one expression of them.

Taste shapes work practices and refines them through negotiation and reflectivity, which suspend the flow of the action in order to intervene and savour the practice and express an aesthetic judgement of it. We may say that practices are constantly refined through the taste-making process, which works both on a sentiment of the perfectible and on repetition as tension toward a never-achieved perfection (Gherardi, 2009, p. 545).

Cooking as a practice is always an interplay between what is traditional – in rigid terms as local ingredients and ways of cooking – and contemporary – ingredients adaptations and new ways of cooking. This apparent "tension" is what changes the cooking practice and keep it "alive" in a process of a continuous taste making (Gherardi, 2009).

Final remarks

This chapter has analysed cooking as a social practice in the light of Strati's organisational aesthetics in two regional food restaurants in João Pessoa/PB. This motivation originated from the gap identified by the researchers of theories that helped to understand cooking and gastronomy beyond the technique and that contemplated its aesthetic, cultural and daily aspects. This way, an activity so common in the daily life of people, such as cooking with its eminently practical character, demands theoretical reflections of the phenomenon in order to contribute to scientific advances in the field.

In this sense, although guided by an epistemology of practices, the great contribution of the work is in the possibility of theorising the practice of cooking and not of carrying a "ready theory" to understand the phenomenon. In other words, it is an effort of theorising from the senses in a way to enable the creation of a sensible knowledge – i.e. a knowledge of the senses – inherent to the practice of cooking and the emergence of aesthetic judgements about the practice itself.

In light of the above, we believe that this chapter presents a theoretical contribution when using organisational aesthetics as a way of understanding the phenomenon of cooking, a methodological contribution in presenting aesthetics as a possibility for empirical investigation. Finally, a practical contribution in presenting and discussing how the learning processes of the cooks occur in order to collaborate with a specific knowledge of cooking practice for the shaping of these professionals that is aligned with the production of their daily "cook". Moreover, it is possible to say that cooking occurs when there is activation of the sensible knowledge through the hands, the eyes, the ears, the nose and the mouth in a continuous process of taste making (Gherardi, 2009).

On the other hand, we also believe that the work may not have covered all the aspects related to restaurant cooking as a regional food practice in the Brazilian Northeast; this fact is basically due to the time constraints to advance research in other restaurants in order to identify possible aesthetic aspects not noted in this research.

This way, when thinking about the future, we think that a research agenda on this theme may involve the expansion of research to other regions with cuisine and gastronomy different from the Northeast to advance in the understanding of the practice of cooking as a regional element producing and produced by culture. In addition to this, the possibility of researching ways of training cooks and chefs, considering the sensible knowledge and the aesthetic judgement as a theoretical basis, could make it possible to better understand the learning processes of these professionals.

Finally, we believe that the theoretical advance on the practice of cooking, and gastronomy may be an opportunity to promote and consolidate the area as a producer of scientific knowledge in a sense attributed by Kurt Lewin (1951, p. 169) that nothing is as practical as a good theory. Cooking theorising is also a contribution to tourism and hospitality fields due to its tight relations, especially when food and gastronomy are key elements of tourists' travel motivation or even an opportunity of welcome a guest at "home".

References

Bahl, M., Gimenes, M.H.S.G. and Nistche, L.B. (2011). Territorialidade gastronômica: as cozinhas regionais como forma de mediação do homem com o meio e como atrativo turístico. *Revista Geográfica de América Central* (online), 2, 1–16.

Bispo, M. de S. (2016). Tourism as practice. *Annals of Tourism Research*, 61, 170–179.

Bispo, M. de S. (2015). Methodological reflections on practice-based research. *Brazilian Administration Review-BAR*, 12(3), 309–323. doi:10.1590/1807-7692bar2015150026.

Braga, V. (2004). Cultura alimentar: contribuições da antropologia da alimentação. *Saúde em Revista, Piracicaba*, 6(13), 37–44.

Carneiro, H.S. (2005). Comida e sociedade: significados sociais na história da alimentação. *História Questões & Debates*, 42, 71–80.

Dufour-Kowalska, G. (1996). *L'art et la sensibilité. De Kant à Michel Henry.* Paris: Librairie Philosophique J. Vrin.

Domaneschi, L. (2012). Food social practices: theory of practice and the new battlefield of food quality. *Journal of Consumer Culture*, 12(3), 306–322.

Essén, A. and Värlander, S.W. (2013). The mutual constitution of sensuous and discursive understanding in scientific practice: an autoethnographic lens on academic writing. *Management Learning*, 44(4), 395–423.

Fine, G.A. (1996). *Kitchens: The Culture of Restaurant Work.* Berkeley: University of California Press.

Flick, U. (2009). *Uma introdução à pesquisa qualitativa.* São Paulo: Bookman.

Furtado, S.M. (2011). Uma reflexão sobre a hospitalidade nos meios de comunicação: um estudo da gastronomia nos programas de TV. *Revista Hospitalidade*, 8(1), 109–130.

Gagliardi, P. (2009). Explorando a Lado Estético na Vida Organizacional. In S.R. Clegg, C. Hardy and W. R. Nord (Eds), *Handbook de Estudos Organizacionais* (Vol. 2). São Paulo: Atlas, 127–149.

Gherardi, S. (2009). Practice? It´s a matter of taste! *Management Learning*, 40(5) 535–550.

Gimenes, M.H.S.G. (2009). O uso turístico das comidas tradicionais: algumas reflexões a partir do Barreado, prato típico do litoral paranaense (Brasil). *Turismo & Sociedade*, 2(1), 8–24.

Gimenes, M.H.S.G. (2011). Viagens, sabores e cultura: reflexões sobre pratos típicos no contexto do turismo gastronômico. In A.M. de P. Possamai and R. Pecceni (Eds), *Turismo, história e gastronomia: uma viagem pelos sabores.* Caxias do Sul: Educs, 19–30.

Gomez, M.-L. and BoutyI. (2011). The emergence of an influential practice: food for thought. *Organization Studies*, 32, 921–940.

Hegarty, J.A. and O'Mahony, G.B. (2001). Gastronomy: a phenomenon of cultural expressionism and an aesthetic for living. *Hospitality Management*, 20, 3–13.

James, L. and Halkier, H. (2014). Regional development platforms and related variety: exploring the changing practices of food tourism in North Jutland, Denmark. *European Urban and Regional Studies*, 23(4), 831–847

Jensen, M.T., Scarles, C. and Cohen, S.A. (2015). A multisensory phenomenology of interrail mobilities. *Annals of Tourism Research*, 53, 61–76.

Kivela, J. and Crotts, J. (2006). Tourism and gastronomy: gastronomy's influence on how tourists experience a destination. *Journal of Hospitality and Tourism Research*, 30(3), 354–377. doi:10.1177/1096348006286797

Lane, C. (2014). *The Cultivation of Taste: Chefs and the Organization of Fine Dining.* Oxford: Oxford University Press.

Leal, W. (2002). *Fragmentos etílicos e gastronômicos: a história do comer e do beber na Paraíba.* 1st edn. João Pessoa: Editora Texto Arte.

Lewin, K. (1951). *Field Theory in Social Science; Selected Theoretical Papers.* D. Cartwright (ed.). New York: Harper & Row.

Lunardelli, T. (2012). Estética do gosto. Dissertation (Master in Arts), Universidade Estadual Paulista.

Meneses, U.T.B. and Carneiro, H. (1997). A História da Alimentação: balizas historiográficas. *Anais do Museu Paulista: História e Cultura Material*, 5 , 9–92.

Miettinen, R., Samra-Fredericks, D. and Yanow, D. (2009). Re-turn to practice: an introductory essay. *Organization Studies*, 30(12), 1309–1327.

Nicolini, D. (2009). Zooming in and zooming out: a package of method and theory to study work practice. In S. Ybema, D. Yanow, H. Wels, and F. Kamsteeg (Eds), *Organizational Ethnography: Studying the Complexity of Everyday Life*. London: SAGE Publications, 120–138.

Reckwitz, A. (2002). Toward a theory of social practices: a development in culturalist theorizing. *European Journal of Social Theory*, 5(2), 243–263.

Schatzki, T.R. (2001). Introduction: practice theory. In T.R. Schatzki, K. Knorr Cetina and E. Von Savigny (Eds), *The Practice Turn in Contemporary Theory*. New York: Routledge, 1–14.

Soares, L.C. and Bispo, M. S. (2014). Contribuições da estética organizacional para a pesquisa em organizações gastronômicas. *Revista Brasileira de Pesquisa em Turismo*, 8(3), 476–493. doi:10.7784/rbtur.v8i3.808

Soares, L.C. and Bispo, M.S. (2017). The learning of cooking in the light of the social practices and the organizational aesthetics. *BBR. Brazilian Business Review* (English Ed.), 14(2), 247–271.

Strati, A. (1992). Aesthetics understanding of organizational life. *Academy of Management Review*, 17(3), 568–581.

Strati, A. (2000). The aesthetics in organization studies. In S. Linstead and H. Höpfl (Eds), *The aesthetics of organization*. London: SAGE Publications Ltd, 13–31.

Strati, A. (2007a). *Organização e estética*. Rio de Janeiro: Editora FGV.

Strati, A. (2007b). Sensible knowledge and practice-based learning. *Management Learning*, 38(1), 61–77.

Strati, A. (2009). 'Do you do beautiful things?': aesthetics and art in qualitative methods of organization studies. In D. Buchanan and A. Bryman (Eds), *The Sage Handbook of Organizational Research Methods*. London: Sage Publications, 230–245.

Strati, A. (2010). Aesthetics understanding of work and organizational life: Approaches and research developments. *Sociology Compass*, 10(4), 880–893. doi:10.1111/j.1751-9020.2010.00323.x

Strati, A. and Montoux, P.G. (2002). Introduction: organizing aesthetics. *Human Relations*, 55(7), 755–766. doi:10.1177/0018726702557001

Tonini, H. (2011). Enoturismo: contemplado vinhos, degustando paisagens. In A.M.P. Possamai and R. Pecceni (Eds), *Turismo, história e gastronomia: uma viagem pelos sabores*. Caxias do Sul: Educs, 127–138.

7 Practising tourism development

The case of coastal destination development policy in Denmark

Laura James and Henrik Halkier

Introduction

In this chapter, we examine the evolution of tourism destination development in coastal destinations in Denmark over the last 10 years. Despite a temperate climate, coastal tourism has been a major component in Danish tourism for decades, accounting for 72% of commercial bed nights and 46% of turnover in 2015 (CRT, 2017; VisitDenmark, 2017). The main attraction is the long sandy beaches, accommodation is mainly self-catering (holiday homes and campsites) and transport is usually self-drive, either domestically or from neighbouring countries such as Germany, Norway and Sweden. After the turn of the century, international visitation has experienced a prolonged period of stagnation and decline, thereby putting destination development high on the political agenda in coastal parts of Denmark (Halkier and James, 2016).

Destination development can be conceptualised as a combination of practices. Two of the most important practices are *promoting* the destination to existing/potential visitors and *creating* new tourist experiences. In recent years there has been increasing debate about the extent to which these practices are undertaken by organisations operating at arm's-length from the public sector and co-sponsored by private firms (Pike and Page, 2014; Beritelli and Bieger, 2014). Such organisations are referred to collectively as destination marketing or destination management organisations (DMO). While the first generation of DMOs essentially consisted of marketing organisations engaged in promoting their destination to existing and potential visitors, subsequent generations of DMOs have had a wider remit. Presenza et al. (2005: 2) argue that "this transition means becoming a destination management organisation instead of just a destination marketing organisation. In this regard, DMOs are becoming more prominent as 'destination developers' by acting as catalysts and facilitators for the realisation of tourism developments". This would suggest that contemporary DMOs are increasingly engaging with a wider range of practices and practitioners. However, there is no consensus over which practices are prioritised by contemporary DMOs or indeed whether management *has* replaced marketing as their main preoccupation (Pike and Page, 2014). Thus, the 'M' in DMO has become increasingly ambiguous.

This chapter contributes to the debate by exploring how destination development – conceptualised as a bundle of practices (e.g. destination marketing, product creation, stakeholder coordination and research) – has changed in coastal destinations in Denmark over the last 10 years. Drawing on the work of Elizabeth Shove and colleagues (Shove, Pantzar and Watson, 2012; Hui, Schatzki and Shove, 2017), as well as Davide Nicolini (2012) we adopt a 'zoomed out' perspective on practices as entities, to analyse the ways in which some of the main elements of destination development practices – and the ways in which they are connected together into bundles – have evolved over time. We argue that studying tourism development using a practice approach helps our understanding of processes of policy change because it provides a framework to explore the 'doing' of tourism policy through the combination of material resources, meanings and competences. A practice approach illuminates the ways in which the constant accomplishment of practice creates path dependent trajectories, which can make it difficult to change practices, and which help to explain the differences between destinations.

Denmark is an interesting case study because local DMOs exhibit a high degree of continuity over time. There is a shared perception of challenge revolving around stagnating/declining international visitation (Halkier and James, 2016), and previous research suggests there has been a shift in DMO practices from promoting towards creating (Henriksen and Halkier, 2009; Jørgensen, 2016).

The chapter proceeds as follows. We begin by reviewing contributions to the literature on DMOs in order to identify key changes in tourism development activities and the way they have been analysed. Following this, a practice-based analytical framework is developed, drawing on key contributions to practice theory. After a presentation of the empirical study and methodology used, we present an analysis of the ways in which some of the main elements of destination development practices – and the ways in which they are connected together into bundles – have evolved over time. The chapter concludes by discussing the role of practices in changing DMO strategies, and the possible contribution of practice theory to our understanding of destination policy development.

Destination development and DMOs

The literature on DMOs and destination development clearly suggests that the nature of destination development activities has changed over time. In the 1980s and 1990s the first generation of local DMOs concentrated almost exclusively on promotion and marketing of the destination and its experience offers to potential visitors, nationally or internationally (Getz et al., 1998; Gretzel et al., 2006; Henriksen and Halkier, 2009; Volgger and Pechlaner, 2014). From the 1990s onwards, however, the activity profile of DMOs gradually widened. Academic writers also began to argue the case for including development of the destination through the introduction of new experiences and services, either in individual firms, by government, or through destination-wide cross-sectoral partnerships between public and private actors (e.g. Getz et al., 1998; Gretzel et al., 2006; Hall, 2008, ch. 2).

Over the last decade several attempts have been made to take stock of the current activity profile of DMOs, and research suggests that while practices associated with destination management – quality improvement, experience development, innovation – are now much more common (Presenza et al., 2005; Henriksen and Halkier, 2009; Pechlaner et al., 2012b; Volgger and Pechlaner, 2014), promotion of the destination to prospective visitors remains important (Bornhorst et al., 2010; Pike and Page, 2014; Dredge and Jamal, 2015; Jørgensen, 2016). However, as shown by Bornhorst and colleagues' (2010) survey of Canadian DMOs, while marketing is "an important measure of success, it certainly is not the only one" (p. 586) in ensuring continued backing from their stakeholders. Meanwhile, the often rather normative discussion about the strengths and weaknesses of marketing and management approaches to destination development has given way to a more pragmatic and analytical approach. Thus promotion and experience development are not seen as opposites but as complementary functions, oriented respectively towards external visitors and internal stakeholders (Presenza et al., 2005, Jørgensen, 2016).

Studies of DMOs and destination development activities have, perhaps unsurprisingly, focused primarily on matters relating to institutions and their relationship to key stakeholders within and outside the destination. One stream of research has explored the remit of individual DMOs and how they fit into the overall institutional landscape within their locality and in relationship to other public bodies (Beaumont and Dredge, 2010; Pechlaner et al., 2012a; Pastras and Bramwell, 2013; Halkier, 2014; Coles et al., 2014). Most tourist destinations are made up by a large number of private firms of varying sizes and public bodies with a wide range of responsibilities (Ioannides and Debbage 1998; Hall and Williams, 2008, ch. 1; Volgger and Pechlaner, 2014).

A second stream of research has explored how DMOs relate to stakeholders within the destination, including the various ways in which stakeholders can be managed and why stakeholders perceive individual DMOs as more or less successful (Getz et al., 1998; Dredge, 2006; Nilsson, 2007; Sheehan et al., 2007; et al., 2009; Bornhorst et al., 2010; Pechlaner et al., 2012b; Volgger and Pechlaner, 2014; Beritelli and Bieger, 2014). This stream has focused on the politics of DMO policy, through the interpretation of strategy documents and interviews with policymakers (e.g. Hall, 2008; Henriksen and Halkier 2009; Weidenfeld et al., 2011; Pastras and Bramwell, 2013; Hristov and Petrova, 2015), the identification of links between DMOs and related policy-making bodies (e.g. Hall, 2008; Pechlaner et al., 2012a; Halkier, 2014) and analyses of the influence of various stakeholder groups on strategy development (e.g. Sheehan and Ritchie, 2005; Sheehan et al., 2007; Pechlaner et al., 2012b; Beritelli and Bieger, 2014).

While normative contestations between political sponsors and industry stakeholders about what is more or less desirable for DMOs to engage in are undoubtedly an important part of the explanation for the slow drift towards a wider range of responsibilities, this seems to have sidelined more low-key issues regarding the practicalities of policy implementation. Although studies of knowledge processes in destinations and reference to DMO management or staff competences are gradually emerging (Getz et al., 1998; Björk and Virtanen, 2005; Halkier, 2010; Dredge, 2014; Sheehan et al., 2016), none of them draw explicitly on practice theory for inspiration, and only to a limited extent on the extensive literature on institutions and organisational culture in political science (North, 1990; Halkier, 2006; Mahoney and Thelen 2010). All in all, this would suggest that studying tourism development using a practice approach could potentially increase our understanding of processes of policy change and how these are furthered or impeded by the need for the actors involved to change the practices they engage in.

Practices, bundles, variation and change

Following Nicolini's (2012) ideas about studying practices empirically, we find it helpful to draw on different practice perspectives in order to conceptualise and analyse the dynamics of destination development practices. Thus we draw on the work of Andreas Reckwitz (2002) and Elizabeth Shove and colleagues (2012). Reckwitz's (2002: 249–50) definition of practice includes "forms of bodily activities, forms of mental activities, 'things' and their use, a background knowledge in the form of understanding, know-how, states of emotion and motivational knowledge". Shove and Pantzar (2007) distinguish between practices as performances and practices as entities – identifiable 'blocks' which consist of different elements which are connected to one other. Shove et al. (2012) identify these elements as *materials* (e.g. bodies, objects, technologies), *competences* (e.g. knowledge, skills, techniques) and *meanings* (aspirations, emotions, ideas). Through the recurrent performance of practices a distinct combination of practice elements become visible over time (practice as an entity), as illustrated by Figure 7.1.

Nicolini (2012) argues that practices may be studied in a zoomed-in perspective, to understand the performance of a practice in a specific context, and/or a zoomed-out perspective to identify practices as 'entities'. A zoomed-out perspective allows an exploration of the connections between practices that 'extend in both space and time, and form a gigantic, intricate, and evolving texture of dependencies and references' (Nicolini, 2012: 229). Nicolini goes on to argue that shifting between both a zoomed in and zoomed out perspective is required to understand practices, which 'can only be studied *relationally*, and … can only be understood as part of a nexus of connections' (Nicolini, 2012: 229).

Various terms have been coined to describe the way in which different practices are connected together into the larger scale 'nexus' identified by Nicolini.

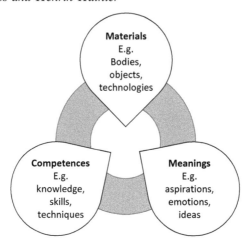

Figure 7.1 Elements of practice according to Shove et al. (2012).

Schatzki (2011) categorises different types of connected practices as arrangements, bundles and constellations. Lamers and van der Duim (2016) draw on this terminology in their analysis of conservation tourism partnerships in Kenya as bundles of livelihood, conservation and tourism practices, mediated by connecting practices of managing the partnership. Taking the example of an airport to illustrate their argument, Shove et al. (2012: 84) refer to 'practice arrangement bundles' as 'loose-knit patterns based on co-location and co-existence', while 'complexes represent stickier and more integrated arrangements including co-dependent forms of sequence and synchronisation'. Schatzki argues that practice bundles can be related to one another in various ways, via "common actions, common organisational elements, or common material entities; chains of action; common motivating events; participants in one bundle being intentionally directed to other bundles", for example (Schatzki, 2017:134).

Our aim is to contribute to debates about practice theory by analysing tourism destination development practice bundles and their constituent elements, including how they have changed over time. Thus, we follow Nicolini (2016: 101) in studying practices as entities where:

> the basic unit of analysis is not a single scene of action or a specific situation or instance of the accomplishment of a practice, but rather a chain, sequence or combination of performances *plus* their relationships – what keeps them connected in time and space.

At the same time it is important to understand the individual practices that make up bundles. In their study of urban food growing, Dobernig, Veen and Oosterveer (2016: 154) caution that using an umbrella concept (such as 'tourism destination management') 'risks losing sight of the multiple logics, dynamics and forms which are present'.

The dynamics of practice

According to Shove et al. (2012), practices emerge and change through novel combinations of new or existing elements – that is, *materials, competences* and *meanings*. They discuss the example of automobility, where the introduction of motor car technology was a material change that prompted the development of new competences (driving, repairs) and meanings (for example, in relation to masculinity), all of which have evolved over time. In addition, different elements may circulate between different practices across time and space. New combinations of elements and their circulation may be the result of deliberate attempts to change existing practices or the result of serendipity. The introduction of new or adapted elements may take place via various mechanisms. Materials can be transported physically; for example, the installation of internet infrastructure has revolutionised the practice of destination marketing by enabling the creation of websites and electronic mail. New competences require research, learning and recontextualisation of different forms of knowledge by practitioners (although some may be transferred in material form, for example in books). Practitioners themselves, by engaging in multiple practices, also circulate multiple meanings.

People, as the carriers of practices, are a crucial link. As Reckwitz (2002: 256) argues 'as there are diverse social practices, and as every agent carries out a multitude of different social practices, the individual is the unique crossing point of practices'. Engagement in multiple practices is therefore a potential source of innovation. As new practitioners are recruited to a practice they bring new knowledge, competences and experiences. In the case of destination development it is clear that many individuals are involved and that they are also engaged in many different related practices such as managing hotels, selling souvenirs, running restaurants, governing a local authority and so on. These practitioners have multiple identities and it is unsurprising that they also may have conflicting priorities and understandings of destination development as a practice bundle. The employees of DMOs have a central role here in that their job is often to link together these different practices and manage multiple stakeholders.

Hui (2017) observes that the distinction between practice as performance and practice as an entity reveals the inherent variation in any practice. The performance of a practice takes place in particular place and time, with a specific set of localised materials, competences and understandings. Thus, practices 'cannot help but encompass differences because of the unpredictable and diverse nature of performances' (ibid: 55). In this sense, every performance of a practice is different and local context is crucial to understanding variation in practice.

Changes to local practices of destination development are also strongly influenced by the wider nexus of practice they are part of. In particular, the practices associated with the governance of tourism and national marketing are crucial. Rules, regulations and targets are set by policy makers located in other places. Funding streams and opportunities to apply for project support shape the relative importance of different practices within destination development and the way in which practices are performed. Moreover, practices of destination development are connected and influenced by many other practices such as transportation (e.g. budget airlines), going on holiday and leisure activities which are critical to the opportunities and challenges that destination development tries to respond to.

The spatial and temporal characteristics of practices are also crucial to understanding both variation and change over time. Destination development is a spatial practice that involves a geographical definition. As Hui (2017) observed, the spatial context of practice is critical to understanding variation. To give a simple example from tourism, we would expect practices of marketing to be different in a beach destination and an urban area due to their different physical and cultural attractions and associated target markets. In Denmark, reorganisation of administrative boundaries has changed the spatial (material) resources that form the basis for destination development as well as the range of stakeholders who are involved in each destination. The temporal dimension is also critical. Shove et al. (2012) make the simple but important observation that not all practices can be undertaken at the same time; in other words, they compete for time resources. Time spent marketing is time that cannot also be spent doing research on new products. The balance between different practices will vary according to the meanings accorded to them by practitioners. Similarly, some (in some cases the majority of) destination stakeholders will only be marginally engaged in development practices. Running a tourism business may be the most important practice they are involved in. Similarly, some 'lifestyle' tourism entrepreneurs may not have any interest in development practices – even if they have the relevant competences and material resources to engage in them. Another important dimension is the temporal rhythm of practice. Thus, some destinations may take a long-term perspective on development while others may be driven by short-term concerns.

Whatever the source of variation and change in practices, it is important to remember than practice is heavily path dependent. Even 'new' practices and bundles are created to some extent from existing elements. Thus, as Schatzki (2002: 226) argues:

> Existing practices have multiple consequences, making courses of action easier, harder, simpler, more complicated, shorter, longer, ill-advised, promising of gain, disruptive, facilitating, obligatory or proscribed, acceptable or unacceptable, more or less relevant, riskier or safer, more or less feasible, more or less likely to induce ridicule or approbation.

The path dependency of practice helps to explain why some practices are resistant to change and certain trajectories are more likely than others.

Methodology

The following analysis is based on an explorative study of 10 coastal destinations in Denmark (see Figure 7.2). The destinations were chosen to represent the variety of Danish coastal tourism, with some having a strong cultural component and most relying mainly on natural attractions such as sandy beaches (see Jørgensen and Halkier, 2013; Halkier et al., 2015). The point is *not* to undertake a systematic comparison of local destinations in order to identify links between particular practice performances and other destination characteristics. Instead, the ambition is to identify common features in destination development practices while allowing for difference in emphasis and change over time.

All the destinations were associated with a nationwide development project, Development of Placed-based Tourism Concepts in Danish Seaside Towns, sponsored by the European Regional Development Fund and Knowledge Centre for Coastal Tourism, and as this policy initiative focused on how to further tourism activities in coastal destinations, local stakeholders had

1. Allinge-Sandvig
2. Sønderborg
3. Møn
4. Hvide Sande/Søndervig
5. Marielyst
6. Hals
7. Skagen
8. Kerteminde
9. Klitmøller/Nørre Vorupør
10. Kongernes Nordsjælland

Figure 7.2 Ten Danish coastal case-study destinations.

already been reflecting on the strengths and weaknesses of many aspects of destination development.

Semi-structured in-depth interviews were conducted with 87 stakeholders, including DMOs, public bodies and private firms, as shown in Table 7.1, and lasted between 60 and 90 minutes. Interviewees were invited to reflect on changes over time in their everyday practices of promoting tourist destinations and creating new tourist experiences. The interviews were analysed with regard to their involvement in, and assumptions about, the two key DMO practices, promoting and creating.

Destination development practices: continuity and change

Destination development is seen as a bundle of practices that include promoting and creating experiences as well as coordinating stakeholders and generating knowledge. In order to illuminate the way in which DMO strategies have evolved, the empirical analysis will focus primarily on the promoting and creating practices because they involve active attempts to influence (potential) visitors, unlike underlying back-office practices like coordinating stakeholder activities or generating market intelligence about customers and competitors. The following two subsections analyse changes and spatial variations by charting the meanings, materials and competences involved in promoting and generating practices. On this basis, the final subsection analyses interactions between practices and the possibly shifting, relative importance of the practices within the destination development bundle.

Promoting destination development

In Denmark promoting tourist destinations to prospective visitors has traditionally been a central activity for DMOs (Presenza et al., 2005; Henriksen and Halkier, 2009). The interviews demonstrate that this practice remains an integrated part of DMO activities in all the ten coastal destinations investigated, while at the same time the elements of this core practice has evolved, as summarised in Figure 7.3.

Table 7.1 Interviews by destination and type of stakeholder.

Stakeholder/ Destination	1	2	3	4	5	6	7	8	9	10	Total
DMO	2	2	1	2	2	3	3	2	3	3	23
Public	2	2	1	2	1	1	1	1	1	2	14
Accommodation/ services	3	0	2	1	3	2	2	4	3	3	23
Attraction	1	3	2	0	3	3	3	4	4	4	27
Total	8	7	6	5	9	9	9	11	11	12	87

Note: Destination numbers refer to numbers used in Figure 1.

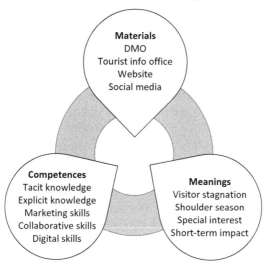

Figure 7.3 Elements of practice: promoting tourist destinations.

Overall, the basic meaning of promoting has been consistent over time: "Attracting international visitors to coastal destination is the key challenge, also because Denmark is relatively expensive" (DMO, Kerteminde), and this requires a joint public-private effort: "No-one can succeed on their own in marketing: we need to work together" (Accommodation, Skagen). It is, however, also clear that nowadays the potential visitors addressed are no longer taken for granted, in the sense that in addition to attempts to maintain the loyalty of existing guests, new markets or segments are also being targeted. The Allinge-Sandvig DMO is, for example, well aware of the need to appeal to different types of visitors: "You can be a couple in many different ways: young active ones and cultural older ones."

The aim of promoting is, in other words, not simply attracting more visitors but also a more selective targeting of specific segments in order to address the stagnating international visitor figures experienced since the late 1990s (Halkier, 2014), for example, by extending the season (VisitDenmark, 2007) and catering for more diverse and individual demands among current travellers (VisitDenmark, 2016/2017). This increasingly selective thinking about promoting can, however, also be contested, especially by attractions that see themselves as being marginalised by the dominant themes used to appeal to prospective travellers, as illustrated by this example: "As an Art Museum, we just don't fit particularly well with the general emphasis on families and coastal pleasures" (Attraction, Marielyst). These tensions are even more pronounced in experience-heterogeneous destinations like Klitmøller/Nørre Vorupør: "For the family- and beach-oriented Nørre-Vorupør, having become part of the Cold Hawaii brand of the neighbouring surf hot-spot Klitmøller is more than complicated" (DMO, Klitmøller/Nørre-Vorupør)

In parallel with this move towards more selective forms of promotion, both the materials and competences involved in promoting Danish coastal destinations have changed, driven by international technology trends and reforms of governance in Denmark.

Since the turn of the century digital technologies have gradually replaced tourist information offices, leaflets and television commercials as the main media of communication, and the interviewees all acknowledge the urgency of promoting destinations digitally, e.g. "We have to prioritise digital platforms, that's where the potential and actual visitors are" (DMO, Nordsjælland), and "We try to be on all platforms, from adverts via websites to social media" (DMO, Skagen). This digitalisation does, however, not only involve setting up promotional DMO websites, but also the emergence of competing channels of digital promotion: individual attractions and service providers are searchable and bookable online, and international sites such as Booking.com and the user-driven TripAdvisor allow tourists to investigate experiences and services from their laptop or phone (Munar et al., 2013). This implies that digital promotion has been added to the tools that individual attractions and service providers need to master. This includes maintaining a lively social media presence and, for DMOs in particular, being able to analyse digital data to inform future destination development initiatives (Ren et al., 2016). From a DMO perspective it is noted that "some of the small actors in the destination struggle with providing the input for our joint promotional website – which then becomes less valuable to visitors because the information is outdated" (DMO, Marielyst).

However, for some of the small private actors, maintaining an effective presence on international websites such as activity-based websites or Booking.com takes precedence over updating their entries on the local DMO website. These channels are seen as adding more value by targeting particular segments – "We mainly promote our activities through social media and specialist fishing media in Germany" (Attraction, Kerteminde) – or providing the key function of online booking in an easy-to-use way: "Booking.com are really good. They even came to our place and trained us in different ways. They are really useful" (Accommodation, Møn).

Digitalisation has, in other words, undermined DMO control, and the task of bringing about joint efforts in promoting destinations now requires not just traditional marketing competences but also access to knowledge about fast-moving digital opportunities that can make collective efforts attractive alongside the individual digital efforts undertaken by visitor attractions and tourist service providers.

Although digital technologies increase the geographical reach of promotional activities, these still have to refer to a particular place. Here it is noticeable that since the mid-2000s the material 'object' of promotion has also been changing, with adjacent local destinations joining forces in order to increase their reach through pooling of resources. One such collaboration includes the entire Danish North Sea coast – "Working together all along the coast for the first time gives us unprecedented clout on the German market" (DMO, Hvide Sande/

Søndervig) – while others operate on a much smaller municipal scale, as argued by the Hals DMO: "Having become part of the large municipality of Aalborg has strengthened a relatively small coastal destination like Hals." Unsurprisingly, the moves towards larger promotional geographies is also being questioned by actors who fear being less visible in the new 'bigger picture' presented to prospective visitors: "The strong promotion of surfing through the Cold Hawaii brand obscures that it is actually nature-related pursuits that unite the destination and backgrounds e.g. the adjacent National Park" (Attraction, Klitmøller/Nørre Vorupør).

The increased digital and geographical flexibility also requires changes in collaboration skills for actors within the destination. Moreover, the reliance on tacit knowledge generated by encountering visitors at tourist information offices, campsites and attractions is now gradually being supplemented or replaced by explicit forms of knowledge about visitation patterns and tourist preferences, although not unequivocally popular with all local stakeholders. While a Skagen attraction manager insist that "I don't need statistics when I constantly meet visitors and speak to others in the tourism business", most stakeholders clearly appreciate the change, as summed up by an accommodation manager in Hvide Sande/Søndervig:

> It is important that there are people that can make numbers available, facts, so everything is not based on a hunch, I don't think that is good for business in the long run. And if you have the numbers, then you can also see if the changes you initiate have an effect.

Moreover, the DMO can no longer rely on well-established routines such as fee-paying when trying to secure private co-funding for the promotion of a much wider geography. As argued by an accommodation provider in Alllinge-Sandvig, "big campaigns are for big players, not for a small pension like us", especially when these efforts can be substituted by individual efforts by private actors acting alone or through international booking portals.

All in all, promoting practices have changed in that on the one hand collective efforts have become more selective, but at the same time the access to international profiling has widened through the relatively easy access to digital platforms. Promoting has moved towards being an ongoing activity rather than a one-big-push activity in preparation of the coming season. The increased geographical flexibility has also meant that there are more promotional possibilities – and, perhaps, less controversially, because individual actors now have more options to promote their activities.

Creating destination experiences

Danish coastal destinations have followed the general European trend in that attempts to develop the visitor experience by improving the quality of existing offers or creating new ones have increasingly become part of what DMOs do

(Presenza et al., 2005; Henriksen and Halkier, 2009; Jørgensen, 2016). The interviews demonstrate that this practice has become an integrated part of DMO activities in all the ten coastal destinations investigated, as summarised in Figure 7.4.

In all the destinations, the practice of creating experiences is built around a wide range of material and cultural resources, ranging from improving down-town ambience by means of flowerpots (Marielyst) and better signage (Skagen), via using culinary cultural heritage for a series of signature events (Sønderborg) to the setting up of a major new visitor attraction, exploring "the powers of nature", close to the North Sea coast and the birthplace of the Danish windmill industry (Hvide Sande/Søndervig)

Like the new selective forms of promotion, improving or creating experiences for tourists not only aims to increase visitor numbers in general, but mostly target specific segments which new experiences are believed to appeal to. For instance, the DMO of Klitmøller/Nørre Vorupør, a destination that has developed itself as a windsurfing destination, argues that it would be easier to attract even more travelling surfers "if we establish better links between surfing-related activities and the national park hinterland". An attraction in Skagen observes that "a programme of monthly events has been a backbone in our attempts to extend the season", thereby aiming experience development towards specific groups of travellers likely to visit Skagen outside the main summer season. It is, however, interesting to note that unlike the practice of promoting, the meaning of the practice of creating has not become internalised by small private stake-holders, especially those involved in accommodation. Instead, they tend to be sceptical about the prospects of bringing about change within the destination, pointing out e.g. planning restrictions as obstacles for experience development,

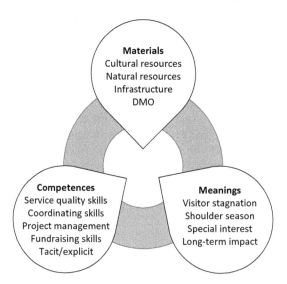

Figure 7.4 Elements of practice: creating tourist destinations.

or insisting that there is little point to their involvement when public bodies are not pulling their weight. As put by an accommodation owner in Marielyst: "The municipality bemoans the lack of private sector efforts but does preciously little themselves to improve the attractiveness of the downtown area."

Major challenges concerning the practice of creating tourist experiences relate to the competences of the private and public stakeholders involved in changing the experience offer. In terms of improving hospitality and creating better 'value for money' for visitors, extensive efforts have been undertaken in order to professionalise firms in general and their service offer in particular. This takes the form of creating networks that focus on developing their businesses (DMO, Møn) and staff training, although the latter is complicated by high levels of staff turnover in a seasonal industry (Public, Hvide Sande/Søndervig) and rules regarding training for the temporary unemployed (DMO, Allinge Sandvig).

Creating new experiences is in several ways a major competence challenge for DMOs and other public bodies. While knowledge about demand for particular new attractions remains difficult to assemble, the new recurring and comparative visitor satisfaction surveys undertaken by the Centre for Coastal and Nature Tourism are generally appreciated as valuable insights that stakeholders should act upon collectively. Rather more challenging is the development of competences related to generating the economic resources needed to sustain investment of resources in new coastal experiences, because the funding for these activities – especially those involving creation of new visitor attractions – typically involves a combination of public and private funding. Public funding for tourism purposes in Denmark has traditionally been largely used to fund the local DMO and its tourist information office(s) (Halkier, 2014; Jørgensen, 2016), and thus development projects have typically been allocated from local one-off tourism initiatives or relied on access to non-tourism programmes for e.g. rural or regional development, whether at the local, regional, national or European level. The discontinuous ad-hoc nature of individual projects therefore requires that DMOs have competences in assembling temporary project partnerships that are willing and able to invest resources in order to improve local visitor experiences. This means that e.g. the general socio-economic development of the area around the destination can determine the extent to which the practice of creating experienced can be engaged in: "In a way, our problem is that we are not located in a peripheral rural area but part of an urbanised municipality: we cannot access the funding that is available for e.g. destinations on the North Sea Coast" (Attraction, Hals).

But generally, it creates, at best, a series of one-off projects that makes it more difficult to engage private stakeholders, as explained by the Hvide Sande/Søndervig DMO:

> In principle this project ends on 31/12, but if the region chooses to provide more funding we will be back in business in half a year. I think that

is unfortunate because it takes a long time to make the artist or the retailer understand why they should participate in our activities – and then it falls to pieces.

(DMO, Hvide Sande/Søndervig)

This is problematic because destination development projects typically have to attract co-funding from private stakeholders while at the same time fitting the aims of the public programmes applied for – and, if successful, that funding will be available only for a specific purposed for a limited period of time. As summed up by an interviewee: "It is a problem that a lot of the development is project based ... and the issue, from the perspective of the local businesses is that as soon as the project ends, then there is no more money and it dies out" (DMO, Klitmøller/Nørre Vorupør).

Moreover, many interviewees claimed that this confuses private firms and undermines confidence in long-term public commitment to individual projects, as recounted by Hvide Sande/Søndervig DMO: "At the moment we have eight different projects. But when we go out and talk to the industry they don't really care where the money comes from. The goal for them is actual development on the ground."

Finally, the stop-go project format which the creating practice is operating through, in turn, makes management of stakeholder relations a key competence for DMO staff, because potential private co-investors need to be identified and kept on board in each of the projects, while at the same time other (non-committed) private actors must be reassured about the overall long-term benefits for the destination. At the same time the temporary projects also constitute a challenge for DMOs as project managers. On the one hand, individual projects have a high risk of turn-over of temporary staff, as illustrated by a public project manager:

My job as a facilitator has been to deliver innovation courses with some of the local tourism actors in order to develop new attractions that can attract tourists outside the main season or make them spend more. However, the facilitator function will end with the project. I hope that a similar actor could be employed by the DMO. I really hope that.

(Public, Møn)

On the other hand, maintaining an overall strategic direction in destination development is clearly complicated by the need to achieve through a portfolio of parallel temporary projects. All in all, the practice of creating experiences in coastal tourist destinations is temporally challenged by a lack of long-term commitment of public and private resources and the need to constantly reinvent public-private partnerships as the organisational vehicle for achieving change.

Conclusions: unpacking the destination development bundle

The analysis above has demonstrated that both promoting and creating destinations can be seen as practices in the sense that they involve recurring patterns of connected *materials, competences* and *meanings* in order to, respectively, tempt visitors to and increase the attraction of, a destination. There is some variation in the materials available, the meanings that engage practitioners and the competences required. In Danish coastal destinations, there have been changes in practices over time, many of which have been driven by destination-external factors such as international competition for tourists (e.g. the need to improve competitiveness through targeted improvement of the experience offer), and the emergence of digital marketing technologies which, along with national changes in the geography of governance, have made it possible to expose both small specialised attractions as well as large-scale destinations to the gaze of would-be visitors. We have argued, following Schatzki, that practices can constitute a bundle if they are related to one another via e.g. "common actions, common organisational elements, or common material entities; chains of action; common motivating events" (Schatzki, 2017: 134). In Danish coastal destinations, significant links exist between the practices of promoting and creating, such that they can be seen as a destination development a practice bundle. However, the relative balance between the two key practices in destination development, promoting and creating, has gradually changed. Unlike the early days of DMOS in the 1990s where M referred to 'marketing' only, experience development has now become an integrated part of the work of local DMOs, with its relative importance continuing to grow also in financial importance since the late 2000s (Kommunernes Landsforening, 2010; 2017).

At the same time, there are significant overlaps between the two destination-related practices, promoting and creating, with regard to meanings, materials and competences. We have seen that the meaning of both practices involves increasing the appeal of Danish coastal destination, often focusing on particular customer segments, underpinned by a shared concern about stagnating or declining visitation. Both practices involve coordination between large number of local actors as a key competence, and the local DMO is the focus point that orchestrates these collective efforts, mobilising tacit and explicit knowledge about visitation patterns and trends.

However, recent developments have exposed fragilities that may destabilise the destination development bundle. Despite the shared meaning – the need to improve and promote coastal destinations in an increasingly competitive market for tourist experiences – several developments within the two practices have disrupted the close alignment with regard to materials and competences question. Firstly, the materials overlap between the two practices is weakened by their increasingly flexible character. Importantly, the geographies addressed when promoting coastal destinations are gradually widened in order to increased international marketing impact, and hence individual destinations and local DMOs risk to fade in importance compared to supra-local entities like e.g. the *West Coast Partnership* or *Destination South Jutland*. At the same time, the creating practice now requires the establishment of frequently changing stakeholder partnerships to execute temporary experience development projects, again questioning the notion of the local destination as a coherent collective. Secondly, the rise of digital marketing has seriously undermined the traditional monopoly of DMO's on international marketing, with individual attractions and service providers increasingly being able to go it alone or rely on alternative commercial (Booking.com) or social media platforms (Facebook, TripAdvisor) to reach potential visitors. Added together, this implies that the destination as a well-defined locality, the key stakeholders who are to engage in destination development practices and, not least, the position of the local DMO as the main focus of stakeholder coordination are being eroded.

These findings on the evolution of Danish coastal DMOs and destination development have been made possible by the adoption of an analytical framework inspired by practice theory. The existing literature, often drawing on organisational theory or political science, has tended to emphasise either a conflictual juxtaposition between destination marketing and management or, more recently, the complementary synergies between the two. Adopting a more fine-grained frame to analyse the practices associated with destination development has allowed us to identify both the gradual coming together of the practice bundle and its possible future unravelling. We do not claim that this is a general feature of destination development and DMOs in e.g. Europe, because the existence and dynamics of practice bundles is an empirical question, and depends on specific local/national circumstances. However, we believe that a practice based analysis opens up new perspectives on the dynamics of destination development.

Acknowledgements

Thanks are due to the Danish ERDF programme and Centre for Coastal Tourism for sponsoring the research, and to research assistant Matias Thuen Jørgensen for his extensive efforts on the road and behind the desk when collecting information and analysing data.

Bibliography

Andersen, J., Jensen, S., Kvistgaard, P. and Therkelsen, A. (2000). *Turistforeningens rolle i fremtidens turisme i Nordjyllands Amt.* Aalborg: TRU, AAU.
Beaumont, N. and Dredge, D. (2010). Local tourism governance: a comparison of three network approaches. *Journal of Sustainable Tourism*, 18(1), 7–28. doi:10.1080/09669580903215139

Beritelli, P. and Bieger, T. (2014). From destination governance to destination leadership – defining and exploring the significance with the help of a systemic perspective. *Tourism Review*, 69(1), 25–46. doi:10.1108/TR-07-2013-0043

Björk, P. and Virtanen, H. (2005). What tourism project managers need to know about co-operation. *Scandinavian Journal of Hospitality and Tourism*, 5(3), 212–230.

Bornhorst, T., Ritchie, J. R. B. and Sheehan, L. (2010). Determinants of tourism success for DMOs and destinations: an empirical examination of stakeholders' perspectives. *Tourism Management*, 31(5), 572–589. doi:10.1016/j.tourman.2009.06.008

Coles, T., Dinan, C. and Hutchison, F. C. (2014). Tourism and the public sector in England since 2010: a disorderly transition? *Current Issues in Tourism*, 17(3), 247–279. doi:10.1080/13683500.2012.733356

CRT. (2017). *Turismens økonomiske betydning i Danmark 2015*. København: VisitDenmark.

Dobernig, K., Veen, E. and Oosterveer, P. (2016). Growing urban food as an emerging social practice. In G. Spaargaren, D. Weenink and M. Lamers (Eds), *Practice Theory and Research: Exploring the Dynamics of Social Life* (pp. 153–178). Oxford: Routledge.

Dredge, D. (2006). Policy networks and the local organisation of tourism. *Tourism Management*, 27(2), 269–280.

Dredge, D. (2014). Tourism-planning network knowledge dynamics. In M. McLeod and R. Vaughan (Eds), *Knowledge Networks and Tourism* (pp. 9–27). London: Routledge.

Dredge, D. (2016). Are DMOs on a path to redundancy? *Tourism Recreation Research*, 41(3), 348–353. doi:10.1080/02508281.2016.1195959

Dredge, D. and Jamal, T. (2015). Progress in tourism planning and policy: a post-structural perspective on knowledge production. *Tourism Management*, 51(C), 285–297. doi:10.1016/j.tourman.2015.06.002

Elbe, J., Hallen, L. and Axelsson, B. (2009). The destination-management organisation and the integrative destination-marketing process. *International Journal of Tourism Research*, 11(3), 283–296. doi:10.1002/jtr.695

Getz, D., Anderson, D. and Sheehan, L. (1998). Roles, issues, and strategies for convention and visitors' bureaux in destination planning and product development: a survey of Canadian bureaux. *Tourism Management*, 19(4), 311–340.

Gretzel, U., Fesenmaier, D. R., Formica, S. and O'Leary, J. T. (2006). Searching for the future: challenges faced by destination marketing organizations. *Journal of Travel Research*, 45(2), 116–126. doi:10.1177/0047287506291598

Halkier, H. (2006). *Institutions, Discourse and Regional Development. The Scottish Development Agency and the Politics of Regional Policy*. Brussels: PIE Peter Lang.

Halkier, H. (2010). Tourism knowledge dynamics. In P. Cooke, C. de Laurentis, C. Collinge and S. MacNeill (Eds), *Platforms of Innovation: Dynamics of New Industrial Knowledge Flows* (pp. 233–250). London: Edward Elgar.

Halkier, H. (2014). Innovation and destination governance in Denmark: tourism, policy networks and spatial development. *European Planning Studies*, 22(8), 1659–1670. doi:10.1080/09654313.2013.784609

Halkier, H. and James, L. (2016). Destination dynamics, path dependency and resilience. Regaining momentum in Danish coastal tourism destinations? In P. Brouder, S. A. Clavé, A. M. Gill and D. Ioannides (Eds), *Tourism Destination Evolution* (pp. 19–42). Abingdon: Routledge.

Halkier, H., Jørgensen, M. T. and Dredge, D. (2015). *Vidensudvikling og destinationsudvikling i kystturismen.* Aalborg: Department of Culture and Global Studies.

Halkier, H., Østergaard, M. Z., Kaae, B., Hvass, K. A. and Jensen, J. F. (2014). Turismeerhvervet i Danmark under forandring: Kvantitet og kvalitet. In L. E. Jønsson and H. Halkier (Eds), *Danmark i det globale turismebillede: Erfaring, tendenser og muligheder* (pp. 23–38). Aalborg: Aalborg Universitetsforlag.

Hall, C. M. (2008). *Tourism Planning: Policies, Processes and Relationships.* 2nd Edition. Harlow: Pearson Prentice Hall.

Hall, C. M. and Williams, A. (2008). *Tourism and Innovation.* Abingdon: Routledge.

Henriksen, P. F. and Halkier, H. (2009). From local promotion towards regional tourism policies: knowledge processes and actor networks in North Jutland, Denmark. *European Planning Studies,* 17(10), 1445–1462.

Hjalager, A.-M. (2000). Tourism destinations and the concept of industrial districts. *Tourism and Hospitality Research,* 2(3), 199–213.

Hjalager, A.-M. (2010). A review of innovation research in tourism. *Tourism Management,* 30(1), 1–12. doi:10.1016/j.tourman.2009.08.012

Hristov, D. and Petrova, P. (2015). Destination management plans – a new approach to managing destinations in England: evidence from Milton Keynes. *Current Issues in Tourism,* 1–21. doi:10.1080/13683500.2015.1070800

Hui, A. (2017). Variation and the intersection of practices. In A. Hui, T. Schatzki and E. Shove (Eds), *The Nexus of Practices Connections: Constellations, Practitioners* (pp. 52–67). London; New York: Routledge.

Hui, A., Schatzki, T. and Shove, E. (Eds) (2017). *The Nexus of Practices Connections: constellations, practitioners.* London; New York: Routledge.

Ioannides, D. and Debbage, K. G. (1998). Introduction: exploring the economic geography and tourism nexus. In D. Ioannides and K. G. Debbage (Eds), *The Economic Geography of the Tourist Industry* (pp. 1–13). London: Routledge.

Jørgensen, M. T. (2016). Developing a holistic framework for analysis of destination management and/or marketing organizations: six Danish destinations. *Journal of Travel and Tourism Marketing,* 1–12. doi:10.1080/10548408.2016.1209152

Jørgensen, M. T. and Halkier, H. (2013). *Samarbejde, Vidensdynamikker og Turismeudvikling i Danske Kystferiebyer.* Aalborg: Institut for Kultur og Globale Studier, Aalborg Universitet. http://vbn.aau.dk/files/95676627/J_rgensen_Halkier_2013_Sama rbejde_vidensdynamikker_og_turismeudvikling_i_danske_kystferiebyer_KUP_rap.pdf.

Kommunernes Landsforening (2010). *Turismen i kommunerne – Overblik og nye turismepolitiske anbefalinger.* København: Kommunernes Landsforening.

Kommunernes Landsforening (2017). *Attraktive Destinationer. Turismepolitiske anbefalinger til regionerne.* København: Kommunernes Landsforening.

Lamers, M. and van der Duim, R. (2016). Connecting practices: conservation tourism partnerships in Kenya. In G. Spaargaren, D. Weenink and M. Lamers (Eds), *Practice Theory and Research: Exploring the Dynamics of Social Life* (pp. 179–201). Oxford: Routledge.

Mahoney, J. and Thelen, K. (2010). A theory of gradual institutional change. In J. Mahoney and K. Thelen (Eds), *Explaining Institutional Change* (pp. 1–37). Cambridge: Cambridge UP.

Morgan, N. and Pritchard, A. (2001). *Advertising in Tourism and Leisure.* London: Routledge.

Munar, A. M. (2016). Surviving metamorphosis. *Tourism Recreation Research,* 41(3), 358–361. http://doi.org/10.1080/02508281.2016.1195961

Munar, A. M., Gyimothy, S. and Cai, L. (Eds) (2013). *Tourism Social Media: Transformations in Identity, Community and Culture.* Bingley: Emerald.

Nicolini, D. (2012). *Practice Theory, Work and Organisation – An Introduction.* Oxford: Oxford UP.

Nicolini, D. (2016). Is small the only beautiful? Making sense of 'large phenomena' from a practice-based perspective. In A. Hui, T. Schatzki and E. Shove (Eds), *The Nexus of Practices Connections: Constellations, Practitioners* (pp. 98–113). London; New York: Routledge.

Nilsson, P. Å. (2007). Stakeholder theory: the need for a convenor. The case of Billund. *Scandinavian Journal of Hospitality and Tourism*, 7(2), 171–184.

North, D. C. (1990). *Institutions, Institutional Change and Economic Performance.* Cambridge: Cambridge UP.

Park, O., Cai, L. A. and Lehto, X. Y. (2013). Collaborative destination branding. In L. A. Cai, W. C. Gartner and A. M. Munar (Eds), *Tourism Branding: Communities in Action* (pp. 75–86). Emerald Group Publishing Limited. doi:10.1108/S2042-1443 (2009)0000001008

Pastras, P. and Bramwell, B. (2013). A strategic-relational approach to tourism policy. *Annals of Tourism Research*, 43, 390–414. doi:10.1016/j.annals.2013.06.009

Pechlaner, H., Herntrei, M., Pichler, S. and Volgger, M. (2012a). From destination management towards governance of regional innovation systems – the case of South Tyrol, Italy. *Tourism Review*, 67(2), 22–33. doi:10.1108/16605371211236123

Pechlaner, H., Volgger, M. and Herntrei, M. (2012b). Destination management organizations as interface between destination governance and corporate governance. *Anatolia*, 23(2), 151–168. doi:10.1080/13032917.2011.652137

Pike, S. and Page, S. J. (2014). Destination marketing organizations and destination marketing: a narrative analysis of the literature. *Tourism Management,* 41(C), 202–227. doi:10.1016/j.tourman.2013.09.009

Presenza, A., Sheehan, L. and Ritchie, J. R. B. (2005). Towards a model of the roles and activities of destination management organizations. *Journal of Hospitality, Tourism and Leisure Science*, 1–16.

Reckwitz, A. (2002). Toward a theory of social practices: a development in culturalist theorizing. *European Journal of Social Theory*, 5(2), 243–263.

Ren, C., Petersen, M. K., Nielsen, T. K. and Halkier, H. (2016). *Smart Tourism i Region Nordjylland – diagnose og fremtidsspor.* København: Aalborg Universitet, Institut for Kultur og Globale Studier.

Schatzki, T. (2002). *The Site of the Social. A Philosophical Account of the Constitution of Social Life and Change.* Philadelphia: Penn State University Press.

Schatzki, T. R. (2011). Theories of practice. In D. Southerton (Ed.), *Encyclopedia of Consumer Culture* (pp. 1447–1451). Thousand Oakes: Sage.

Schatzki, T. R. (2017). Sayings, texts and discursive formations. In A. Hui, T. Schatzki and E. Shove (Eds), *The Nexus of Practices Connections: Constellations, Practitioners* (pp. 126–140). London; New York: Routledge.

Sheehan, L. R. and Ritchie, J. R. B. (2005). Destination stakeholders exploring identity and salience. *Annals of Tourism Research*, 32(3), 711–734. doi:10.1016/j.annals.2004.10.013

Sheehan, L., Ritchie, J. R. B. and Hudson, S. (2007). The destination promotion triad: understanding asymmetric stakeholder interdependencies among the city, hotels, and DMO. *Journal of Travel Research*, 46(1), 64–74. doi:10.1177/0047287507302383

Sheehan, L., Vargas-Sánchez, A., Presenza, A. and Abbate, T. (2016). The use of intelligence in tourism destination management: an emerging role for DMOs. *International Journal of Tourism Research*, 18(6), 549–557. doi:10.1002/jtr.2072

Shove, E. and Pantzar, M. (2007). Recruitment and reproduction: the careers and carriers of digital photography and floorball. *Human Affairs*, 17(2), 275.

Shove, E., Pantzar, M. and Watson, M. (2012). *The Dynamics of Social Practice*. London: SAGE.

Therkelsen, A. and Halkier, H. (2010). Branding provincial cities: the politics of inclusion, strategy and commitment. In A. Pike (Ed.), *Brands and Branding Geographies* (pp. 200–212). Cheltenham: Edward Elgar.

Therkelsen, A. and Halkier, H. (2012). Destination branding challenges – or why getting the right umbrella can be difficult. In T. Furunes, R. J. Mykletun and E. Marnburg (Eds), *Current Research in Hospitality and Tourism*. Bergen: Fagbokforlaget.

VisitDenmark (2007). *Kystferiestrategi i retning mod helårsturisme*. København: VisitDenmark.

VisitDenmark (2016). *Kyst- og naturturister i Danmark*. København: VisitDenmark.

VisitDenmark (2017). *Turismen i Danmark – skaber vækst og arbejdspladser* (pp. 1–21). København: VisitDenmark.

Volgger, M. and Pechlaner, H. (2014). Requirements for destination management organizations in destination governance: understanding DMO success. *Tourism Management*, 1–12. doi:10.1016/j.tourman.2013.09.001

Weidenfeld, A., Williams, A. M. and Butler, R. W. (2011). Why cluster? Text and Subtext in the engagement of tourism development policies with the cluster concept. In D. Dredge and J. Jenkins (Eds), *Stories of Practice: Tourism Policy and Planning* (pp. 335–358). Farnham: Ashgate.

8 Tourism innovation by bundling practices

A genealogy of the 'Zeelandpas' destination card

Timo Derriks, René van der Duim and Karin Peters

Introduction

In recent decades, destination cards have become quite common, especially in larger cities, facilitating, for example, free entrance or discounts on major attractions and free or low-priced public transportation. The Dutch coastal province of Zeeland, the Netherlands, introduced four regional destination cards in 2014 and branded them as the 'Zeelandpas'. The cards themselves had their own names and specific offers but were all part of the Zeelandpas innovation project and were promoted as such. In 2015, the regional destination cards became unified into one Zeelandpas destination card that could be used across the entire state province.

In this chapter we examine the history of this regional tourism destination card and develop a specific and detailed analysis of its development as a 'bundling of practices' (Lamers and Van der Duim, 2016). As we will argue, in this 'bundling' process three existing practices (destination branding, market research and public transportation) are combined. We examine the development of this destination card genealogically by historically following its actors and their actions. We reconstruct how connections between practices have been achieved (Nicolini, 2006) and how constituent practices have changed accordingly.

The Zeelandpas connects practices in a new hybrid form (Shove et al., 2012) and can be seen at the same time as a service, process, marketing, management and institutional innovation (Hjalager, 2010). Studies that particularly focus on innovation in tourism are relatively young, scattered and fragmented (Paget et al., 2010). Hjalager (2010) therefore argued for more research on innovation at the destination level and stressed the need to study the interplay between innovation processes and the wider governance contexts in which they take place (Halkier et al., 2014). In order to better satisfy the more and more experience-centric tourist, who also has more destinations to choose from (Halkier et al., 2014), Maggioni et al. (2014) claim that collaboration between service providers is crucial. Destination cards can be seen as examples of collaborative, public-private, service bundling initiatives (Zoltan and Masiero, 2012).

Innovation by tourism destination cards so far has only been investigated in the German and Italian speaking context (Zoltan and Masiero, 2012). Angeloni (2016) recently reviewed literature and examined an Italian tourism kit. In her study she shows that implementing a multi-application smart card is a complex process as it requires synchronised activity of heterogeneous actors through integrated and interoperable electronic solutions.

Similarly, this study will examine the process of creating, realising and implementing a destination card in a Dutch context. It aims to contribute to literature on tourism destination cards by presenting a detailed understanding of its associated processes. To do so, we first introduce practice theory as an alternative and at the same time promising approach to study innovation processes within a tourism destination. By genealogically studying how practices are affected, constrained or enabled over time by other practices and the related material consequences (Nicolini, 2012), we aim to provide a better understanding and detailed insights of the unfolding and realisation of tourism innovation (Pantzar and Shove, 2010).

In this chapter, we particularly focus on which 'doings and sayings', rules and materials played an important role in connecting existing practices into this destination card and how this bundling affected existing practices. We will examine the different stages in which this bundling took place, and how as a result the deployment of a destination card emerged. Besides offering detailed insights in how different practices were connected and disconnected, we also discuss the conditions that supported or hindered the development of the destination card.

The chapter proceeds as follows. First, we briefly introduce practice theory, the case and the methods used. Second, by studying the genealogy of this card we will show how practices were connected and the card was developed. We will conclude with a brief discussion of our results.

Innovation by bundling practices

Practice theories focus both on ordinary activities such as cooking or cleaning as well as practice-arrangement bundles, i.e. interconnected social practices and material arrangements of different sizes. In this respect Nicolini (2009, 2012) makes a distinction between a 'zoomed-in' and a 'zoomed-out' position. In the first position practice theorists study specific social phenomena, such as daily routinised activities and face to face interactions (Lamers et al., 2016). Studies on these situated practices normally lead to 'thick descriptions' of social practices which are already familiar to many people. According to Shove et al. (2012) these everyday life practices are constituted by three elements: materials, meanings and competences. These are not only interdependent, but are also mutually shaping. When treating these elements as building-blocks of practices, emergent patterns, connections and their history can be identified and used to describe processes of transformation, diffusion and circulation (Shove et al., 2012). Innovation in this zoomed-in position can be seen as the introduction of new things or methods (Shove et al., 2012), involving changing combinations of symbolic and material ingredients and of competences or know-how (Pantzar and Shove, 2010; Lamers et al., 2016).

In the case of Nordic walking, Pantzar and Shove (2010) showed how the practitioners involved, including managers, manufacturers and consumers, all played their part in actively integrating the elements in question and how connections between the defining elements were made as well as sustained. Innovation therefore should not be seen as an outcome of managerial intervention but as "the varied contributions many actors and histories make to what is, as a result, an inherently uncontrollable process" (Pantzar and Shove, 2010: 459). These practitioners can be more or less faithful, and individuals can drop out and take up different practices as their lives unfold. Consequently, practice theories appreciate the active and creative role of the practitioners themselves. With their analysis, Pantzar and Shove (2010) provided a new sense of the theoretical potential of conceptualising innovation in terms of practices instead of only in terms of products and services, which is normally the case in tourism innovation studies.

Whereas Pantzar and Shove (2010) 'zoom in' and study innovation of a singular practice, namely Nordic-walking, innovation can also be studied from a 'zoomed-out' perspective. Although according to practice theorists ontologically there are no differences between micro and macro phenomena as the social happens at only one level (see Lamers et al., 2016; Schatzki, 2005), from a 'zoomed-out' position it makes sense to look at bundling of practices and material arrangements that mutually affect and precondition one another. For example, Lamers and Van der Duim (2016) have shown in their study how conservation tourism partnerships should be seen as practice-arrangement bundles and have conceptualised these as deliberate attempts to create distinct nexuses of practices and material arrangements to tackle societal challenges. In studying the process of bundling, the interlinking through the introduction of connecting practices is emphasised (Lamers and Van der Duim, 2016). In this way Lamers and Van der Duim (2016) 'zoom out' and specifically focus on connections between practices resulting in new practice-arrangement bundles. Whereas 'zooming in' on innovation emphasises the changing and integration of (new) elements in one practice, 'zooming out' considers why and how these elements changed in relation to the practices they originate from, how these practices mutually affect or enable each other, and the roles of practitioners in making these connections.

In this chapter a destination card is seen as a new bundle of practices by including new things and methods based on the integration of existing (bundles of) practices that in turn might possibly (have to) change as well. Schatzki (2017) highlights that practices and arrangements are linked by relations such as causality, constitution, intentionality, intelligibility and prefiguration. Resulting bundles are also related to one another in various ways, via:

> common actions, common organisational elements, or common material entities; chains of action; common motivating events; participants in one bundle being intentionally directed to other bundles; overlapping, orchestrated or mutually referring places and paths; orchestrations of (i.e. mutual dependencies among) actions, material entities and organisational elements of different types in different practice-arrangement bundles; and physical connections and causality.
>
> (Schatzki, 2017: 134)

A comparative and historical perspective on the trajectory of all related practices and their changing embeddedness in wider practice-arrangement bundles is crucial for analysing change in tourism practices and therewith innovation as all innovations requires change to some extent (Lamers et al., 2017).

To study these trajectories, Lamers et al. (2017), suggest using the conceptual framework provided by Schatzki (2002; 2016). According to Schatzki, practices consist of 'doings and sayings' and material arrangements that hang together, organised by practical understanding, general understanding, rules and teleo-affective structures. Whereas practical understandings denote particular abilities that relate to the actions composing a practice, general understanding is the shared idea of what a practice entails and what the meanings of the practice are. Rules, according to Schatzki (2002: 79), consist of:

> explicit formulations, principles, precepts, and instructions that enjoin or direct people to perform specific actions. To say that rules link doings and sayings is to say that people, in carrying out these doings and sayings, take account of and adhere to the same rules.

Finally, practices are organised by teleo-affective structures, the property of a practice linking its 'doings and sayings' to a range of acceptable ends, purposes, beliefs and tasks that ought to be accomplished, including the manner in which these projects and tasks should be executed. As we will see, when connecting practices manage to survive and prosper, the original practices undergo gradual changes as they become more and more directed to the rules and teleo-affective structures of the larger practice-arrangement bundle (Lamers et al., 2016).

Based on the above, this study concentrates on reconstructing the genealogical path of how the practices associated and required for the new practice-material arrangement of a destination card were combined. Following this line of thought, the objective of this study is not only to identify and describe the new practice-arrangement bundle associated with the Zeelandpas destination card creation in terms of its realisation and implementation, but also to understand how bundling happened and affected constituting practices as for example destination branding or doing market research. In this way, this study aims to offer a detailed understanding of difficulties and successes related to introducing a destination card in a particular region.

Selected case and study design

In this chapter we conceptualise the destination card as a bundling of practices. The destination card is now known as the 'Zeelandpas' in the province of Zeeland, the Netherlands. The state province of Zeeland is located in the south-west of the Netherlands and divided into 13 municipalities.

Although it is now believed to benefit destination competitiveness, the Zeelandpas destination card development was also a long, challenging and complex process of combining practices and related collaboration between tourism entrepreneurs and other stakeholders. Its history can be traced back to early 2000s. The Zeelandpas was for many years limited to the northern island of Schouwen-Duiveland and better known as the SchouwenDuivelandPas. The evolution of this card resulted in four regional destination cards in 2014, branded as the Zeelandpas but with distinct offers. Only in 2015 did it become a card for the entire province and it is still operating as such today.

The genealogic approach taken in this study concentrates on the life of practices. We focus on how connecting and bundling practices emerged, were perpetuated, changed and sometimes disappeared (Nicolini, 2017). Questions were concerned with how recurrent scenes of actions have been historically constituted. We break down big stories into smaller stories that can be traced empirically. We examine what elements were being brought in and changed each other, and how the innovation was unfolding. Practice theory provides the language to do so (Nicolini, 2017; Shove et al., 2012) and to answer the questions of which practices were being put together and to what effect; how practitioners were recruited and how (the bundling of) practices evolved over time.

In order to reconstruct the path of connecting and bundling towards the realisation of this 'Zeelandpas', the first author collected data in various ways. As participant observation, often used in analysing practices, was impossible, the qualitative method of interviewing was the most appropriate method. Most information therefore stems from interviews with those involved in the card's development. These informants were found in related documents and by means of snowballing. A total of 20 people were interviewed. Questions and topics to discuss were prepared beforehand and based on the literature review on practice theory and innovation. These topics and questions concerned the role the interviewees played, how they perceived the process and what according to them were major influences on performance and progress as well as how the implementation of a destination card influenced related practices and commitments of related practitioners.

Following the interviewing of informants involved in the development of the card, entrepreneurs whose services could be accessed via the destination card were asked to give oral or written feedback on how they for example got in touch with the card, what their motivation was to get involved, how special deals were created and how they thought their customers appreciated the use of the card and its specific offers. Also, they were asked what they appreciated in terms of organisation and what might have been done differently or should be improved in the future. In total 13 entrepreneurs replied, eight in writing; five were met in person. All interviews were recorded and transcribed, resulting in a total of 25 transcripts of recorded interviews and 8 e-mails with written answers. Besides conducting interviews, a total of 32 related documents were analysed. These documents varied from internal and progress reports to published plans. In addition, we examined 27 collected media announcements that mentioned the 'Zeelandpas' or regional variations of them, mostly in local newspapers and retrieved online from local newspaper's archives using search words such as 'tourist card', 'destination card' and 'Zeelandpas'.

Data was collected until the point of saturation and analysed in NVivo10 qualitative data analysis software, which also enabled to code the data in terms of practices and its constituting elements. As the destination card developed over time and the elements of practice – meanings, competences and materials – changed along the way, a chronological 'thick description' was created that allowed the identification of practices and their constitutive elements. To understand the innovation process, emphasis in the analysis was thereafter placed on the bundling of practices and the genealogical path of the innovation.

Bundling practices to realise the Zeelandpas

Based on our analysis, we identified four different periods in the bundling of practices. During these four periods, the development of the destination card combined – in various ways – three practices: destination branding, conducting market research and facilitating public transportation. To a lesser extent and more sporadically, other practices, as for example improving customer services at a campsite, improving resident services in the municipality and levying tourist taxes, were also associated and perceived as required for the success of the destination card.

Period 1: First destination card ideas and realisation efforts (2001–2005)

In 2001, the municipality of Schouwen-Duiveland announced the introduction of a tourist card that could combine holiday park services and giving discounts on activities. The original goal was to stimulate collaboration between entrepreneurs offering tourism related services and products and those accommodating the tourists, as illustrated by a municipality representative: 'How do we team up somebody who is selling cheese in

Nieuwerkerk with a campsite in De Westhoek, accommodating people that might want that cheese?'

The municipality of Schouwen-Duiveland hired an external organisation to organise this collaboration in such a way that it would on the one hand benefit branding the isle of Schouwen-Duiveland and at the same time allow market research to take place. In addition, the improving of customer services at holiday parks, levying tourist taxes and expanding resident services within the municipality were also explored as possible future aims to be included in this collaboration.

The basic idea was that tourists would, ideally, become more loyal to the destination as a result of being enabled to undertake more activities and being stimulated by discounts and special offers. At the same time, the ease of holiday making would increase as the card could for instance be used to access a campsite, a swimming pool or turning on the showers. To do so, the card needed to include technological features which would for example enable opening campsite entry barriers or the possibility to make use of certain discounts and packages as created by means of a digital back office software platform. Exploring these technological possibilities and putting effort in convincing entrepreneurs to engage and collaborate with the project required certain expertise and materials and with that financial resources. The municipality provided funding through a subsidy of the European Union and invited organisations to make a bid. As a result a software developing organisation was given the opportunity to investigate the feasibility of the project, including the technological features involved.

In order for a card to function properly, tourism organisations needed to create offers, issue and accept the card, thereby changing their existing business practices. Implementation of the card prompted practical as well as general understandings of what to do for and with the card and for which reason, materials such as scanners and printers and particular skills to be able to use the cards. The feasibility study resulted in a final report in which the end goals of the destination card were described: the card should stimulate tourists to undertake more activities, should ease their holiday making and should also allow the monitoring of tourist behaviour to improve marketing activities.

A specific recommendation was to create a foundation to facilitate synergy and cooperation, also by operating an Internet site that would handle visitor bookings and act as back-office for entrepreneurial cooperation. The foundation should be managed by a new organisation as part of the existing Tourism Information Bureau (in Dutch: VVV), a public organisation concerned with promoting the region. All related enterprises within hospitality, recreation and retail would ideally have equal representing voices to cooperate and strengthen each other instead of competing with each other. A small office would be occupied with the back-office tasks such as promotion and marketing, data collection and engaging stakeholders.

Although it took time and effort for the entrepreneurs to understand the benefits, technology and required skills and efforts to be made, the larger holiday parks eventually embraced the idea of the destination card and planned integrating it in their practices once the card was implemented. Based on this commitment a final report was presented to discuss subsequent steps. During the meeting in which the report was presented, the city's council demanded more insights in the social and economic impacts of a card and commissioned a study. The idea of an impact study conflicted with the opinions of entrepreneurs who were willing to be involved, arguing that it would delay the implementation process and because of it, the momentum would be lost. In this way, at the end of this period, the bundling of destination branding and conducting market research by means of a destination card failed and stopped. As one of the interviewees stated: 'After the council's decision for an impact study it became silent for a while, supported by the question; "who will take the lead?" And it remained silent.'

The impact study was not carried out. The software development company decided to withdraw and as a consequence the bundling of practices by means of a destination card halted.

Period 2: Card realisation and first efforts in digitalisation (2006–2010)

In 2006, a newly created foundation entitled 'Stichting SchouwenDuive-landPas' resumed the process of developing a destination card capitalising on a changed mind-set of entrepreneurs, now more focused on collaboration than on competition. The foundation adopted the feasibility plan. It consisted of only entrepreneurs, especially managers of campsites and bungalow parks. According to one of the founders of the SchouwenDuivelelandPas foundation this proved to be a solid base to start.

The foundation distributed a paper tourist card that eventually had to evolve into one with digital features. The card was dispensed by several accommodation providers. The regional bus company was also included in the business model so that tourists would enjoy free bus transportation on the island. A fixed amount of transportation costs was yearly billed by the bus company to the foundation.

The central aim for bundling practices in this period was again a practical tourist card, but somewhat smaller in scope than previously suggested. While the municipality approved the foundation to take the lead role, they decided neither to join the foundation nor to get operationally involved until the card functioned properly. At a later stage extra features for residents, as for example access to garbage disposal points, could be added making the card of value for residents as well. Until that point, the municipality only provided financial resources for the foundation.

With financial resources being scarce, the foundation also looked at new subsidy opportunities in order to further develop the digital system. In the process of moving towards a digital tourist card, the foundation had to include new practices and hence capture new stakeholders, as it was believed current participants did not have enough time, knowledge and competences to successfully develop the project. A researcher from the Research Centre for

Coastal Tourism joined due to her background on knowledge creation and sharing. In addition, an IT professor was enrolled to play an active role in digitalisation, especially to develop methods to eventually monitor and use digital traces left behind by card users. A technology consultant also joined as it was believed he could advise the entrepreneurs in the foundation during the process.

With the inclusion of these experts as carriers of practices (see Shove et al., 2012), new skills were enrolled in the bundling process. Eventually, a digital pilot was launched which enabled the card to be scanned. Computer hardware, printers and scanners had to be bought, installed and used in order to link products to and to enable the scanning of the cards. This also required new practical understandings, skills of loading, printing, registering and scanning and hence 'ways of doing' of the entrepreneurs involved. However, scanning cards in busses was not yet possible. In order to make use of public transportation, the cards needed to be shown so the bus driver could check the printed date of validity.

The digital traces left by registering the card use never reached the critical mass at this stage to deliver market information of any value to the isle's relevant industry players. Concerning this pilot and the difficulty in achieving a sufficient amount of data, a respondent explained:

> You have to start somewhere. If you would be able to scan the card in the bus, you would have much information directly. It is necessary entrepreneurs will be involved and actually scan as well. That requires support for entrepreneurs ... but the reports will be valuable. It is difficult to convince the entrepreneurs themselves, as they hardly see the benefits of such reports for their business.

In September 2011 however, media announced that the SchouwenDuivelandPas had received a serious boost due to a subsidy of 400.000 euros granted by the Rotterdam Harbour Company as part of a Delta development program as compensation for the expansion of the harbour of Rotterdam (Maasvlakte II). From here onwards, the foundation started exploring and implementing other digital applications.

Ideas about expanding the practice-arrangement bundle in the form of a destination card beyond the Schouwen-Duiveland isle's borders were obstructed by differences in meanings between various practitioners linked to different business models. The founding entrepreneurs, as initiating practitioners, felt their aims and goals were too different from the newly enrolled practitioners acting as innovators. In a final effort to create a shared 'teleoaffective structure' (Schatzki, 2005) all organisations and people involved were invited to a meeting that was perceived as being crucial for the continuation of the project.

The meeting was a failure because the various practitioners were not able to speak each other's language. Those with digital expertise espoused the benefits of technological possibilities and open source programming but were confronted by others pointing at the loss of ownership and undesirable sharing of business data. It appeared that the foundation's management perceived actions by other stakeholders – who joined because of the technological features, research possibilities and business opportunities resulting from upscaling the card to other regions – as being dubious. They accused the latter of having 'hidden agendas'. The IT professor, for example, was accused of 'making profit' as an end goal instead of focusing foremost on improving marketing based on market research.

The feeling of existing hidden agendas and accusations made it impossible to come to a common understanding and develop shared rules. Thus, although there was a strong collaboration of entrepreneurs propelling the bundling, their lack of technological knowledge forced them to incorporate other skills and competencies and hence practitioners. As a result, general and practical understandings supporting the bundling process dwindled, also because of a lack of trust associated with privacy concerns and financial gains which resulted again in broken links. The card continued to be in place for the same destination, having the original features, but without technological developments as planned. The collaboration with related experts ended.

Period 3: Towards one destination card for the entire delta region (2011–2013)

Despite all these challenges, the SchouwenDuivelandPas destination card remained operational. While earlier explorations in upscaling failed, the entrepreneurs chairing the SchouwenDuivelandPas foundation now crossed paths with another group of entrepreneurs pursuing the creation of a booking portal for the entire Delta region, including the entire state province of Zeeland and the western part of neighbouring province Noord-Brabant. A regional bank initiated a subsidy program through which entrepreneurs were stimulated to innovate. A group of entrepreneurs operating in the hospitality industry applied for funding and presented an idea to promote tourism within this Delta area. As a result, the SchouwenDuivelandPas was integrated in the 'Deltaleven' project, merging organisations with a different professional background, namely those from hotels on the one side to those from campsites and bungalow parks on the other.

The original focus of the Deltaleven project was to create a business-to-business platform that also included a booking site tailored to this area. Following this idea, tourist offers and public transportation could be packaged and monitored, for example through data traces of a digital tourist card. In pursuing this, the newly created Deltaleven foundation invited the director of Promotion Zeeland Delta (PZD) to get involved as a means to include destination branding in the bundling process. Nevertheless, although the SchouwenDuivelandPas foundation acknowledged the added value of the Deltaleven project, they made clear from the beginning that they would still maintain their own destination card at Schouwen-Duiveland.

In the meantime, new practitioners were involved in the Deltaleven project bringing in new practical understandings, materials and skills. The Austrian system of Feratel was introduced to act as the digital infrastructure supporting the Deltaleven project, because of its possibilities to link a booking portal with a tourist card. Since the entrepreneurs that participated in the Deltaleven project realised the project took much of their scarce time, they also decided to appoint and hire a former hotelier to act as project leader. The realisation and especially the organisation of a booking portal and a destination card were delayed since the subsidy grant required the involvement of various other parties. For example, Impuls, the region's economic stimulation agency, was involved to keep track of the progress related to the subsidy criteria. The Research Centre for Coastal Tourism became involved, as the subsidy agreement required collaboration with a research centre. As a result, communication was perceived to be difficult, hindered by the lack of common practical understandings between practitioners with varying backgrounds. One of the interviewees argued that the amount of people involved was too big for quick progress and fast response to market developments:

> Deltaleven wanted to be a fast running organisation. Anticipating on market demands and customer needs in order to offer added value whenever the customer stays in Zeeland. To be fast, having a foundation executive board of twenty-six people is not desired. You have to have a foundation of five, that's it.

At one point, public actors made the choice to focus first on improving the development of the destination card instead of the portal system. The portal system, however, was favoured by the foundation and its private actors. Pursuing the card first instead of the portal affected the central objective of the foundation's and thus the practitioners' commitment, since the entrepreneurs realised their envisioned portal was not to be realised anytime soon. At this point, the connecting practitioners were divided into those with entrepreneurial backgrounds from those with public interests. As a result, the project outcomes did not meet the subsidy grant's criteria as an important part of the subsidy was to study and test appropriate technology. Because of a quick decision to work with the 'Feratel' company as software supplier, the normally essential stage of studying and testing a variety of possible technologies was ignored. One of the interviewees confirms:

> They [the entrepreneurs] skipped the whole required phase concerning research anyway since they just decided to go with Feratel. A large part of the subsidy program, noteworthy, was about studying technology, making blue prints and test it. That entire phase had been neglected.

Impuls initiated and coordinated an exit strategy for Deltaleven, as they believed not enough progress had been made: besides the disagreement on prioritising the card over the portal and the neglecting of testing multiple digital infrastructures before choosing one, the end goals were not completely clear and financial resources almost exhausted. Parallel to the Deltaleven project, a bundling of tourist information service practices was taking place in the region of Zeeland. Here, previously separate and somewhat independent, operating local offices, responsible for branding their own destinations, were merged into one regional tourist information services organisation, promoting the entire state province. One practitioner was active in both constellations: the PZD director. Soon after the Deltaleven project stopped, the destination card idea was adopted by this new regional VVV tourist information service, with the PZD director as its new director.

Period 4: Adoption by the VVV tourist information services (2014–2015)

This merging had important consequences. The VVV tourist information became responsible for the further development of the destination card by creating a new organisational structure based on a clear and transparent hierarchical business format. Part of the plan was to create specific cards per region with their own foundations in place and regional coordinators appointed and responsible for increasing the amount of card issuers and adopters. In this way, the implementation of regional destination cards was believed to be more capable of directing practices in destination branding, market research and public transportation in accordance with the rules and the central ideas behind the Zeelandpas. Besides the Schouwen-Duivelandpas and the card in West-Zeeuws Vlaanderen (from this moment on the 'ZeeuwsVlaanderenPas'), the regions Veere (VeerePas) and Noord-Beveland (NoordBevelandPas) joined this Zeelandpas practice-arrangement bundle. With these cards in place, emphasis was on promoting the state province by creating special offers in each region and collaboration between entrepreneurs. Another important aspect concerned the enticing of visitors to spread and discover other places by means of using the card for certain free transportation possibilities offered in each region.

During the start-up phase, conducting market research, i.e. the scanning of cards and using digital traces for marketing purposes, was not yet an explicit end goal. Emphasis was on creating special deals or new combinations of existing tourism products and services, something which was in the beginning rather challenging. Besides difficulties in presenting appealing special offers, the transportation discounts varied between the regions, which caused some confusion amongst tourists. After operating for a few months, entrepreneurs as well as regional coordinators themselves soon expressed a desire to move to one uniform card in the following season. Having one Zeelandpas instead of several destination dependent cards would also make marketing more effective:

> Right now, it is not efficient as each card has its own offers, which makes it hard to communicate clearly about the regional destination card. Still,

it is the Zeelandpas and the concept is the same; offering experiences. However, when you want to explain the offer on a card, separate flyers or posters are needed to be shown.

In 2014 the card fee was three euros in all regions, except in Schouwen-Duiveland: their business model was different since issuing organisations paid monthly fees and cards were given away for free, just like they did in the earlier years. Changing business practices to increase selling of the card was challenging, as the card faced promotional difficulties, related to the short time available for preparing and distributing promotional material. Furthermore, the training and manuals that were offered did not entirely make up for the poor commercial skills of accommodation reception employees during check-in procedures.

   Activities to support the implementation and address these difficulties, such as sales training, were funded by leftovers from prior periods, private funding and a financial injection by the province, not by a new subsidy. Whereas digital traces and sharing of data at first was something entrepreneurs were somehow scared of and not eager to believe in, this gradually changed, probably because sharing available data was perceived to be safe and secure and could indeed produce meaningful marketing insights. The data collected, however, proved to be limited as not many cards were personalised at issuing offices or registered at accepting organisations.

   Realisation of one general Zeelandpas destination card was still something for the future, but at least an operational card was in place in various regions. Although the collecting of digital data to be used for market knowledge generation was included, it was not set at the foreground as the use of the card in general was seen as the biggest priority. Table 8.1 summarises the Zeelandpas innovation as the bundling of practices.

Conclusion and perspectives: innovation as bundling of practices

This case of the Zeelandpas illustrates that the bundling of practices – in this case destination branding, conducting market research and facilitating public transportation – by means of a destination card as a practice-material arrangement is full of obstacles. As Shove et al. (2012: 64) argue, the contours of *any* practice, let alone a bundle of practices, "depend on changing populations of more and less faithful carriers or practitioners". In order to bundle practices with different meanings, clear end goals and intentions – a common teleo-affective structure – practical and general understandings and clear rules have to be developed by the varied contributions of actors. Concerning the genealogy of the Zeelandpas destination card, bundling the distinct practices by trying to create a common understanding, clear rules, a shared way of implementing, was arduous. Organisational principles such as teleo-affective structures, general and practical understandings and rules were partly missing as meanings, materials and competences of the practices to be bundled were

Table 8.1 Key characteristics and practical concerns of each identified period.

	P1. 2001–2005	P2. 2006–2010	P3. 2011–2013	P4. 2014–2015
Bundling as distinct practice				
Central meaning	Branding the isle of Schouwen-Duiveland by improving loyalty due to increased service marketing	Increase tourist spending by packaging, stimulating public transportation	Providing a bookings portal to experience the Delta area and foster loyalty with destination card integration	Implementing a comprehensive marketing model emphasising the card as the way to explore Zeeland
Main practitioners	A software development agency (private)	Foundation SchouwenDuivelandPas, representing and being chaired by campsite and bungalow park entrepreneurs (private)	Foundation Deltaleven, representing and being chaired by hotel and hospitality entrepreneurs (private)	VVV Tourist information services, responsible for regional tourism marketing and communication (public)
Project title	Toeristenpas Schouwen-Duiveland	SchouwenDuivelandPas	Deltaleven (card: DeltaPas)	Zeelandpas
Original teleo-affective structure directing practice-arrangement bundle	Branding the destination by triggering entrepreneurs to collaborate	Enabling public transportation using a tourist card that also holds few special offers for activities	Destination branding, by the stimulating of bookings and collaboration by means of an online platform; Allowing the use of the card to access special offers and free transportation	Destination branding by fostering collaboration that result in joint marketing activities; Keep public transportation discounts running; Collecting digital data for market knowledge
Scale of practice-arrangement bundle	Isle of Schouwen-Duiveland	Isle of Schouwen-Duiveland	Delta region, pilot cards in West-Zeeuws-Vlaanderen and Schouwen-Duiveland	Schouwen-Duiveland, West-Zeeuws-Vlaanderen, Noord-Beveland, Veere

	P1. 2001–2005	P2. 2006–2010	P3. 2011–2013	P4. 2014–2015
Dynamics of bundling practices	Teleo-affective structures between private and public practices did not match.	Rules and understanding of connecting practices did not match, nor was there one clear teleo-affective structure. Efforts to align elements failed.	Rules related with a material change in the form of a new subsidy required various practitioners to be involved. End goals were prioritised differently by various practitioners	New practitioners carried the bundling practice onwards, emphasising clearer rules, understanding and priorities. Emphasised end goal was branding the destination and offer public transportation: less priority was given to market research
Changes in the connected practices				
Destination branding	Bundling efforts resulted in a variety of entrepreneurs understanding the need and benefits of joint marketing activities. A business plan was created	Only a small number of cards were issued and a limited number of discounted activities were offered by a small and local selection of entrepreneurs. Cards could be scanned and digital traces could be displayed through open source systems	The Schouwen-Duiveland bus card continued to operate, just as a transportation card in Zeeuws-Vlaanderen. Pilot studies on the digital platform of Feratel allowed to register, load and scan the card	The VVV launched a campaign in which four regional cards were branded as Zeelandpas: SchouwenDuivelandPas, ZeeuwsVlaanderenPas, VeerePas, NoordBevelandPas. Each with slightly different offers and business model variations
Market research	A business plan was created that included possibilities to conduct market research	Experimenting with open source systems allowed for some preliminary analysis	More options were available but entrepreneurs were still hesitant about sharing their business data	Market research was not prioritised but still possible due to the continuation of the Feratel system
Public transportation	A business plan was created that included possibilities to offer public transportation	It was possible to use the card at a bus line by showing the card and presenting valid dates	Two pilots were realised that allowed (digital) card use at but lines in the two regions	Agreements in each of the four regions allowed the card to be used for public transportation

too diverse. The various practitioners hardly succeeded in overcoming these differences, struggling to explain or convince why and how to match and align associated practices. Nevertheless, during the entire period and despite the difficulties, the Zeelandpas destination card not only continuously changed, but also matured resulting from the forging of new relations (Shove et al., 2012) and countless recurrent and situated enactments (Lamers and van der Duim, 2016; Schatzki, 2016) which we subdivided in four periods.

By sharing these insights, this study has also contributed to the existing literature on tourism destination cards. It highlights practical implications of introducing a destination card (Zoltan and Masiero, 2012) and illustrates in detail the challenging processes involved. In this way, it adds to Angeloni's (2016) overview of important factors related to the destination cards by showing how these factors fostered or hindered the realisation of a regional destination card in a Dutch context. Practice theory helps us to understand how bundling in this context happened and has proved to be a promising approach to study tourism innovations.

References

Angeloni, S. (2016). A tourist kit 'made in Italy': an 'intelligent' system for implementing new generation destination cards. *Tourism Management*, 52, 187–209. doi:10.1016/j.tourman.2015.06.011

Halkier, H., Kozak, M. and Svensson, B. (2014). Innovation and tourism destination development. *European Planning Studies, 22*(8), 1547–1550. doi:10.1080/09654313.2013.784571

Hjalager, A. M. (2010). A review of innovation research in tourism. *Tourism Management, 31*(1), 1–12.

Lamers, M. and van der Duim, R. (2016). Connecting practices: conservation tourism partnerships in Kenya. In G. Spaargaren, D. Weenink and M. Lamers (eds), *Practice Theory and Research: Exploring the Dynamics of Social Life* (pp. 179–201). London: Routledge.

Lamers, M., van der Duim, R. and Spaargaren, G. (2017). The relevance of practice theories for tourism research. *Annals of Tourism Research, 62*, 54–63.

Lamers, M., Weenink, D. and Spaargaren, G. (2016). Conclusion: the relevance of practice theory for researching social change. In G. Spaargaren, D. Weenink and M. Lamers (eds), *Practice Theory and Research: Exploring the Dynamics of Social Life* (pp. 229–242). London: Routledge.

Maggioni, I., Marcoz, E. M. and Mauri, C. (2014). Segmenting networking orientation in the hospitality industry: An empirical research on service bundling. *International Journal of Hospitality Management, 42*, 192–201.

Nicolini, D. (2006). Knowing in practice. The case of telemedicine. OLKC (Organizational Learning, Knowledge and Capabilities), Warwick, 20–22 March.

Nicolini, D. (2009). Zooming in and out: Studying practices by switching theoretical lenses and trailing connections. *Organization Studies, 30*(12), 1391–1418.

Nicolini, D. (2012). *Practice Theory, Work, and Organization: An Introduction.* Oxford: Oxford University Press.

Nicolini, D. (2017). Is small the only beautiful? Making sense of 'large phenomena' from a practise-based perspective. In A. Hui, T. Schatzki and E. Shove (eds), *The Nexus of Practices Connections: Constellations, Practitioners* (pp. 98–113). London; New York: Routledge.

Paget, E., Dimanche, F. and Mounet, J.-P. (2010). A tourism innovation case: an actor-network approach. *Annals of Tourism Research, 37*(3), 828–847.

Pantzar, M. and Shove, E. (2010). Understanding innovation in practice: a discussion of the production and re-production of Nordic Walking. *Technology Analysis and Strategic Management, 22*(4), 447–461.

Schatzki, T. (2002). *The Site of the Social. A Philosophical Account of the Constitution of Social Life and Change.* Philadelphia: Penn State University Press.

Schatzki, T. R. (2005). Peripheral vision: the sites of organizations. *Organization Studies, 26*(3), 465–484.

Schatzki, T. (2016). Practice theory as flat ontology. In G. Spaargaren, D. Weenink and M. Lamers (eds), *Practice Theory and Research: Exploring the Dynamics of Social Life* (pp. 28–42). London: Routledge.

Schatzki, T. R. (2017). Sayings, texts and discursive formations. In A. Hui, T. Schatzki and E. Shove (eds), *The Nexus of Practices Connections: Constellations, Practitioners* (pp. 126–140). London; New York: Routledge.

Shove, E., Pantzar, M. and Watson, M. (2012). *The Dynamics of Social Practice: Everyday life and How It Changes.* London: Sage.

Zoltan, J. and Masiero, L. (2012). The relation between push motivation and activity consumption at the destination within the framework of a destination card. *Journal of Destination Marketing and Management, 1*(1), 84–93.

9 Smart Tourism

A practice approach

Carina Ren, Morten Krogh Petersen and Tanja Knoblauch Nielsen

Introduction

In recent years, an increasing number of researchers have explored the emerging phenomenon of Smart Tourism (e.g. Buhalis and Amaranggana, 2013; Gretzel, Sigala, Xiang and Koo, 2015a; Gretzel, Werthner, Koo and Lamsfus, 2015b). According to Gretzel et al. (2015a), the concept describes "the increasing reliance of tourism destinations, their industries and their tourists on emerging forms of ICT that allow for massive amounts of data to be transformed into value propositions" (Gretzel et al., 2015a, p. 179). As the digital opportunities and solutions following this digital transformation carry great promises towards improving the user experience and raising tourism consumption, researchers have been concerned with how big data is currently – and potentially – improving marketing, flow regulations and product development in tourism (Boes, Buhalis and Inversini, 2015; Gretzel et al., 2015b). What remains rather neglected is how these digital opportunities impact organisational roles and identities in what we may term the 'Smart Tourism Destination' (Boes et al., 2015).

In this chapter, we are interested in exploring how new digital and technological opportunities challenge, sustain and are incorporated into already existing organisational practices in tourism. Building on the idea of Smart Tourism as an ecosystem (Gretzel et al., 2015b; Werthner et al., 2015), we argue in this chapter that a better understanding is needed of how destination actors engage with digital technologies on a daily basis and how such practices are often 'more-than-digital'. Such a practice-oriented approach, we argue, allows for a less 'datacentric' understanding of how technology is integrated and becomes meaningful in the daily lives of users.

In order to explore this, we 'zoom in' on the everyday practices of developing a Smart Tourism Destination and how Smart Tourism is imagined and developed in conjunction with everyday practices of tourism actors. With its focus on how the social comes about as "ongoing routinised and recurrent accomplishment[s]" (Nicolini, 2012, p. 3), we invite practice theory as our theoretical companion. In this approach, developing the Smart Tourism Destination is not merely a question of 'more data' or of increasingly using or developing new technologies – it is not a question of going from 'less Smart' to 'more Smart' in technological terms. Rather, integrating 'smartness' into tourism organisations is understood as an accomplishment enabled through its bundling (Lamers and Van der Duim, 2016) with already existing organisational practices. We examine this bundling by following destination actors, their daily actions and how connections between practices are achieved (Nicolini, 2006) – in some cases with success, in others not.

In what follows, we show how Smart Tourism is addressed at an organisational level in the first and tentative stages of development in the North Denmark Region (hereafter, the Region). The material on which we base our analysis is drawn from a research project mapping regional Smart Tourism undertaken by the authors. It was generated during joint meetings and collaborative workshops with representatives from destination management organisations (DMOs) and the tourism industry, as well as through observations and interviews in the field. By exploring 'imaginaries' as well as 'mundane everyday practices' of Smart Tourism, we were able to grasp the day-to-day development of Smart Tourism and to sketch out several ways in which Smart Tourism was configured.

The insights from our study enabled us to develop an understanding of how innovation can take different trajectories and thus how Smart Tourism is not a uniform and homogeneous endeavour. In our final discussion, we argue that technology, the digital, and data cannot do anything 'on their own' to develop Smart Tourism but need to be connected to ongoing tourism practices which are continuously created and reproduced by tourism actors. This underlines the argument that Smart Tourism should be seen not as a purely technological achievement but as an ongoing, networked and distributed activity (Ren and Jóhannesson, 2018) and that such achievements are always situated in specific organisational (and other) contexts.

Smart Tourism in theory

Gradually, tourism researchers have begun to work with the notion of 'Smart Tourism'. One of the departure points is a focus on innovative applications of smart technologies that allow businesses and consumers to become more interconnected in the travel process (Neuhofer et al., 2012), and create more personalised tourism experiences (Neuhofer et al., 2013). Pushing forward this ambition, researchers and practitioners strive to enhance the level of personalisation to design the right service or experience for real needs, at the right time and place.

Inspired by the principles of Smart Cities, Smart Tourism is made possible through the use, integration and distribution of mobile information and communication technologies, which provide targeted information and efficient services to tourists (Buhalis and Amaranggana, 2013). Such endeavours are facilitated by technologies and digital platforms such as sensors, big data and open data (Xiang, Tussyadiah and Buhalis, 2015). Smart Tourism suggests new ways to connect and exchange information between different actors (Wang, Li and Li, 2013).

In this chapter, we will take another approach to Smart Tourism, which deals only indirectly with the ideal of personalised tourism experiences, as we focus on the challenges for tourism organisations in developing Smart Tourism. Institutional and organisational actors are currently searching for ways of harnessing the potential of new kinds of data, technologies and connectivity. The promise is that this will lead to resource optimisation, increased sustainability, more innovation and entrepreneurship, and enhance competetiveness (Gretzel et al., 2015b; Nam and Pardo, 2011; Wang, Li, Zhen and Zhang, 2016).

As argued by Afsarmanesh and Camarinha-Matos (2000), smart organisations must "join their skills and resources in order to either offer an integrated and aggregated service, or to better answer to a business opportunity, and whose cooperation is supported by the computer networks" (p. 456). Smart Tourism thus entails new organisational and collaborative practices.

The joining of skills and resources may be seen as crucial to the further development of Smart Tourism, but how is this to happen in practice? One way to approach this question is the Smart Tourism Ecosystem (Gretzel et al., 2015b; Werthner et al., 2015), defined as "a tourism system that takes advantage of smart technology in creating, managing and delivering intelligent touristic services/experiences and is characterised by intensive information sharing and value co-creation" (Gretzel et al., 2015b, p. 560).

Tourism actors interact with information, technologies and each other in new kinds of ways, which have yet to be fully described and understood. The ecosystem approach highlights the importance not to see Smart Tourism as driven exclusively by technological developments and data. As pointed out by Gretzel et al. (2015b, p. 184) data lies at the core of all Smart Tourism activities, but data is, as also illustrated in our case, far from seamlessly generated and distributed between tourism actors.

The ecosystems approach shows how Smart Tourism is composed neither of purely technical devices, data and digital platforms nor of 'purely social' interactions. Rather, Smart Tourism emerges in the joining of the two, which foregrounds a socio-technical approach. As suggested in our short literature review, there is also a need for new ways to conceptualise Smart Tourism, which zoom in on the 'backstage' of tourism, paying particular attention to how Smart Tourism is imagined and performed in everyday organisational practices. In order to proceed in such a direction, we take inspiration from practice theory, especially sociologist Elizabeth Shove's work on innovations in daily practice, that is, how (new) practices are produced and reproduced.

Grasping Smart Tourism development – a practice approach

An increasing number of social science scholars including anthropologists, sociologists, geographers, historians and philosophers have recently taken a "turn to practice" (Savigny, Knorr-Cetina and Schatzki, 2001). This turn problematises the explanation of human action through structuralist, individualistic or mentalist models and focuses instead on the practices we inevitably participate in when going about our daily business as social beings, whether at work or in our leisure time. Practice theoretical approaches give priority to the study of embodied actions, emotions, things, technologies, interactions, encounters, performances and actual use (Buch, Andersen and Klemsdal, 2015, pp. 1–2; see also Nicolini, 2012; Reckwitz, 2002; Schatzki, 1996; Savigny, Knorr-Cetina and Schatzki 2001).

Within tourism studies, practice theory has recently been addressed conceptually (de Souza Bispo, 2016; Lamers et al., 2017) and in the exploration of a variety of tourism-related activities, such as practices of sleeping (Valtonen and Veijola, 2011), air-travel (Cohen et al., 2011), and wilderness guiding (Rantala, Valtonen and Markuksela, 2011). An understanding of these as cultural practices and, thus, markers of social distinction (Bourdieu, 1984) has been put forward. More recently, the practices of developing – as well as consuming – tourist experiences have also been explored through the lens of practice theory (James and Halkier, 2016).

The sociologist Elizabeth Shove is instructive in our exploration of how 'Smart practices' are sustained and incorporated into already existing organisational practices in tourism. In her work, Shove combines explorations of what elements constitute a given mundane practice with organisational innovation theory. Organisational innovation theory defines entrepreneurs as persons "who combine, relate and organise pre-existing but previously separate elements or components in novel ways" (Pantzar and Shove, 2010, p. 449), resulting in new ways of going about everyday life. Shove takes "all practitioners to be entrepreneurs" (Pantzar and Shove, 2010, p. 449), resulting in a novel analytical apparatus to explore how everyday activities such as cooking, exercising or communicating are developed and transformed.

As suggested in the work of Shove, practices can be construed as processes "involving the active and performative integration of symbolic and material ingredients and of competence or know how"(Pantzar and Shove, 2010, pp. 448–449). Practices comprise three constitutive elements: "*materials* – including things, technologies, tangible physical entities, and the stuff of which objects are made; *competences* – encompassing skill, know-how and technique; and *meanings* – in which we include symbolic meanings, ideas and aspirations"(Shove, Pantzar and Watson, 2012, p. 14). For a practice to emerge, links between these three elements have to be made. For a practice to be sustained, the links are also to be continuously performed. As a consequence, if the links between the three elements are broken, the practice in question dies, which Shove and Pantzar has captured with the term 'fossilisation' (Shove and Pantzar, 2006). In our research, we particularly tended to the presence of these three elements.

One illustrative example of analytical work that this model for studying transformations may perform is a study of the practice of Nordic Walking conducted by Shove and colleague Mika Pantzar (2010). To fashion Nordic Walking as a recognisable and meaningful fitness practice is quite a feat – it is basically a reinvention of something the human species has done for millions of years, namely walking. On top of this, performers of Nordic Walking do look pretty "silly"(Pantzar and Shove, 2010, p. 452). So how did this practice become established and how is it maintained?

To Pantzar and Shove, the practice of Nordic Walking is the outcome of the circulation and linking of the constituting elements of this practice. These constituent elements – walking poles, knowing how to use these poles while walking, and the meaningfulness of walking, for instance, as a healthy or social activity – are not only produced, circulated and linked by producers and manufacturers who have a financial incentive to promote associations between them. They are also produced, circulated and linked by "practitioners (those who do) who ultimately make such integrations happen. Although these roles are different, both are involved in the (re)production of practice"(Pantzar and Shove, 2010, p. 452).

The transformation of a practice is thus described as an achievement that hinges upon the continuous linking of constitutive social and technical elements. Translating these insights into the phenomenon of Smart Tourism, it firstly emerges as something more than a technical phenomenon, as a bundling of socio-technical practices. Second, for such practices to become established, the three constituent elements of materials, competencies and meanings need to be produced, circulated and connected. This entails that not only technical and digital solutions and data need to be available (*materials*). Also managerial, technical and collaborative skills to work with and make sense of Smart Tourism (*competencies*) are necessary, as is the willingness to develop Smart Tourism for instance for the sake of business or regional development (*meanings*). Third, the linking of constituent elements is not a one-off event, as these have to be continuously related by practitioners performing and bundling the socio-technical practices of Smart Tourism. In the following, we describe how we explored these achievements and their constitutive elements in our research.

Methodology and case description

The research project that originally prompted the theoretical reflections on Smart Tourism described above came together through the collaboration of a regional development fund and the University of Aalborg, which is an important regional actor in educating and researching in tourism. Over a period of six months, the project co-funded by the two institutions mapped ideas and initiatives on Smart Tourism among public and private tourism actors within five municipalities in the Region, which had been identified as particularly relevant to the development fund. As destinations, the municipalities are geographically distributed, different with regard to their tourism characteristics (city, coastal, nature and attractions) and with a varied degree of urbanisation, where Aalborg stands out as a larger city.

The tourism consultants in the development fund also pointed to a number of organisations, attractions and networks which they saw as relevant to include in the study. The regional tourism actors were chosen either because of their size (such as large attractions), their first-mover reputation or their relevancy as public or private stakeholders in a municipal or regional context (for instance as a DMO). The actors preselected by the development fund were either asked to take part directly in the project by serving as members of an advisory group, who meet three times during the project, or through consultation, where they advised on relevant interviewees or local Smart Tourism cases of interest.

The understanding of Smart Tourism as the bundling of socio-technical practices led to the adoption of a research methodology concerned with exploring the situated everyday practices of Smart Tourism. Based on our interest in exploring Smart Tourism through practice, our research aim was to gain insights from a broad spectrum of tourism actors through a combination of visits, meetings and research interviews. Our interview guides were built up around the three constitutive elements of competencies, materials and meanings pinpointed by the work of Shove and Pantzar (2006; Pantzar and Shove 2010). In our interviews we probed how our informants went about their daily tasks (also asking them to show us how and when this was done), how they made use of or lacked certain skills, what new kinds of technologies, data and connectivities between tourism actors were or were not integrated into the daily working practices of the informants and how they related this work to broader 'digital' or 'smart' visions or goals in relation to their business or destination. Besides these preselected actors, others were gradually included in the study as they became known to us through interviews and conversations, documents or in the press.

In many cases, initial interviewees helped to connect us with other smaller tourism actors, such as attractions and hotels. All selected informants worked with tourism related activities on a daily basis either on a strategic and/or operational level. They occupied positions such as webmasters, marketing directors, project managers and head of destination management organisations (DMO). Some of our informants played more than one role at the destination. For instance, a head of DMO could also be a board member of a regional or national DMO, a business council or other organisations. Because of the broad distribution in professional functions, their experiences with using (for instance) digital platforms and social media in their daily work varied, offering different views on the materials, competencies and meanings that existed within the regional tourism landscape.

In total 13 semi-structured interviews were conducted, recorded and transcribed. Also a number of informal conversations and email exchanges took place during and after meetings and visits to attractions and organisations. As part of the research design, two workshops were also held with participating tourism actors and informants. The workshops were held mid-way and after the fieldwork and were used to discuss and provide input to our analytical results and most importantly to help us work to design future trajectories for Smart Tourism in the region.

Our analysis of the material generated was guided by practice theory, as described in the above, and by its understanding of how practices emerge, are reproduced and disappear. We focused on how, why, when and where Smart Tourism emerges (or not) as a practice as defined by the actors themselves and on how Smart Tourism could become further developed in the future through a reshuffling or strengthening of constitutive elements. In analysing our material we looked for accounts of, for instance, daily service tasks, the introduction of new technologies or engagements in collaborative projects and how our informants attributed meaning or value (or not) to such practices. We sought, in other words, to describe different ways in which links were forged or cut between the materials, competencies and meanings of Smart Tourism practices. The different ways in which tourism actors become carriers of Smart Tourism practices and how the constitutive elements were present in different organisations resulted in very different configurations. We argue that four configurations are central in understanding the situated practices of developing Smart Tourism.

Four configurations of Smart Tourism

In relation to Smart Tourism, we very soon found out that the situation in the Region was characterised by a paradox. Interest in the phenomenon was high amongst the tourism actors we approached in our research, but when interviewed, very few could identify what they themselves regarded as examples of 'smart' practices. In other words, the willingness and interest to engage with 'Smart Tourism' was high, but the performance was not – at least in our interlocutors' very 'technical' understanding of what constitutes Smart Tourism. However, when deploying the broader understanding of Smart Tourism as an ecosystem of sustained socio-technical and collaborative achievements, and by focusing on the practices that the tourism actors are engaged in today, it was still possible to discern different kinds of Smart Tourism practices.

In our analysis, we abstained from an evolutionary approach, classifying actors on a technological scale (from 'less' to 'more' use of digital data for instance). Instead we worked to identify and structure Smart Tourism practices by exploring the variations in time and space in how Smart Tourism was practised. By doing so, we were able to show how Smart Tourism practices did not evolve in any unilinear way from 'less' to 'more' technical or digital, but that rather oscillated between different spaces and at different times of the week, the seasons, the year, etc.

In our material, we looked firstly at *when* Smart Tourism takes place: does it happen occasionally and based on sudden, arising needs or in a more cyclical, recurrent way? Second, we identify differences in *where* the work around Smart Tourism takes place: does the work stem from one central actor (such as an attraction) or in and through the collaboration of different actors (for instance a collaborative effort to establish a booking platform)? When combining these two 'axes of difference', four configurations of Smart Tourism practices emerge: as *ad hoc* (one-off, mono-sited), as *project based* (one-off, multi-sited), as *routine* (recurrent, mono-sited) and as *network* (recurrent, multi-sited) (see Table 9.1).

The four ways in which Smart Tourism unfolds in the daily work of tourism actors are not constant or even stable. They may not either be attributed to particular types of companies, attractions or organisations. While only one particular configuration can be found in some tourism organisations or businesses (for instance working project based), traces might be found in most organisations, of more than one manifestation, either simultaneously or alternating. In the following, we offer examples of how the four configurations of Smart Tourism unfold in the daily work of tourism actors as it was described to us during interviews.

Smart Tourism as ad hoc

The configuration of Smart Tourism practices as ad hoc is characterised by sporadic initiatives taken by individual tourism actors. There are no set routines or strategies to guide these initiatives of, for instance, collecting existing or generating new kinds of data, analysing or visualising these. These initiatives are set in motion by an emerging challenge or opportunity, which may be handled or taken by consulting with digital data. What, for instance, do people post about our attraction or destination on social media right now and how might we use such digital traces to address a given problem? This manifestation of Smart Tourism is experimental by nature. It is marked by a trial and error approach where the tourism actors seek to work with different kinds of new media, technology and data, separately or in combination. Through this work, the tourism actors seek to discern how Smart Tourism can address specific challenges and opportunities of their organisation and hence, how it may be meaningful and valuable to them.

When the tourism actors tell us about Smart Tourism as ad hoc, they often list various kinds of initiatives. Characteristically, there is seldom a systematic follow-up on results. As Gretzel et al. point out: "data is mindlessly captured and storage/retrieval/information management costs are not calculated" (Gretzel et al., 2015a, p. 184). Tourism businesses do not necessarily think about what data is generated and in what way it could be made useful. So

Table 9.1 Four configurations of Smart Tourism.

Time/space	Mono-sited	Multi-sited
One-off	*Ad hoc*	*Project based*
Recurrent	*Routine*	*Network*

while materials and to some degree competences are present, a clear idea or aspiration (meaning) seem to be lacking.

In this example, a communications manager at a public attraction talks about their experiments with digital technologies:

> At the moment we are developing an application, which we've received funding for. We've taken several other initiatives. Physical computing, where you can go to a big screen and move around a little and then the exhibit react in accordance to the movements of people. We've had different kinds of small games and also touch screens. That communication, however, was a little one-way, as we have not really taken in the data produced, right? We also use Google Analytics so we could, actually, look at the data and say: 'We can see that people move this way through the application and the use so and so much time here and there.' And then use that data to change the content of the exhibition if that was what we wanted to do. But to change the basic structure of the exhibition is expensive and time-consuming. So we haven't done that.

While this lack of utilisation of the data produced could be understood as a missed opportunity, we could also assert that in this case it is simply not seen as meaningful to work with Smart Tourism in any other way than ad hoc as it is too expensive and time-consuming.

A similar argument can be made concerning the widespread technology of various kinds of loyalty programs. These produce data about the flow and consumption of tourists, which potentially allow tourism organisations to better predict for instance when tourists will visit what attractions. However, and as mentioned by the webmaster of a DMO, "these kinds of data are difficult to translate into something useful". He adds that the software for analysing data is not that expensive anymore, but "you have to think and implement it in the right way from the beginning", and it is challenging to find the resources to do that.

These examples show how technology and data do not single-handedly drive the creation of Smart Tourism practices. Existing practices and infrastructures – here in the guise of time and money – hamper engagement with Smart Tourism practices in any other way than on a case-by-case basis. The constitutive elements of a Smart Tourism practice are, in other words, all present, but so are other concerns (time, money, other responsibilities in the business) inhibiting them to be linked in any other ways than ad hoc.

Smart Tourism as project-based

Smart Tourism initiatives and development in Northern Denmark – and elsewhere – are often funded by private and, predominantly, public research and development projects, the project we report upon in this very chapter being a case in point. Through such projects, tourism actors are brought together in the attempt to share and create knowledge and new kinds of digital platforms, and collaborations that might drive the development of Smart Tourism. Being organised as projects, these initiatives and development activities have fixed beginnings and endings. They focus on the completion of a predetermined task, and are expected to yield specified outcomes.

Assessed through our practice theoretical approach, one problem with this specific way of configuring Smart Tourism is the focus on developing new digital platforms and technologies rather than initiating the production and re-production of Smart Tourism *practices*, in which – following Shove's innovation model – the materials are better linked with the other constituent elements of competencies and meanings. One of our interlocutors, a destination development team leader of a national tourism development organisation, alludes to this in the following quote, where he frames a technology developed within a project as 'evidence' that the project actually did produce something:

> If a project is to develop an application or a website then this very concretely proves that the project produced something. If you measured how many guests that actually download the application or visit the site in question, then I think you'd get a quite disappointing result.

This statement touches upon how such projects may produce or engage with technologies, but rarely succeed in producing, circulating and linking the constituent elements of Smart Tourism practices. In the above, the presence of a digital solution does not by itself make tourists able or willing to download an application or to visit a website developed through (and for the purpose of) a Smart Tourism project. Informed by the work of Shove and Pantzar, we might say that the materials, such as a website or an application, are in place, but not the meanings nor the competences to connect it to a Smart Tourism practice.

This critique of organising and seeking to establish Smart Tourism through the configuration of projects is rather outspoken amongst our interlocutors. Private but also public sector tourism actors describe such projects as not really hitting the mark. As one of our informants, marketing manager at a large attraction, remarks,

> you cannot get angry with private actors who do not support the community, but you can get angry with a municipal or regional project if it spends money on things that are not giving to the community or tourism in Northern Denmark.

Often, more mundane issues are brought to the fore – rules and regulations for the handling of tourism products, administrative and organisational borders of municipalities, a lack of understanding and trust amongst tourism actors of different sizes, sectors and fields – as hindering collaboration and the establishing of Smart Tourism practices. Again, this points to the necessity to take such mundane issues, often a jumble of material, competencies and meaning, and not only new technology or data opportunities, into consideration when seeking to develop Smart Tourism.

Smart Tourism as routine

Smart Tourism as routine is a systematic and automated practice where working with digital platforms and data has found its rhythm in the broader ecology of daily practices of the tourism organisation. Because of its clear links to digital technology and data, the manifestation of routine is the one that comes closest to the tourism actors' own understanding of what Smart Tourism is and what it should entail. In our interviews, conversations and reading, many actors point to the potentials of working with data to monitor, measure, analyse and manage all aspects of the destination and of tourism behaviours. While most of the regional actors are still in the early phases of engaging with and harvesting the outcomes of digital opportunities, many of the smaller public and private tourism actors express a wish to work with data in this particular way in order to better get to know the desires and behaviour of the tourists and to activate this intimate information in relation to their tourism business.

An example of routinised Smart Tourism practices is how digital data are drawn at set intervals – every year, month, day or hour – into the completion of tasks such as managing flows of tourists or optimising marketing efforts. The carriers of this practice of Smart Tourism as routine are primarily large and private tourism actors such as attractions and amusement parks. Below is an example, where an employee responsible for marketing at a large attraction tells us about her work with data:

> We have a lot of raw data, which tells us something about where our guests come from, how far they are willing to drive by car, and their nationalities – those kinds of things. When the season ends, I consult with this information. I receive one complete report at the end of the season, which I of course use when I'm, for instance, considering leaving out the German text in our folder. Maybe we don't have that many German guests? Or maybe the Germans, that visit, do not mind reading in English?

Here we have an example of a yearly cycle of deciphering and acting upon changes in the behaviour of the guests of the attraction. The person responsible for marketing goes on to tell us how this also works in a daily cycle through survey of customer satisfaction conducted daily:

> We can consult the customer survey daily. We can see that there were bad reviews of the experience by the ticket sales yesterday, for instance. What

happened? Where they arguing with someone or had someone gotten out on the wrong side of the bed and should have stayed at home? We ask those questions in the units involved in those things.

Smart Tourism as routine is the practice in which the materials, competencies and meanings of Smart Tourism as an everyday innovation in the tourism organisation have been shaped, connected and transformed most profoundly. The examples discussed here show that making better operational decisions does not only rely on large data set, complex analytics and modelling, but are also about bundling Smart Tourism practices to other daily or cyclical activities in the organisation.

Smart Tourism as network

The fourth and last manifestation of Smart Tourism as a socio-technical practice connects itself to and feeds off existing tourism networks. Like the routine manifestation, the network is characterised by recurring activities and events but also entails a broader range of activity with the participation of a more or less set number of tourism actors. A recent initiative is described by a webmaster at a city DMO:

> A year or two back, we [the city DMO] took the initiative to create a network or experience group together with some of the larger cultural institutions and attractions who are doing well in terms of the digital. One of our motives was to make new connections. We entailed some exciting collaborations enabled by us talking together.

Smart Tourism as network is, however, not only about Smart Tourism narrowly defined, but about harnessing the potential of combining different kinds of data, experiences and knowledge through sequential deliberations. Many tourism actors in the Region describe how they regularly meet with others to deliberate about overall challenges and potential in many different networks and identify this as a valuable and recurrent part of their everyday organisational practice. As the manager of a DMO puts it, "we meet, we deliberate on issues, get some feedback, and then we can move on with these issues".

Smart Tourism as network can unfold in a network of private tourism actors as the following quote from a marketing employee at a large attraction shows:

> We share our user surveys within the Top Attractions network. We can benchmark one another. All the attractions share their data with each other so that we can compare ourselves to the other attractions on different parameters. So it's a transparent sharing, you could say, of important information.

The discussions at network meetings are informed by different kinds of data, experiences and knowledge, ranging from national measurements of the tourism industry to the situated data and experiences of individual actors. The value of sharing can be related to the smart tourism ecosystem which first and foremost implies a "focus on a shared goal or purpose related to the production and consumption of touristic value, culminating in meaningful touristic experiences" (Gretzel et al., 2015a, p. 560). These networks may, however, also be less business-oriented and more issue-oriented, meaning that the partners meeting up span different sectors but discuss a shared concern for the industry. The network supports collective knowledge and competitiveness. In that sense, it encourages "co-opetition, where a combination of collaboration and competition offers greater opportunities (Buhalis, 2000; Ritchie and Crouch, 2003)" (Boes et al., 2016, p. 116).

What marks Smart Tourism as network is the continuous and rhythmical 'testing of the water' through deliberations in which digital solutions were often pointed to as a common interest. The materials of this practice are not limited to what is most commonly defined as 'smart' materials – new technologies and digital data – but is highly socio-technical and collaborative as it constantly merges with rising concerns, custom practice and joint resources. Everything that may qualify the handling of a given and situated issue is included. Understood with the resources from Shove, it is the manifestation of Smart Tourism that most directly respects and draws upon existing materials, competencies and meanings. As a reason for this, and in spite of the obvious lack of direct focus on digital innovation, it may also hold the most promise for a strong linking of constituent elements towards the future development of Smart Tourism in the Region.

Conclusion

In this chapter, we have seen how tourism actors envision and grapple with the phenomenon of Smart Tourism in tourism organisations through an exploration of the daily undertakings of tourism practitioners in the region of Northern Denmark. Rather than seeing Smart Tourism as a unilineal technological or digital evolution, Smart Tourism was defined as a socio-technical ecosystem. We explored attempts to develop Smart Tourism in the Region as a construction of sustained practices. As a way to understand Smart Tourism innovation, we took inspiration from the work of Shove on how new practices are produced and sustained. We used her understanding of the three constitutive elements of materials, competencies and meanings to probe the everyday organisational practices of local tourism actors.

Based on insights from our interview and field material, we see how Smart Tourism practices were organised around two axes. One showed differences in when or how often these activities took place – as either 'one-off' or 'recurrent'. The other displayed a difference in where the activities took place – either at a single or at multiple sites. Based on these findings, we were able to develop four configurations of Smart Tourism; *ad hoc, routine, project based* and *network.* Returning to Shove's work on the constitutive elements of practice, some of these configurations consisted of strong singular elements, for instance apps or access to digital data (materials), while other elements seemed to be lacking, such as a strong sense of purpose (meaning) or skill sets in the organisations (competencies). This underlines, firstly, that Smart Tourism innovation should not be understood merely as a technical innovation process but also an organisational process. And, secondly, that this innovation is not purely technical, but rather socio-technical and bundled with other ongoing organisational practices.

Contrasting more radical understandings of Smart Tourism, which see the future as a 'rupture' from current ways of working with tourism, we propose that successful development should engage in linking, or what we called bundling, new tourism practices to existing ones. This could be done, for instance, within existing tourism networks and as part of ongoing deliberations of issues and concerns relating to regional tourism. Developing Smart Tourism requires a continuous tinkering with imaginaries and technical solutions in order to situate them as meaningful practices of a destination. It is our hope that more effort will be put into conducting such studies of situated Smart Tourism development practices along and across the proposed research and development trajectories in the years to come.

Bibliography

Afsarmanesh, H. and Camarinha-Matos, L. M. (2000). Future smart-organizations: a virtual tourism enterprise. In *Web Information Systems Engineering, 2000. Proceedings of the First International Conference* (Vol. 1, pp. 456–461). IEEE.

Aalborg Municipality (2016). Smart Aalborg. Retrieved from www.aalborg.dk/om -kommunen/strategisk-vaekst/smartaalborg.

Boes, K., Buhalis, D. and Inversini, A. (2015). Conceptualising Smart Tourism destination dimensions. In I. Tussyadiah and A. Inversini (Eds), *Information and Communication Technologies in Tourism 2015* (pp. 391–403). Cham: Springer International Publishing.

Boes, K., Buhalis, D. and Inversini, A. (2016). Smart Tourism destinations: ecosystems for tourism destination competitiveness. *International Journal of Tourism Cities*, 2 (2), 108–124.

Bourdieu, P. (1984). *Distinction: A Social Critique of the Judgement of Taste*. Cambridge, MA: Harvard University Press.

Buch, A., Andersen, V. and Klemsdal, L. (2015). Turn to practice within working life studies. *Nordic Journal of Working Life Studies*, 5(3a), 1.

Buhalis, D. (2000). Marketing the competitive destination of the future. *Tourism Management*, 21(1), 97–116.

Buhalis, D. and Amaranggana, A. (2013). Smart Tourism Destinations. In Z. Xiang and I. Tussyadiah (Eds), *Information and Communication Technologies in Tourism 2014* (pp. 553–564). Cham: Springer International Publishing.

Cohen, S. A., Higham, J. E. and Cavaliere, C. T. (2011). Binge flying: behavioural addiction and climate change. *Annals of Tourism Research*, 38(3), 1070–1089.

de Souza Bispo, M. (2016). Tourism as practice. *Annals of Tourism Research*, 61, 170–179.

Graziano, T. (2014). Boosting innovation and development. The Italian Smart Tourism. A critical perspective. *European Association of Geographers*, 5(4), 6–18.

Gretzel, U., Sigala, M., Xiang, Z. and Koo, C. (2015a). Smart Tourism: foundations and developments. *Electronic Markets*, 25(3), 179–188.

Gretzel, U., Werthner, H., Koo, C. and Lamsfus, C. (2015b). Conceptual foundations for understanding smart tourism ecosystems. *Computers in Human Behavior*, 50, 558–563.

James, L. and Halkier, H. (2016). Regional development platforms and related variety: exploring the changing practices of food tourism in North Jutland, Denmark. *European Urban and Regional Studies*, 23(4), 831–847.

Lamers, M. and van der Duim, R. (2016). Connecting practices. *Practice Theory and Research: Exploring the Dynamics of Social Life*, 75.

Lamers, M., van der Duim, R. and Spaargaren, G. (2017). The relevance of practice theories for tourism research. *Annals of Tourism Research*, 62, 54–63.

Lamsfus, C. and Alzua-Sorzabal, A. (2013). Theoretical framework for a tourism internet of things: Smart destinations. *TourGUNE Jounal of Tourism and Human Mobility*, 2, 15–21.

Marres, N. (2005). Issues spark a public into being: a key but often forgotten point of the Lippmann-Dewey debate. In B. Latour and P. Weibel (Eds), *Making Things Public* (pp. 208–217). Cambridge, MA: MIT Press.

Nam, T. and Pardo, T. A. (2011). Conceptualizing smart city with dimensions of technology, people, and institutions. In *Proceedings of the 12th Annual International Digital Government Research Conference: Digital Government Innovation in Challenging Times* (pp. 282–291). ACM.

Neuhofer, B., Buhalis, D. and Ladkin, A. (2012). Conceptualising technology enhanced destination experiences. *Journal of Destination Marketing and Management*, 1(1–2), 36–46.

Neuhofer, B., Buhalis, D. and Ladkin, A. (2013). *High tech for high touch experiences: a case study from the hospitality industry*. In *Information and Communication Technologies in Tourism 2013* (pp. 290–301). Berlin, Heidelberg: Springer.

Nicolini, D. (2006). Knowing in practice. The case of telemedicine. OLKC (Organizational Learning, Knowledge and Capabilities), Warwick, 20–22 March.

Nicolini, D. (2012). *Practice Theory, Work, and Organization*. Oxford: Oxford University Press.

Pantzar, M. and Shove, E. (2010). Understanding innovation in practice: a discussion of the production and re-production of Nordic Walking. *Technology Analysis and Strategic Management*, 22(4), 447–461.

Rantala, O., Valtonen, A. and Markuksela, V. (2011). Materializing tourist weather: ethnography on weather-wise wilderness guiding practices. *Journal of Material Culture*, 16(3), 285–300.

Reckwitz, A. (2002). Toward a theory of social practices: a development in culturalist theorizing. *European Journal of Social Theory*, 5(2), 243–263.

Ren, C. and Jóhannesson, G. T. (2018). Collaborative becoming. Exploring tourism knowledge collectives. In C. Ren, G. T. Jóhannesson and R. van der Duim (Eds), *Co-creating Tourism Research. Towards Collaborative Ways of Knowing*. Oxon: Routledge.

Ritchie, J. R. B. and Crouch, G. I. (2003). *The Competitive Destination: A Sustainable Tourism Perspective*. Wallingford: CABI Pub.

Savigny, E. V., Knorr-Cetina, K. and Schatzki, T. R. (2001). *The Practice Turn in Contemporary Theory*. London: Routledge.

Schatzki, T. R. (1996). *Social Practices: A Wittgensteinian Approach to Human Activity and the Social.* Cambridge: Cambridge University Press.

Shove, E. and Pantzar, M. (2006). Fossilization. *Journal of European Ethnology,* 35(1–2), 59–63.

Shove, E., Pantzar, M. and Watson, M. (2012). *The Dynamics of Social Practice: Everyday Life and How It Changes.* London: Sage Publications.

Valtonen, A. and Veijola, S. (2011). Sleep in tourism. *Annals of Tourism Research,* 38 (1), 175–192.

Wang, D., Li, X. (Robert) and Li, Y. (2013). China's "smart tourism destination" initiative: a taste of the service-dominant logic. *Journal of Destination Marketing and Management,* 2(2), 59–61.

Wang, X., Li, X. (Robert), Zhen, F. and Zhang, J. (2016). How smart is your tourist attraction? Measuring tourist preferences of smart tourism attractions via a FCEM-AHP and IPA approach. *Tourism Management,* 54, 309–320.

Werthner, H., Koo, C., Gretzel, U. and Lamsfus, C. (2015). Special issue on Smart Tourism systems: convergence of information technologies, business models, and experiences. *Computers in Human Behavior,* 50, 556–557.

Xiang, Z., Tussyadiah, I. and Buhalis, D. (2015). Smart destinations: foundations, analytics, and applications. *Journal of Destination Marketing and Management,* 4 (3), 143–144.

10 Bringing together tourism practices

Experiences from the international student competition of Fermo (Italy)

Giovanna Bertella, Cristina Santini and Alessio Cavicchi

Introduction

The overall purpose of this study is to use practice theory to describe and discuss learning in tourism. The focus is on the potential of experiential and location-based educational methods. More precisely, this study applies the practice lens to the planning and evaluation of a student event with the aim to better understand its potential and uncover possible critical factors and challenges.

Several studies concerning entrepreneurship and tourism highlight the opportunity to adopt experiential learning methods (Ruhanen, 2005; Bennett, 2006). These methods imply a shift from traditional teaching and learning methods where the teachers, usually in the classroom, "deliver" knowledge to the students, to methods based on the active engagement of students in real life problems. In this context, the learning location can assume an important role as the context where the educational activities occur and as the object of study (Croy, 2009). The location, and more specifically the local community, can become an integrated part of the educational context.

Experiential learning for the students can be viewed as related to the development of new capabilities for the entrepreneurs along a sort of community-based developmental path toward becoming a learning destination (Mooney and Edwards, 2001; Schianetz et al., 2007; Kelliher and Reinl, 2014). This way to frame education in tourism is also in line with the position of those scholars who argue that an action-oriented approach has the potential to improve the dialogue between stakeholders and facilitate knowledge diffusion (Johannisson et al., 1998; Gibb, 2002; Rasmussen, 2006).

Adopting central concepts from the Communities of Practice (CoP) framework as presented by Lave and Wenger (1991) and Wenger (1998), this study elaborates on the ideas underpinning the design of a student event arranged in 2016 by the University of Macerata and the Piceno Laboratory on the Mediterranean Diet. It discusses and reflects on the related learning lessons, with particular attention paid to the emergence of destination-based relationships and to the students' and entrepreneurs' perspectives on how such relationships have contributed to their respective practices and identities.

The content of this chapter is the following. The next section presents the main concepts of practice-based learning, location-based learning and community of practice. In particular, the concepts of self and community identity, peripheral participation, constellation of CoPs, boundary and brokering are discussed. The case study relative to the student event arranged by the University of Macerata and the Piceno Laboratory on the Mediterranean Diet is then described, in relation to the adopted method and the findings. These are discussed and, finally, conclusions about the experiences gained from the specific student event are presented.

Theoretical background

Scholars from various disciplines have discussed the emergence of a practice turn as a revitalised interest in a conceptualisation of knowledge and learning where action and reflection blend in and contribute to both task performance and identity building (Schatzki, 2001; Gherardi, 2009; Corradi and Gherardi, 2010). Among these, Raelin (2007) takes an epistemological perspective and critically presents the positivistic theory-practice divide. This divide is considered having clear limitations as it implies a view of learning as a process of transferring information, leaving little space for reflection and creativity. As a valid alternative, the author proposes work-based learning environments where practitioners use theory to frame their challenges, and educational learning environments where students and teachers are co-inquirers in search for a better understanding of reality and feasible solutions to possible challenges (Raelin, 1997, 2007).

A practice turn can also be observed within organisational studies. Here, practice-based approaches to learning are discussed, emphasising the social and contextual aspect of knowledge and the relevant dynamic interactions among individuals and organisations on the basis of shared visions and through language, tools and procedures (Brown and Duguid, 1991; Orlikowski, 2002; Sole and Edmondson, 2002; Cox, 2005; Østerlund and Carlile, 2005). Similarly, in educational studies, a practice turn has occurred. Several scholars have called for an approach to learning that could improve the dialogue between the industry and the relevant educational and research institutes (Johannisson et al., 1998; Gibb, 2002; Fuller et al., 2005; Bennett, 2006; Rasmussen, 2006; Landri, 2012).

This trend concerns also tourism and hospitality educational studies (Ruhanen, 2005; Albrecht, 2012). Here, practice-based learning is often related to experiential learning that, according to Kolb (1984), can be defined as "a holistic integrative perspective on learning that combines experience, perception, cognition and behavior" (p. 2) (Conceição and Skibba, 2008; Maier and Thomas, 2013). A similar concept used in the hospitality and tourism education literature is the one of authentic learning, a type of learning where the disciplinary aspects of learning meet the situated lived experience of the students in a process that is described as interactive, reflective and focused on both doing and being (Paddison and Mortimer, 2016).

With an approach to learning strongly influenced by the concepts of practice-based, experiential and authentic learning, Croy (2009) reflects on the location dimension. Location-based learning (LBL) is described as a type of learning characterised by an active involvement of a destination community cooperating with the education institution, a marked student centeredness and responsibility and a learning unit that includes learning objectives that are relevant to both students and community members. Differently from other approaches, LBL views the destination not only as the context that can provide the students with valuable experience but also as a partner (Croy and Hall, 2003). The centrality of the location and the community can be viewed in terms of proximity, understood in spatial and relational terms. Ren et al. (2014) adopt the proximity concept in discussing learning events where students can receive insights on their future working life and the related challenges and, at the same time, might function as knowledge brokers, linking research-oriented knowledge and practice. Similarly, LBL methods are argued to potentially lead to the development of a sort of partnership among the teachers, the students and the destination community, with the result of contributing to the development of a learning destination. The latter is here understood as a destination characterised by learning as a social goal for the community, including individuals and organisations, and collaboration among the tourism, civic, voluntary and education sectors (Schianetz, 2007).

Based on these considerations, our focus is on the structural and procedural aspects of educational methods that can facilitate the emergence of a learning destination where students, entrepreneurs and scholars can become better in their present and future practices. These aspects are identified using the Communities of Practice (CoP) framework.

Communities of Practice

Lave and Wenger's (1991) book *Situated Learning. Legitimate Peripheral Participation* has heavily contributed to make the concept of Communities of Practice quite popular in the business management literature as well as in the education literature (Tigh, 2015). We refer to the theoretical framework presented in this book, and in the later book by Wenger (1998) *Communities of Practice. Learning, Meaning, and Identity*, in order to describe the following concepts relevant to the practice-based approach to learning adopted in the student event object of our investigation:

- self and community identity;
- peripheral participation;
- constellation of CoPs;
- boundary and brokering.

Lave and Wenger understand learning as "an integral part of generative social practice in the lived-in world" (Lave and Wenger, 1991: 35). According to this position, learning is essentially social and situated as it does not take place in the learners' head but occurs mainly through people's mutual engagement in an activity that belongs to a certain domain – called domain of interest. Moreover, learning is viewed as meaningful for the individuals' sense of identity: learning is not only a process of acquiring knowledge and skills but also a process of identity development (Lave and Wenger, 1991; Wenger, 1998).

According to this position, learning is about becoming a practitioner or a better practitioner. Moreover, learning is a matter of belonging to a community of people who, on the basis of a shared domain of interest, engage in a relevant practice. In addition to mutual engagement, the sense of belonging of community members develop through the processes of imagination and alignment. Imagination is defined as "creating images of the world and seeing connections through time and space by extrapolating from our own experience" (Wenger, 1998: 173). Alignment is the coordination of the various activities within a community so that they can contribute to a broader enterprise that is an advancement in terms of doing and knowing. In this context, Lave and Wenger introduce the concept of peripheral participation, a process through which unexperienced practitioners gradually become practitioners and join communities of practice. Thus, a CoP can be described as the social arena where processes of becoming occur, formally and informally, as individuals interact with each other and reflect on their practical doing and on its meaning in the specific context.

Although characterised by a strong sense of belonging, CoPs are not isolated and important relations can develop with other CoPs on the basis of some common interest. Here, the processes of boundary and brokering are particularly important. According to Wenger (1998), boundaries are not only unavoidable but also useful in relation to sense of identity and learning, especially when they are crossed and re-arranged. Boundary processes, understood here as those processes of being aware of a social group's boundaries and eventually re-thinking such arrangement, can enable intra- and inter-coordination.

In particular, boundary encounters – exemplified by Lave and Wenger (1991) in meetings, conversations and visits – can act as fora for mutual engagement. This includes both the development and reinforcement of reciprocal relations among people and the use of objects, such as artefacts and documents. Some of these objects can be qualified as boundary objects as their use facilitates the coordination of different perspectives: boundary objects can act as connections between practices.

When relations among CoPs are created by individuals, these act as brokers who can connect communities and also "open new possibilities for meaning" (Lave and Wenger, 1991: 109). Brokering is described as a complex process: it involves the translation of ideas into practices, the application and coordination of new ideas in relation to different practices and, finally, the alignment between such renewed practices. According to Lave and Wenger (1991), brokering requires legitimacy and the ability to link practices and negotiate with practitioners so that the elements of a practice can be introduced into another practice.

Although boundary encounters are quite common, Lave and Wenger (1991) observe that there is the risk that, with time, such encounters acquire a sort of independence and become something else from the practices that they were supposed to connect.

Communities of Practice and LBL

Lave and Wenger (1991) reflect on the local dimension of CoPs. In particular, the authors specify that practices are located and outline the possibility that relations of proximity can facilitate or hinder learning. With such considerations as starting point, the CoP approach can be viewed in relation to location-based learning (LBL).

Applying the LBL approach, the location is here viewed as the destination, more precisely the relevant context and the competent partner that gives meaning to the mentioned CoP aspects and processes. The destination refers to the specific geographical area as well as the local host community. The latter includes a variety of actors, such as entrepreneurs, teachers and students of local education institutions. Moreover, the destination also temporarily hosts tourists and, among these, tourism students visiting the destination.

All the aforementioned actors can be viewed as learners engaged in different but related practices concerning tourism theory and practice. The main idea of the student event object of this study is inspired by the concept of boundary encounter and concerns the creation of a forum for possible social interactions and mutual engagement that can facilitate tourism learning. No matter who the learner is – entrepreneur, student or scholar – it is her/his experience of the destination that can provoke and trigger reflections and actions in its complexity, including the various potentials and challenges in terms of tourism development. These experiences can be relevant to self and community identity building, sense of belonging to the centre or the periphery of specific social groups and the possibilities to cross these social groups' boundaries.

Such learning experiences can be particularly important for the students who can learn more about and explore in practice their future possibilities. Through social interactions with tourism scholars and entrepreneurs and through location-based problem solving, students are stimulated to use their imagination. As stated by Lave and Wenger (1991), imagination is "a process of expanding our self by transcending our time and space and creating new images of the world and ourselves" (p. 176). Students engaged in educational and ludic activities are stimulated to consider alternative life choices and explore possible lifestyles.

Method

Our research can be qualified as a case study where the case is chosen on the basis of its "key-ness" and the researchers' familiarity with it (Thomas, 2011).

The case concerns an international event arranged in 2016 by the University of Macerata and the Piceno Laboratory on the Mediterranean Diet: the International Student Competition (ISC). The "key-ness" of the case can be explained by this event being an ideal set where tourism students, scholars and practitioners meet and learn together. Being an event structured as an experiential and location-based form of education including both theoretical and practical sections, the ISC case can contribute to some interesting insights on the emergence of CoPs in tourism. Moreover, the ISC case study investigates a variety of tourism-interested individuals not limited to entrepreneurs, as in previous tourism studies adopting the CoP framework (Bertella, 2011).

With regard to the researchers' familiarity with the case, we have personally participated in the ISC planning, implementation and evaluation. Most of the data derives from personal participation and observation, conversations and discussions with the event stakeholders. Our approach is in line with Community Based Participatory Research (CBPR), i.e. "a collaborative approach to research that equitably involves all partners in the research process and recognises the unique strengths that each brings" (Kellogg Health Scholars, 2016 in Deale, 2017, p. 55). In accord with the methodological dialogic engagement between theory and practice advocated for instance by Rule and John (2015), our belief is that this participatory approach can stimulate the dialogue and active participation of all the stakeholders. This can lead to benefits such as a better understanding of research, learning opportunities, service to the community and connections with partners (Minkler, 2004; Santini et al., 2016; Deale, 2017).

In addition to the data sources mentioned above, additional primary data has been collected through surveys before and after the event. Such surveys were directed to the participating students, the entrepreneurs, the Piceno Laboratory on the Mediterranean Diet and some public agency representatives. With the aim to gain a broader understanding of the event and its effects, and in particular to investigate the local community's perspective, secondary data has been collected. Secondary data consists of articles from the local press, reports on local economic outlook delivered by regional research institutes and universities, as well as datasets available in local chamber of commerce websites.

The International Student Competition (ISC) of Fermo

Background context

The event took place in the Marche region, in Central Italy, in the municipality of Fermo. The Municipality of Fermo has 38,000 inhabitants. It is the leading city of the province, a reference point for 39 provincial municipalities. The Province of Fermo has 180,000 inhabitants and covers about 800 km^2, from the Sibillini Mountains to the Adriatic Sea, with a density of 230 inhabitants/ km^2. The local economy includes the footwear and leather goods industry that has recently experienced a decline, and agriculture (cereals, vegetables, grapes, olives and livestock).

Tourism and gastronomic tourism represent a fundamental axis of development both for Fermo Province and for the whole Marche region. Nevertheless, numbers of incoming flows are still limited, if compared to other Italian areas. For instance, the total number of tourist arrivals in Fermo in 2012 was 82,759 with 889,627 overnights. Only 5,400 were international arrivals corresponding to 30,000 overnights. The peak season is July and August, which comprises 34% of annual arrivals.[1]

The agri-tourism sector has been the foundation for the development of gastronomy and rural tourism in the region, allowing the development of the food and wine sector for the past 20 years. Wine and food supply chain potential is considered an important development axis to support eno-gastronomic tourism. For this reason, over the past 25 years, Fermo Municipality has funded and supported *Tipicità*, a festival about the typical local products, especially food and wine, held every year and attracting more than 10,000 visitors.

In 2013, Fermo Municipality took part in a European project to advance its gastronomic ambitions. The result is URBACT, a network of five European "gastronomic cities". The aim of URBACT is to work together in order to develop and implement strategies and actions that leverage gastronomy as a tool for urban development (URBACT, 2013). These includes the facilitation of exchange of experiences and learning among city policymakers, decision-makers and practitioners and the assistance to policy-makers and practitioners to define and put into practice Local Action Plans (LAPs) with long-term perspectives. LAPs represent the final outcome of the whole project for each city: a strategic document that identifies needs, analyses problems, and proposes feasible sustainable solutions.

During the LAP creation process, the weakness of the Fermo eno-gastronomic tourism offer emerged: the main problem was identified in Fermo lacking an iconic product that could be used for branding the city based on its eno-gastronomic culture. On the other hand, a strength was identified in Fermo being one of the places where the so-called Seven Countries Studies was carried out. This is one of the major studies to investigate diet and lifestyle for cardiovascular diseases across different countries and cultures over an extended period of time.[2] According to this study, there is a clear link between the Mediterranean Diet and the development of a healthy nutritional program. This can be viewed in relation to the key role that eno-gastronomy can play in the development of tourist routes and, more in general, tourist products (Hall and Mitchell, 2000). The idea that emerged during the LAP process was that tourists could be attracted to the extent the local destination managed to brand itself as the cradle of the Mediterranean Diet.

As a result, the Piceno Laboratory on Mediterranean Diet, an association of doctors and actors within the health and gastronomy sector, was established. It is from the dialogue between these stakeholders, local tourism entrepreneurs and the University of Macerata that the proposal of the ISC emerged as a possible way to carry on the stakeholders' engagement independently from the "Gastronomic Cities" EU project, train students starting from real problems and challenges and promote the whole Fermo territory. Thus, the ISC was viewed as the starting point for building a sustainable development for Fermo and the nearby rural settings on the basis of the critical aspects identified in the LAP document. In this sense, URBACT was the trigger of a process where local actors could use their competence and their non-local relations to arrange annual events adapted to the specific circumstances of their areas of origin and aiming to develop the destination.

Planning the ISC, its participants and objectives

The ISC was arranged by the University of Macerata and The Piceno Laboratory on Mediterranean Diet as a five-day event where teams of students across different schools and countries compete for a prize. The ISC included in total 60 students from Italy (University of Macerata and University San Raffaele in Rome), Belgium (Ephec Business School in Brussels and PXL University College in Hasselt), Norway (University College Southeast Norway in Tønsberg), Poland (University of Poznan) and Czech Republic (College of Polytechnics of Jihlava). The students included both bachelor and master students. In addition to the students, other event participants were scholars and local stakeholders (40 participants in total). Among the latter were members of the Piceno Laboratory on the Mediterranean Diet, local entrepreneurs and public agency representatives.

The idea underpinning the design of the ISC is to promote the formation and reinforcement of three CoPs within the event context. The event organisers designed the event so that three potential CoPs could meet and interact. One CoP refers to the local tourism and agri-food entrepreneurs. These are strongly motivated to acquire better professionalism. The need of an upgrade of their skills and competences emerged clearly during the "Gastronomic Cities" EU project (URBACT, 2013). This need was the starting point to develop the event and, more specifically, the tasks for the students. The latter were focused on branding and ICT as these were the aspects that the local entrepreneurs felt as important but not particularly developed yet. The main objective identified for the local stakeholders was to use the event to reflect on and elaborate innovative developmental paths to increase the international reputation of the destination.

The scholars form a second CoP. These scholars can be viewed as practitioners that share the practice of researching and teaching tourism. Most scholars participated to the event as tutors of the students coming from their institutions, and some were invited as keynote speakers. Especially among the tutors of scholars, a particular interest in experiential teaching methods can be identified as a common element. Some scholars already knew each other from a previous student competition held in Milan during the EXPO 2015. Other participating scholars knew the organisers personally. Before the ISC, this group lacked the strong sense of belonging characterising a CoP. So, one of the objectives of the event was identified in the strengthening of these relations. The event was viewed as a meeting point facilitating the emergence and reinforcement of relations for future cooperation. The main objective for the community of scholars was to share knowledge and experience whilst planning future research and teaching activities.

The third CoP refers to the students. Their engagement is motivated by their life project of becoming tourism entrepreneurs or/and scholars. In this sense, they can be viewed as peripheral members of the two afore-mentioned communities. The objectives for the students were: discovering linkages between gastronomy, events and place branding; understanding the potential of food and gastronomy for sustainable development; devel-oping skills for destination management challenges mainly through the use of ICT for place branding activities; and experiencing a full-immersion week in the Italian culture and tourism activities in Marche. Moreover, in a sort of role-playing style, the students had as main task for the compe-tition to act as consultants for the local stakeholders, using their skills and imagination to develop a branding plan for the location. The entrepre-neurs were expected to help the students to understand the local context and the challenges related to their job, and the scholars to provide them with the theoretical background necessary to understand and analyse the specific context, including the main task relative to ICT tools for destina-tion branding.

Expectations: the ISC as a boundary encounter and the students as brokers

In addition to the objectives mentioned above, the idea underpinning the event was to create connections between these three CoPs. Identifying tourism as the common domain of interest, these CoPs can be viewed as a potential constellation. Here, the event can function as a boundary encounter among the various members. This can be illustrated as in Figure 10.1.

It can be observed that, usually, students, scholars and entrepreneurs have several occasions to meet. For many students and scholars, the meetings are quite frequent and usually framed in the educational program of the institu-tions they belong to. Sometimes, students meet tourism entrepreneurs, for example during fieldwork tours and as guest lectures. Scholars and entrepre-neurs tend to meet during the aforementioned student activities and during research fieldwork.

The idea of the ISC was then to encourage and reinforce these partly already existing relations, providing a unique educational and entertainment experience and, ultimately, promote a safe and creative learning environment for all the individuals involved. With such aim, the following activities were arranged:

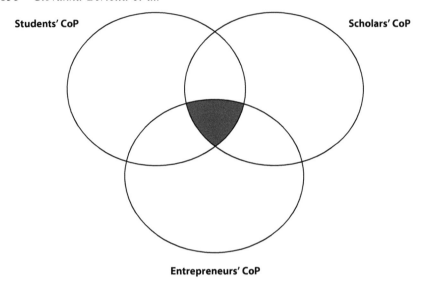

Students' CoP   Scholars' CoP

Entrepreneurs' CoP

Figure 10.1 The ISC as a boundary encounter between three CoPs.

- seminars led by academics and performed in historical theatres and buildings;
- daily competitions where students had to use ICT to promote the destination;
- main competition with the task of prepare a strategic plan for branding the destination;
- fieldtrips in local wineries and farms;
- educational tasting and show cooking sessions;
- meetings and workshops with local public and private stakeholders (mayors of a dozen municipalities, the association Piceno Lab on Mediterranean Diet, food and wine producers, food producers, hospitality operators);
- meals based on the local gastronomy in historical towns and villages.

The students and the scholars were accommodated in local B&Bs and guest farms. Here, conversations arose spontaneously among participants, regardless of their role. The daily communal dinners were arranged at the restaurant of a close collaborator of the Piceno Laboratory on the Mediterranean Diet. Also at this occasion, spontaneous conversations among all the involved individuals emerged. Moreover, during the dinners ludic and entertainment activities (master chef cooking shows, local music), educational activities (meeting local food producers) and briefing meetings were arranged.

During the event, the students were expected to act as potential brokers. Their presence and their activities were expected to facilitate the communication between the tourism scholars and practitioners. Moreover, due to their age and familiarity with social media, the students were also viewed as potential important contributors to find innovative branding possibilities. This was interpreted as an important element in terms of imagination, one of the main processes for learning CoPs. Imagining the future of the destination and possible ways to influence it could not only contribute to introduce new practices but also start important discussions about a shared vision. The open discussion of the students' ideas with scholars and entrepreneurs was identified as having important potentials in terms of alignment, a process that could lead to the strategy development for Fermo as a tourism destination branded as the Mediterranean Diet cradle.

Evaluating the ISC

The organisers evaluated the ISC, both informally through conversations and formally through meetings and surveys with all the participants. This occurred at the beginning, during and after the event itself. In the entrepreneurs' answers, the passion for the territory and their job, communication and collaboration are the key-words. All the entrepreneurs highlight the importance of communicating and collaborating within the local tourism context but also across sectors and adopting a broader perspective. For example, a practitioner wrote:

> This is the first time I collaborate with academicians in such an ambitious project (...) everybody has his/her own competence: the path to collaboration is long and not easy but together we can do it! I'll always be available for such initiatives!
>
> (Wine producer)

The entrepreneurs' expectations in relation to the scholars and the students concerned the potential insights for possible strategies for the territory, and the possibility to gain an understanding about how the territory is perceived by outsiders, its strengths and its weaknesses. Similar to the entrepreneurs' comments were the considerations made by public agencies representatives and by the members of the Piceno Laboratory on the Mediterranean Diet. From the students' perspective, the expectations and motivations to join the event vary, from gaining credits useful for the study program, to the educational and fun aspects of the event. The answers show also a marked interest in meeting local people and tourism entrepreneurs. The post-event data from the entrepreneurs' perspective show that the expectations in regard to the local collaboration were met. Many comments concerned the contribution that the event had given in terms of reinforcing the local network of relations. Here, also the planning meetings are reported as extremely useful:

the group discussion for the planning and coordination have been useful in creating work groups that can be used for the future student competition as well as for other joint projects.

(Guest farm owner)

the theoretical and potential collaborative relations relative to the local network have become reality (...) the relations between the Piceno Lab, the producers, the restaurants and the accommodation facilities have evolved, becoming stronger and broader.

(Piceno Lab member)

These results suggest that the event contributed to the reinforcement of the entrepreneurs' CoP and, to a certain extent, also to the reinforcement of the relations between the entrepreneurs and the scholars, in particular those belonging to the local university.

Still in the perspective of the entrepreneurs, a clear sense of empowerment emerges. As has been previously underlined, these rural areas have a limited flow of tourists, and the fact to be the object of a student competition, hosting visitors from several EU countries, made the local people feel proud of their tradition and lifestyle.

The entrepreneurs' answers show appreciation and respect in relation to the work performed by the students, with some respondents highlighting the opportunity that the event gave them in relation to be oriented on new communication channels and "young" ways to perceive a destination. A sense of affection toward the students can also be observed in some of the answers by the entrepreneurs who seem to be impressed by the genuine interest shown by the students in relation to the territory and also to the individual businesses.

The latter aspect seems to have been clearly perceived by the students, with some open comments during the last dinner about the feeling of having received a warm and genuine welcome by the local people. Based on their answers collected after the event, and their discussion with their accompanying teachers, the students can be said to be overall very satisfied with the event both as a learning experience and a tourist experience. With regard to their learning, it can be said that their role in the students' CoP was perceived as less peripheral. In particular, the meeting with local entrepreneurs and the active role they were invited to play seems to be very much appreciated. In relation to these aspects, some students have reported the event as important in gaining insight for their possible future working life.

Still with regard to the students, the local ones have reported feeling a sort of responsibility towards the other students and the local entrepreneurs. With regard to the latter aspect, the event seems to have reinforced these students' attachment to the territory. As a confirmation of this, some of these students who had finished their master studies the year that the first competition

(2016) was arranged, have then decided to participate in the second competition, in 2017, in some cases as experienced PhD students.

Finally, scholars evaluated the competition positively, something that is confirmed by the participation of several scholars also to the second edition in 2017. During the competition, informal relations among scholars have developed and common research and teaching related interests were discussed. The results of such discussions are common research projects across institutions. For the scholars belonging to the local University, better insights in the work of the colleagues and their positions in relation to pedagogical methods and regional development were mentioned in the post-event discussions as positive outcomes of the competition. For some scholars also the contact with the local entrepreneurs working in agriculture and tourism was viewed as improved after the event.

Lessons learned

The ISC created many meeting points and formal and informal discussion fora, involving tourism entrepreneurs, scholars and students. The experience gained from the ISC shows that the event can be viewed as a boundary encounter as conceptualised by Lave and Wenger (1991) and hoped for by the event organisers, with many potentials for learning to become a better student, entrepreneur and scholar. Some of these potentials emerged during the event quite clearly while others did not, indicating then directions for future similar events.

For the students, the combination of the educational and the ludic aspects, the experience of the destination as tourists but also as consultants triggered a strong engagement. This seems to have contributed to their sense of identity as better practitioners in the sense of engaged students and as future entrepreneurs in the tourism sector. This can be viewed as an important result in line with Lave and Wenger's understanding of learning as becoming and belonging.

With regard to the expectation of the students acting as brokers, it can be concluded that, to a certain degree, this expectation was met and the students contributed to translate some theoretical ideas and tools in to concrete plans for the local destination. This was quite evident during the daily ICT-related competitions. With regard to this, the entrepreneurs showed appreciation and enthusiasm for the students' work. This can be explained by the legitimacy recognised to the young students by the not-so-young entrepreneurs in relation to ICT.

On the other hand, the expectation concerning the students' contribution as creative brokers was not met. This can be explained by referring to a prerequisite identified by Lave and Wenger in relation to brokering, namely the ability to link practices. The main competition results do not show any particular innovative solutions proposed by the students. Moreover, the results of the main competition were quite limited in relation to the reflection and use of the theory introduced in the initial lectures. The latter element can also explain the lack of creativity and can depend on the fact the students were at different levels of their studies (bachelor, master) and some might lack the necessary background and maturity. Using Lave and Wenger's framework, this might indicate a too peripheral position of some students in relation to the practice related to tourism studies. With regard to this, future events might select the students differently, and/or provide them with some study material in advance, in addition to arranging a creativity workshop at the beginning of the event.

Another element that might have influenced the limited role that the students had in terms of creative brokering concerns cultural proximity. During the event, the cultural dimension, and more specifically the cultural differences among the participants, emerged. Here, the local students played a central role. They were very familiar with the local area, the related challenges and, in addition, they were already established as a working group led by their teacher. Due to this, they acted as mentors for the foreign students, often facilitating the communication with the teachers and clarifying the expectations in relation to the competition and how to approach and behave with the local people. It can be noted that the foreign students met difficulties in acting as brokers due to their cultural distance in relation to the entrepreneurs' CoP and the lack of a deep contextual understanding of the local tourism.

It can be asked whether the organisers' initial conceptualisation of the students' CoP as a homogenous group was correct. Based on the experience gained from the event, the cultural proximity and distance of the various CoP members are very relevant factors. The hypothesised students' CoP composed by local and foreign students lacked the sense of belonging that CoPs have according to Lave and Wenger's framework. Such sense of belonging was observed among the local students, but was not particularly evident among the students as a whole.

In line with Lave and Wenger's framework, another important element of boundary encounters are boundary objects. In relation to the ISC, these can be identified in the proposals that were elaborated by the students and presented to the entrepreneurs and the scholars. The creation of boundary objects could have been better structured. In particular, a collection of written documents and pictures following the event as a sort of journal and a final report on the students' work could have contributed to organise the interconnections among the three communities and reinforce their sense of belonging to one constellation. Such journal and report could also include the scholars' perspectives. Here, it can be noted that the hectic timing of the various activity and, in some cases, the priority given to the implementation and discussion of the students' activities limited the dialogue among some of the scholars and the entrepreneurs. The latter commented on this, asking explicitly how the scholars would have solved the task given to the students.

One of the peculiarities of the ISC was the lack of a shared cultural background due to the different countries of origin. The experience gained from the ISC shows that although challenging, as commented above in the case of the students, this element is not necessarily problematic, confirming that a shared domain of interest and a relational proximity created and supported by several activities can, at least in part, compensate for possible cultural differences. In fact, the multicultural aspect has been indicated by the entrepreneurs as a positive element, potentially important as the local community is interested in exploring opportunities relative to foreign markets.

An important lesson learned concerns the local community. The findings suggest that the event contributed to the reinforcement of the entrepreneurs' CoP, in particular their sense of belonging to a community of particularly engaged economic actors and, to a certain extent, their relation with other local actors and with scholars, in particular those belonging to the local university. As it has been previously underlined, these rural areas have a limited flow of tourists, and being the object of a student competition, hosting visitors from several EU countries, made the local people feel proud of their traditions and lifestyle. It can be added that the local newspapers and TV programmes played an important role. The local press was interested in the event, and the daily coverage of the activities performed by the students together with international scholars and local entrepreneurs had the effect of promoting the ISC as an event particularly relevant to the local territory and highlighting the possibilities of an increase in professionalism in the local hospitality sector.

Moreover, the local actors expressed a strong sense of empowerment gained by the event. Background research has shown that community based research can play an effective role for improving stakeholders' empowerment: some educational models have been replicated and adopted by other institutions given their efficacy in improving participants' empowerment (Strand et al., 2003). Even if most of the research exploring the linkages between community-based research and empowerment focuses on social change, some considerations that underline the efficacy of community-based research, including its participatory-based research methods, can be extended to the specific examined case.

This aspect relative to local pride and sense of empowerment can now be viewed as a critically important in relation to the earthquake that occurred in the area some months after the student event and that forced the local entrepreneurs and more in general communities to find and implement joint actions in order to minimise the negative economic impacts.

With regard to the scholars' community, the student event has mainly reinforced already existing relations, with the results of plans for joint research and teaching projects. Another result for the involved scholars can be identified in a deeper understanding of the specific context.

Conclusion

Adopting the Communities of Practice (CoP) framework and the location-based learning (LBL) approach, this chapter has presented the case of the International Student Competition of Fermo (Italy). The findings confirm that a practice-based approach to learning that has its focus on experiencing a location and is implemented through collaboration with local stakeholders has important learning potential.

The main findings of the case suggest that the specific event has had positive outcomes especially for the students involved and local entrepreneurs. For the students, the event seems to have contributed to their sense of belonging to a constellation of communities of tourism-interested people and their sense of becoming more engaged members of such a broad community. Among the students, local students have had a central role, facilitating communication and relations with both local teachers and, even more, with entrepreneurs. Within the event, students have played the role of brokers connecting the theory and the practice of tourism. Such process has not been particularly creative and, in this regard, some improvements for future events have been identified in relation to the possible stimulation of imagination processes. Other improvements have been identified in relation to a better structured creation of boundary objects and alignment processes.

Another important result of this study concerns the effects of the event on the local community. The latter, and in particular the local entrepreneurs, has felt empowered by the event and this has led to a particularly high motivation to continue the collaboration especially with local actors, including the University.

This study concludes that the CoP framework can be fruitfully adopted to design and evaluate events that aim to facilitate the emergence or the reinforcement of tourism communities of students, scholars and entrepreneurs and these communities' reciprocal relations. Critically important factors that have emerged from the investigated case include in particular: the challenging but also potentially enriching aspect related to the multicultural dimension of boundary encounters and the importance of the relative position of the members within their respective practices. These factors can limit the learning and innovating outcomes of the event, and influence future events in the sense that these might continue to be arranged with positive effects but without contributing particularly to the creation of connections among tourism related practices.

The combination of the concepts of CoP and LBL allowed broadening the perspective of a student event so to include the local community and, in particular, the local entrepreneurs. In the specific case, this has resulted in the tasks that the students were asked to solve being perceived as particularly relevant from the perspective of the local people. This led to a lively engagement of both entrepreneurs and students. More in general, the LBL approach turned out to be an important contribution to the CoP framework applied to tourism due to its focus on the destination, and consequently on potentials in terms of regional development. In the case investigated, the results related to this aspect concern mainly the sense of empowerment infused by the event to the local host community. Moreover, the conceptualisation of the event as an encounter between CoPs where learning is linked to the specific area contributed to theoretically frame and practically implement the role of higher education institutes in correspondence to the so-called Third Mission, i.e. higher education institutes as key players in regional economic development and knowledge transfer. Future longitudinal studies might explore whether and to which extent the event and its following edition in 2017 have contributed to the emergence of new practices.

Notes

1 www.urbistat.it/adminstat/it/it/demografia/dati-sintesi/fermo/109/3
2 www.sevencountriesstudy.com/

References

Albrecht, J. N. (2012). Authentic learning and communities of practice in tourism higher education. *Journal of Teaching in Travel & Tourism*, 12(3), 260–276.

Bennett, R. (2006). Business lecturers' perceptions of the nature of entrepreneurship. *International Journal of Entrepreneurial Behavior & Research*, 12(3), 165–188.

Bertella, G. (2011). Communities of practice in tourism: learning and working together. An illustrative case study from northern Norway. *Tourism Planning & Development*, 8(4), 381–397.

Brown, J. S. and Duguid, P. (1991). Knowledge and organization: a social-practice perspective. *Organization Science*, 12(2), 198–213.

Conceição, S. C. O. and Skibba, K. A. (2008). Experiential learning activities for leisure and enrichment travel education: a situative perspective. *Journal of Teaching in Travel & Tourism*, 7(4), 17–35.

Corradi, G. and Gherardi, S. (2010). Through the practice lens: where is the bandwagon of practice-based studies heading? *Management Learning*, 41(3), 265–283.

Cox, A. (2005). What are communities of practice? A comparative review of four seminal works. *Journal of Information Science*, 31(6), 527–540.

Croy, W. G. (2009). Location-based learning: considerations for developing and implementing destination-partnered authentic-experiential learning. *Journal of Hospitality and Tourism Education*, 21(1), 17–23.

Croy, W. G. and Hall, C. M. (2003). Developing a tourism knowledge: educating the student, developing the rural area. *Journal of Teaching in Travel & Tourism*, 3(1), 3–24.

Deale, C. S. (2017). Learning through engagement: undergraduate students engaging in community-based participatory research (CBPR) in hospitality and tourism education. *Journal of Teaching in Travel & Tourism*, 17(1), 55–61.

Fuller, A., Hodkinson, H., Hodkinson, P. and Unwin, L. (2005). Learning as peripheral participation in communities of practice: a reassessment of key concepts in workplace learning. *British Educational Research Journal*, 31(1), 49–68.

Gherardi, S. (2009). Practice? It's a matter of taste. *Management Learning*, 40(5), 535–550.

Gibb, A. (2002). In pursuit of a new 'enterprise' and 'entrepreneurship' paradigm for learning: creative destruction, new values, new ways of doing things and new combinations of knowledge. *International Journal of Management Reviews*, 4(3), 233–269.

Hall, C. M. and Mitchell, R. (2000). Wine tourism in the Mediterranean: a tool for restructuring and development. *Thunderbird International Business Review*, 42(4), 445–465.

Johannisson, B., Landstrom, H. and Rosenberg, J. (1998). University training for entrepreneurship – an action frame of reference. *European Journal of Engineering Education*, 23(4), 477–496.

Kelliher, F. and Reinl, L. (2014). Learning in action: implementing a facilitated learning programme for tourism micro-firms. *Irish Business Journal*, 9(1), 5–16.

Kellogg Health Scholars. (2016). History. Retrieved from www.kellogghealthscholars.org/about/vision.php

Kolb, D. A. (1984). *Experiential Learning: Experience as the Source of Learning and Development*. Englewood Cliffs, NJ: Prentice-Hall.

Landri, P. (2012). A return to practice: practice-based studies of education. In P. Hager*et al.* (eds), *Practice, Learning and Change: Practice-Theory Perspectives on Professional Learning* (pp. 85–100). London, New York: Springer.

Lave, J. and Wenger, E. (1991). *Situated Learning. Legitimate Peripheral Participation*. Cambridge, MA: Cambridge University Press.

Maier, T. A. and Thomas, N. J. (2013). Hospitality leadership course design and delivery: a blended-experiential learning model. *Journal of Hospitality & Tourism Education*, 25(1), 11–21.

Minkler, M. (2004). Ethical challenges for the "outside" researcher in community-based participatory research. *Health Education & Behavior*, 31(6), 684–697.

Mooney, L. A. and Edwards, B. (2001). Experiential learning in sociology: service learning and other community-based learning initiatives. *Teaching Sociology*, 29(2), 181–194.

Orlikowski, W. J. (2002). Knowing in practice: enacting a collective capability in distributed organizing. *Organization Science*, 13(3), 249–273.

Østerlund, C. and Carlile, P. (2005). Relations in practice: sorting through practice theories on knowledge sharing in complex organizations. *Information Society*, 21(2), 91–107.

Paddison, B. and Mortimer, C. (2016). Authenticating the learning environment. *Journal of Teaching in Travel & Tourism*, 16(4), 331–350.

Raelin, J. A. (1997). A model of work-based learning. *Organization Science*, 8(6), 563–578.

Raelin, J. A. (2007). Toward an epistemology of practice. *Academy of Management Learning and Education*, 6(4), 495–519.

Rasmussen, E. A. and Sørheim, R. (2006). Action-based entrepreneurship education. *Technovation*, 26(2), 185–194.

Ren, C., Gyimóthy, S., Jensen, M. T., Krizaj, D. and Bratec, M. (2014). Proximity of practice: student-practitioner collaboration in tourism. In G. Alsos, D. Eide and E. Lier Madsen (eds), *Handbook of Research on Innovation in Tourism Industries* (pp. 325–348). Cheltenham: Edward Elgar Publishing.

Ruhanen, L. (2005). Bridging the divide between theory and practice. *Journal of Teaching & Tourism*, 5(4), 33–51.

Rule, P. and John, V. M. (2015). The necessary dialogue: theory in case study research. *International Journal of Qualitative Methods*, 1–11.

Santini, C., Marinelli, E., Boden, M., Cavicchi, A. and Haegeman, K. (2016). Reducing the distance between thinkers and doers in the entrepreneurial discovery process: An exploratory study. *Journal of Business Research*, 69, 1840–1844.

Schatzki, T. R., Knorr-Cerrina, K. and Von Savigny, E. (eds) (2001). *The Practice Turn in Contemporary Theory*. London: Routledge.

Schianetz, K., Kavanagh, L. and Lockington, D. (2007). The learning tourism destination: the potential of a learning organisation approach for improving the sustainability of tourism destinations. *Tourism Management*, 28(6), 1485–1496.

Sole, D. and Edmondson, A. (2002). Situated knowledge and learning in dispersed teams. *British Journal of Management*, 13(2), 17–34.

Strand, K. J., Cutforth, N., Stoecker, R., Marullo, S. and Donohue, P. (2003). *Community-based Research and Higher Education: Principles and practices*. San Francisco: Jossey-Bass.

Thomas, G. (2011). A typology for the case study in social science following a review of definition, discourse, and structure. *Qualitative Inquiry*, 17(6), 511–521.

Tigh, M. (2015). Theory application in higher education research: the case of communities of practice. *European Journal of Higher Education*, 5(2), 111–126.

URBACT (2013). The URBACT II Local Support Group Toolkit. Available at www.urbact.eu.

Wenger, E. (1998). *Communities of Practice. Learning, Meaning, and Identity*. Cambridge, MA: Cambridge University Press.

11 Tourism and theories of practice

Key themes and future directions

Laura James, Carina Ren and Henrik Halkier

In their recent article on the relevance of practice theories for tourism research, Machiel Lamers, René van der Duim and Gert Spaargaren (2017) identified three main ways in which practice-based approaches could contribute to tourism studies and policy. Firstly, they suggest that theories of practice allow in-depth analysis of tourism consumption and production; secondly they suggest that practice theories contribute an understanding of change in tourism and; thirdly, they suggest that practice theories can be used to trace and 'unravel' networks of tourism practices that stretch across space. The preceding chapters of this book provide examples of all three of the potential contributions identified by Lamers, van der Duim and Spaargaren, and also extend our understanding the intersection between practice theory and tourism in new ways.

The authors who have contributed to this collection have drawn on wide variety of practice theories and theorists, using concepts such as communities of practice, popularised by Lave and Wenger (1991), Schatzki's (2002) conceptualization of practice-arrangement-bundles, Shove et al.'s (2012) three elements of practice, and Nicolini's (2012) ideas about the nexus of practice and the importance of 'zooming in' and 'zooming out', to name some of the most prominent. The sheer diversity of practice-based approaches is perhaps one reason why they have, until recently, received relatively little attention within tourism (Souza Bispo, 2016). As many commentators have noted, there is no one single theory or methodological framework which is suitable for all applications, but rather a loose 'family' of theories and concepts which share some central assumptions regarding the importance of practices as the fundamental unit through which social life is enacted (Spaargaren, Lamers and Weenink, 2017).

As Lamers, Van der Duim and Spaargaren (2017) noted in their review, many researchers who have used practice based approaches in their studies of tourism have focused on in-depth explorations of individual practices (e.g. Rantala, 2010; Valtonen and Veijola, 2011) and, more recently, the ways in which various tourism activities can be conceptualised as a bundle or nexus of different practices (e.g. Lamers and Pashkevich, 2018). The contributions in this book have also, in different ways, demonstrated how practice theories can be used in empirical analyses of a wide range of tourism related phenomena, from the everyday micro-practices of individual tourists, to the governance of destination development and processes of tourism-related socio-technological innovation. However, they have also illuminated some of the conceptual and methodological opportunities and challenges that practice theories present to researchers of tourism. In this concluding discussion, we would like to discuss some of the implications of the preceding chapters for future research in tourism studies. These are divided into four themes: the temporal dynamics of tourism practices; networks of tourism practices; practices of learning and innovation in tourism; and the materiality of tourism practices. Finally, we reflect on the contribution that studies of tourism might make to the development of practice-based approaches, and suggest areas in which further work needs to be done.

The temporal dynamics of tourism

Many practice theorists have focused on the temporal dynamics of practices, particularly the tension between reproduction and change in practice over time. Many definitions of practice emphasise the importance of repetition and the continual re-enactment of everyday routines, as in Reckwitz's (2002, 249) frequently cited definition of practice as 'a routinised type of behaviour which consists of several elements'. As Larsen (Chapter 2) has argued, this may be another reason for the slow adoption of practice-based approaches in tourism studies, where traditionally tourism has been associated with 'exotic' and 'out of routine' experiences. Hui notes that even routines are subject to changes because each time practices are enacted they take place in a specific context and are performed by a specific practitioner such that they 'cannot help but encompass differences because of the unpredictable and diverse nature of performances' (Hui, 2017, 55). Warde (2005, 140), similarly argues that: "the sources of changed behaviour lie in the development of practices themselves. The concept of practice inherently combines a capacity to account for both reproduction and innovation". Beyond the variations in tourism practices that are an inherent part of their reproduction, studies of the temporal dynamics of practice offer new insights into everyday rhythms, long-term development, adoption and adaptation by practitioners. Potentially fruitful avenues for future research in this direction have been discussed in several chapters of this book.

In Chapter 2, Fuentes and Svingstedt, for example, have used the concepts of *recruitment, career* and *defection*, to explore how practitioners of slow tourism are recruited into slow travel practices and become committed to certain modes of travel such as walking and cycling. They trace the development of slow travelling careers and how individual practitioners sometimes defect to other kinds of travel practices (notably air travel), either temporarily or permanently. Their chapter provides a clear demonstration of the utility of a practice-based approach to understanding the relations – and tensions –

between different types of mobility. Their study shows that slow travel – like other tourism practices – is dynamic and changes over time and they provide a framework that other researchers could use to study the development of a wide variety of tourism activities.

Ren, Petersen and Nielsen (Chapter 9) consider the temporal dynamics associated with the development of smart tourism practices. Rather than seeing smart tourism in terms of linear technological evolution, or a 'rupture' from current practices, they suggest that such development involves linking, or bundling, new tourism practices to existing ones. Based on a case study of smart tourism activities in North Jutland, Denmark, they develop a typology drawing on the temporality of the practices, looking at how the temporal nature of Smart Tourism practices – ad hoc, routine, networked and project based – plays a crucial part in how it is linked to the daily work of managing and developing tourism at local destinations.

Rantala provides a different perspective on the temporal dynamics of practice in Chapter 5, where she uses case studies of nature-based holidays in Finland and Norway to explore the rhythms of practice. Her analysis, which highlights the aesthetic and affective qualities of practice, explores the ways in which materialities, embodiments and representations follow a range of cyclical and linear rhythms that disrupt the supposed dualism between everyday life and holiday time. By taking rhythm and the dynamics between time and space as the starting point, Rantala is able to explore process of becoming (Edensor, 2010) as human practices and their tempos are shaped by the cycles of nature, weather and the seasons. Thus, the nature holiday is built around the rhythms and frictions of the complex relationships between the body and the environment.

In contrast to Rantala's in depth focus on the micro-rhythms of practices, James and Halkier (Chapter 7), draw on Nicolini (2012) in using a zoomed-out perspective to trace the evolution of bundles of tourism development practices over time. Drawing on Shove et al.'s (2012) conceptualisation of practices as combinations of materials, competences and meanings, their study of coastal destinations in Denmark shows how practices of promotion and experience creation have changed over time. Furthermore, their analysis shows how the relations between these practices have evolved within destination development practice bundles. They also argue that the constant accomplishment of practice creates path dependent trajectories, which can make it difficult to change practices, and which help to explain the differences between destinations. This chapter demonstrates the ways in which practice-based approaches could help our understanding of destination governance practices and the challenges to changing them.

Studies of the temporal dynamics of tourism practices intersect with other debates within tourism studies, such as the evolution of tourism destinations (Brouder, 2017). Evolutionary approaches in tourism studies have drawn heavily on concepts and theories from economic geography, such as resilience and path dependence (Halkier and James, 2017). The difficulty of changing the direction of tourism destination development is a key theme, and researchers exploring this issue have pointed to the role of institutions, entrepreneurship, economic crises and environmental disasters as factors that could explain why change does or does not occur (e.g. Sanz-Ibáñez et al., 2017; Gill and Williams, 2017). As the contributions in this volume have shown, a practice-based approach could contribute to this debate by showing how deeply embedded, and often only incrementally changing, social practices help to explain why it is difficult to escape path dependency.

Practices of learning and innovation in tourism

The tension between reproduction and change in social practices is underlined in debates about practice-based theories of learning and innovation (James and Halkier, 2016). The classic communities of practice theory of learning set out by Lave and Wenger (1991) described how learning can be conceptualised as a process through which new recruits to a practice participate in a community defined by a particular practice and gradually master the knowledge and skills to become a full participant. In this way, the community and the practices that define it are reproduced over time as new generations of practitioners are enrolled and develop practice incrementally. Many writers have emphasised the difficulty of sharing knowledge between practices because knowledge is bound up in the tools, understandings and rules that govern practices (Carlile, 2002). Nevertheless, established ways of practising may be contested and potentially transformed by the introduction of new technologies or concepts (Magaudda et al, 2011). In his later work on communities of practice, Wenger (1998) explored the learning possibilities of overlaps and connections between different communities of practice as a source of learning and innovation. This could happen, for example, when individuals are engaged in multiple practices, thereby acting as boundary spanners who transfer knowledge between communities.

Bertella, Santini and Cavicchi (Chapter 10) build on the communities of practice framework and location-based learning (LBL) approaches, in their study of a collaborative student competition that brought together students of tourism with local entrepreneurs. Interestingly, their analysis indicated that the event increased the students' sense of identity as participants in a constellation of communities of tourism practices. They also found that students acted as 'brokers' bringing theoretical knowledge to the everyday practices of the entrepreneurs. Nonetheless they also found that the collaborative processes were not especially creative and in the future such events could benefit from better alignment processes and the structured creation of boundary objects to facilitate learning.

Derriks, van der Duim and Peters (Chapter 8) also engage with issues of learning and the connections between different practices through their study of the development of a regional destination card in the Dutch province of Zeeland, offering free entrance or discounts on major attractions and free or low-priced public transportation. The process of innovation is conceptualised as the bundling of previously separate practices such as destination branding, conducting market research and facilitating public transportation. The study, which traces the bundling process over time, demonstrates the difficulties of developing common understandings and rules due to the diversity of the meanings, materials and competencies associated with the individual practices.

In Chapter 4, Larsen presents a different perspective on learning by using Reckwitz's conceptualisation on practices as skilful bodily performances. Thus 'a social practice is the product of training the body in a certain way: when we learn a practice, we learn to be bodies in a certain way' (Reckwitz, 2002, 251). In his discussion of marathon running as a social practice, Larsen notes that people need to train their bodies in order to acquire the physical and mental competences required to run long distances. His discussion of the popularisation of marathon running shows how the inclusion of novice and less-experienced runners has changed the meaning of marathon running as a practice and spurred the development of marathon tourism, as the races have become major events attracting runners and spectators alike.

Networks of tourism practices

The adoption of a practice-based approach has important implications for our understanding of scale and the interconnectedness of tourism actors and activities. Most practice theories operate with a flat ontology which does not distinguish between social 'layers' (micro/macro, small/big). Rather, size and scale is defined by to the extension of bundles of practices in time and space, for instance through the concept of 'practice-arrangement bundle' (Schatzki, 2016a, 2016b). As practice-arrangement bundles practices, such as traveling, walking and running (to take three examples related to tourism that are featured in this book), are comprised of groups of practices that are linked together. Thus everyday, mundane and 'simple' practices are connected into complex distributed networks that stretch across space. In Chapter 3, for example, Hannam and Witte show how walking as a recreational and touristic practice in China draws on and adapts Western Romantic narratives of recreational hiking in nature. They argue that walking practices are learnt through interaction in online communities that stretch across the globe.

Lamers et al. (2017, 62) argue that 'understanding how tourism products, as well as extensive tourism networks more widely, are connected to, and embedded in, practice-arrangement bundles helps to unpack the complexity of tourism and to identify innovative and robust ways of governing tourism development'. This is illustrated by James and Halkier (Chapter 7), whose study of coastal tourism destination development in Denmark shows how 'local' practices are inextricably connected to governance practices at a 'regional' and 'national' level, which have a direct impact on the meanings, competences and materials that make up destination development in any given place.

As many contributions to the debates on practice theory have underlined, the tracing and unpacking of the complex relations that connect different practices together is crucial (Hui, Schatzki and Shove, 2017; Shove et al., 2012; Nicolini 2012). As we have noted, many practice-based studies in tourism have focused on the detail of practice as performance rather than practice as entity. As the contributions to this book have shown, practice theory also offers a conceptual framework that can be used to research 'larger' phenomenon that extend across regional, national or international boundaries.

The materiality of tourism practices

The materiality of practices is a theme that runs through all contributions in this book and underlines the importance of taking the materiality of tourism seriously. This is the case for contributions that focus on individual performances of practice and those that take a more 'zoomed out' perspective on practices as entities.

Hannam and Witte (Chapter 3), for example, draw on the work of Edensor (2010) to explore the way in which understanding walking as a touristic practice requires us to pay attention to the affordances of the surrounding environment, and the visual, tactile and sonorous senses through which the walker interacts with the landscape. Rantala's (Chapter 5) analysis of the environmental sensitiveness that emerges when we become tourists in natural settings and use 'marginal', simplified outdoor living tactics, shows the value of exploring the dynamic between humans and the more-than-human world. De Souza Bispo, Cunha Soares and Chavez Cavalcante (Chapter 6) use an evocative interpretative approach based on the work of Strati (2009) to explore the ways in which the senses and aesthetic judgement are crucial to the 'doing' of cooking as a social practice in tourism and hospitality. They show how the practice of regional cooking involves a complex mixture of touch, taste and smell. Their chapter shows how cooks produce 'sensible knowledge': that is, a knowledge of and through the senses that is inherent to the practice of cooking and the development of aesthetic judgments about the quality of the food produced.

In his contribution, Larsen (Chapter 4) emphasises the role of material objects and technologies in the recruitment of practitioners to marathon running and individuals' journey from novices to experienced members of the running community of practice. He notes, for example, that the popularity of running shoes as casual wear since the 1970s meant that many people had the basic equipment required to start running. He also discusses the role of specialised clothing and running watches that assist runners to train their bodies and improve their performances.

Ren, Petersen and Nielsen (Chapter 9) also explore the role of technology in supporting new practices – in their case Smart Tourism practices. They show how the adoption of a particular technology or digital solution does not by itself make tourists change their own practices (e.g. by downloading an app or using a website). They draw on the work of Pantzar and Shove (2010) to argue that materials, meanings and competences must be linked together in order for a tourism innovation to develop. They show that Smart Tourism is not a singular practice, but can rather be configured in many different ways by connecting them to other practices relevant to a tourism organisation or destination. James and Halkier (Chapter 7) also draw on the work of Shove and colleagues, in arguing for the importance of the material in destination development practice bundles. Their chapter, for example, highlights the importance of natural and human resources in forming the material basis of tourism practices such as marketing and experience creation.

Final thoughts

We began this concluding chapter with reference to Lamers, van der Duim and Spaargaren's (2017) suggestions for how practice-based approaches could contribute to tourism studies. They highlighted in depth analyses of individual practices, changes over time and spatial networks of practice as key areas of interest. We believe that the contributions in this volume have further demonstrated the value of practice theory for understanding tourism as a phenomenon and indicated new avenues for research taking a practice-based approach. But we would also argue that the bringing together of tourism studies and practice theory has implications for the latter, namely by strengthening the emphasis on the temporal, material, dynamic and inter-connectedness of practices.

We hope that this book will inspire others to continue this work in all areas of tourism studies.

References

Brouder, P. (2017). Evolutionary economic geography: reflections from a sustainable tourism perspective. *Tourism Geographies*, 19(3), 438–447.

Carlile, P.R. (2002). A pragmatic view of knowledge and boundaries: Boundary objects in new product development. *Organization Science*, 13, 442–455.

Edensor, T. (2010). Introduction. Thinking about rhythm and space. In T. Edensor (ed.), *Geographies of Rhythm. Nature, Place, Mobilities and Bodies* (pp. 1–18). Surrey: Ashgate.

Gill, A. and Williams, P. W. (2017). Contested pathways towards tourism-destination sustainability in Whistler, British Columbia: an evolutionary governance model. In P. Brouder, S. A. Clavé, A. Gill and D. Ioannides (eds), *Tourism Destination Evolution* (pp. 43–64). Abingdon: Routledge.

Halkier, H. and James, L. (2017). Destination dynamics, path dependency and resilience. Regaining momentum in Danish coastal tourism destinations? In P. Brouder,

S. A. Clavé, A. Gill and D. Ioannides (eds), *Tourism Destination Evolution* (pp. 19–42). Abingdon: Routledge.

Hui, A. (2017). Variation and the intersection of practices. In A. Hui, T. Schatzki and E. Shove (eds), *The Nexus of Practice. Connections, Constellations, Practitioners* (pp. 52–67). Abingdon: Routledge.

Hui, A., Schatzki, T. and Shove, E. (eds) (2017). *The Nexus of Practices. Connections, Constellations, Practitioners*. Abingdon: Routledge.

James, L. and Halkier, H. (2016). Regional development platforms and related variety: Exploring the changing practices of food tourism in North Jutland, Denmark. *European Urban and Regional Studies*, 23, 831–847.

Lamers, M. and Pashkevich, A. (2018). Short-circuiting cruise tourism practices along the Russian Barents Sea coast? The case of Arkhangelsk. *Current Issues in Tourism*, 21(4), 440–454.

Lamers, M., van der Duim, R. and Spaargaren, G. (2017). The relevance of practice theories for tourism research. *Annals of Tourism Research*, 62, 54–63.

Lave, J. and Wenger, E. (1991). *Situated Learning: Legitimate Peripheral Participation*. Cambridge: Cambridge University Press.

Magaudda, P., Halkier, B., Katz-Gerro, T. and Martens, L. (2011). When materiality 'bites back': digital music consumption practices in the age of dematerialization. *Journal of Consumer Culture*, 11(1), 15–36.

Nicolini, D. (2012). *Practice Theory, Work, and Organization*. Oxford: Oxford University Press.

Pantzar, M. and Shove, E. (2010). Understanding innovation in practice: a discussion of the production and re-production of Nordic Walking. *Technology Analysis and Strategic Management*, 22(4), 447–461.

Rantala, O. (2010). Tourist practices in the forest. *Annals of Tourism Research*, 37, 249–264.

Reckwitz, A. (2002). Toward a theory of social practices: a development in culturalist theorizing. *European Journal of Social Theory*, 5(2), 243–263.

Sanz-Ibáñez, C., Wilson, J. and Clavé, S.A. (2017). Moments as catalysts for change in the evolutionary paths of tourism destinations. In P. Brouder, S. A. Clavé, A. Gill and D. Ioannides (eds), *Tourism Destination Evolution* (pp. 81–102). Abingdon: Routledge.

Schatzki, T. (2002). *The Site of the Social. A Philosophical Account of the Constitution of Social Life and Change*. Philadelphia: Penn State University Press.

Schatzki, T. (2016a). Keeping track of large phenomena. *Geographische Zeitschrift*, 104(1), 4–24.

Schatzki, T. (2016b). Practice theory as flat ontology. In G. Spaargaren, D. Weenink and M. Lamers (eds), *Practice Theory and Research. Exploring the Dynamics of Social Life* (pp. 28–42). London: Routledge

Shove, E., Pantzar, M. and Watson, M. (2012). *The Dynamics of Social Practice*. London: SAGE.

Souza Bispo, M. (2016). Tourism as practice. *Annals of Tourism Research*, 61, 170–179.

Spaargaren, G., Lamers, M. and Weenink, D. (2017). Introduction: using practice theory to research social life. In G. Spaargaren, D. Weenink and M. Lamers (eds), *Practice Theory and Research. Exploring the Dynamics of Social Life* (pp. 3–27). London: Routledge.

Strati, A. (2009). 'Do you do beautiful things?': aesthetics and art in qualitative methods of organization studies. In D. Buchanan and A. Bryman (eds), *The Sage Handbook of Organizational Research Methods* (pp. 230–245). London: Sage Publications.

Valtonen, A. and Veijola, S. (2011). Sleep in tourism. *Annals of Tourism Research*, 38 (1), 175–192.

Warde, A. (2005). Consumption and theories of practice. *Journal of Consumer Culture*, 5(2), 131–153.

Wenger, E. (1998). *Communities of Practice. Learning, Meaning, and Identity.* Cambridge, MA: Cambridge University Press.

Index

For Product Safety Concerns and Information please contact our EU
representative GPSR@taylorandfrancis.com
Taylor & Francis Verlag GmbH, Kaufingerstraße 24, 80331 München, Germany